THE POLICE, ACTIVISTS, AND KNOWLEDGE

The Police, Activists, and Knowledge

THE STRUGGLE AGAINST RACIALIZED POLICING IN FRANCE

MAGDA BOUTROS

STANFORD UNIVERSITY PRESS
Stanford, California

Stanford University Press
Stanford, California

Library of Congress Cataloging-in-Publication Data
Names: Boutros, Magda, author.
Title: The police, activists, and knowledge : the struggle against racialized
    policing in France / Magda Boutros.
Description: Stanford, California : Stanford University Press, 2026. |
    Includes bibliographical references and index.
Identifiers: LCCN 2025033682 (print) | LCCN 2025033683 (ebook) |
    ISBN 9781503645059 (cloth) | ISBN 9781503645066 (paperback) |
    ISBN 9781503645073 (ebook)
Subjects: LCSH: Racism in law enforcement—France. | Police brutality—
    France. | Social movements—France. | Political activists—France. |
    Knowledge, Theory of—Political aspects—France.
Classification: LCC HV7936.R3 B68 2026 (print) | LCC HV7936.R3
    (ebook)
LC record available at https://lccn.loc.gov/2025033682
LC ebook record available at https://lccn.loc.gov/2025033683

Cover design: Michel Vrana
Cover photograph: Laurent Gayer, Demonstration against police brutality
in Paris, June 2, 2020

The authorized representative in the EU for product safety and compliance
is: Mare Nostrum Group B.V. | Mauritskade 21D | 1091 GC Amsterdam
| The Netherlands | Email address: gpsr@mare-nostrum.co.uk | KVK
chamber of commerce number: 96249943

Contents

Tables and Figures

Preface

This book is about activism against racialized policing in France, but the questions that drove my inquiry emerged when I was working in Egypt during the 2011 revolution. At the time, I was a researcher in an Egyptian human rights organization, focusing on issues of policing, fair trial rights, and prison conditions. After graduating from university with an undergraduate degree in law and a master's in criminal justice, I had moved back to Egypt, from where my family had migrated to France when I was a child.

As my colleagues and I joined the massive protests that marched toward Tahrir square on January 25 and in the days that followed, we realized that, as human rights advocates, we had a role to play in this revolutionary moment. In addition to joining the protests, we could contribute through our skills and expertise in documenting rights violations, initiating lawsuits, proposing reforms, and launching public campaigns. With my colleagues in the criminal justice unit, we set out to document police abuses, including the killing and maiming of protesters, torture in police custody, and the mass killings of incarcerated people. We published research reports, spoke to the media, represented victims in court, and made reform recommendations. We continued this work after Hosni Mubarak stepped down, as the country engaged in a rocky (and ultimately unsuccessful) transition to democracy.

But no matter how many witness testimonies we collected, how many

medical records, death certificates, and hours of video footage we presented, every time we published a report about police abuses, the response
from law enforcement was the same: they flatly denied all our claims. I
remember one TV talk show I was invited to intervene in, where the other
guest was a high-ranking police officer. I spoke about our latest research
on the police killings of protesters in front of the Interior Ministry in
November 2011. Police snipers positioned on building rooftops had shot
at protesters with live bullets, killing at least fifty people, while officers
on the ground shot at the protesters with rubber pellets, injuring hundreds, including at least sixty documented cases of people who lost an
eye. On the talk show, I detailed our research, which relied on our own
observations during the protests as well as on witness testimonies, doctors'
accounts, medical records, and hours of video footage showing officers
shooting directly at protesters. On air, my interlocutor dismissed everything I said with a condescending tone, saying, "this young woman doesn't
know anything about the police." He denied that the police were targeting
protesters' eyes, and added, "I've spent my whole career in the police, and
I can tell you, officers during protests don't have live ammunition, so if
people were really killed, then the shots must have come from infiltrators."
For all the documentation work we did, we had no way of accessing police
records that would demonstrate that the snipers shooting live ammunition
were police officers, or that riot police were given instructions to target
protesters' eyes.

Of course, it wasn't surprising that police leaders would try to deny
engaging in unlawful practices. What was infuriating, however, was that,
more often than not, they got away with it. The police officer knew he was
lying (he admitted as much after we got off air, telling me, "the police are
like my family, I'd do anything to defend them"). But I wondered how
many viewers believed him, a high-ranking male officer who spent his
career in the police, over "a young woman who doesn't know anything
about the police." By virtue of his status as a policeman, my interlocutor
was perceived to be more reliable than a young female researcher, and
more credible than the protesters who testified about being shot at. He and
other high-ranking officers were regularly given a platform in the mainstream media, which was rarely granted to the targets of police abuses.

In the courts, too, police officers routinely got away with blatant lies and dissimulation, escaping accountability for killing, torturing, and injuring thousands of protesters, political prisoners, and criminal defendants. In most cases, when victims filed complaints, officers denied wrongdoing and covered for each other. Investigators told complainants that it was impossible to identify the perpetrators, and the cases were dismissed for lack of evidence. Without access to police records, our lawyers could not identify the officers involved or prove that they acted under instructions from their supervisors.

My frustration at the police's systematic denial of wrongdoing led me to think more deeply about what it takes to organize against an institution like the police, which can kill, maim, and injure, but also has the power to conceal these actions, lie when challenged, and for the most part, get away with it. While the Egyptian police are particularly brutal and prone to dissimulation, I knew that movements organizing against policing across the world grappled with similar issues. Everywhere, the police have significant control to shape what is known and what remains hidden about their practices.

As I continued thinking about how to build effective resistance strategies, another set of questions emerged. Along with colleagues in Egypt, we grappled with a tension between our human rights work and our involvement in the revolution. On one hand, as human rights advocates, we promoted a reformist approach that sought to improve existing state institutions, calling for police reform and for independent and impartial investigations into violations. On the other hand, as revolutionaries, we demanded nothing less than a complete overhaul of the justice and security apparatus. We cheered when protesters stormed state security offices, and we participated in direct-action efforts that sought to preserve public safety without the police, such as antiharassment intervention teams. At a time when legal and political structures were being fundamentally challenged, we debated whether it still made sense to document violations, engage in litigation, and call for reforms.

This led me to question the potential and limitations of various models of activism. I was increasingly aware of NGOs' constraints and of the limits of the human rights discourse to combat structural oppressions, but I also understood that slow, incremental change was often our only avenue. I admired radical, grassroots initiatives that sought to build alternative models of public safety without the police, but I witnessed how exhausting and traumatic this work can be, how difficult it is to sustain it, and how vulnerable it made activists to state repression. I started asking myself what the costs and trade-offs of various approaches are, and whether the coexistence of expert-led reformist efforts and community-led radical action is an asset or a hurdle for the cause.

When I switched to academia in 2013, I planned to examine these questions in postrevolutionary Egypt. But by the time I was due to start fieldwork, conducting research in Egypt had become unsafe, so I kept the same research interests and shifted my attention to my other home country. France provided a good case study to examine activism against oppressive policing: it has a persistent problem with racist policing, police brutality, and impunity, and there were various activist groups attempting to combat these issues, both through professionalized NGOs and victim-led, grassroots movements.

I moved to Paris for my fieldwork in 2016 and got involved with two mobilization efforts that exemplified the models of activism I wanted to study: a campaign against racial profiling led by a coalition of nongovernmental organizations and lawyers, and a protest movement led by families of victims of police killings demanding "Truth and Justice." Shortly after I started the fieldwork, I was introduced to a neighborhood mobilization in the twelfth arrondissement of Paris, which I incorporated in my analysis as a third model, neither fully top-down nor completely bottom-up, but structured around a coalition of local actors, who called on outside experts for support. I got involved in all three activist groups, attending meetings, participating in public events and protests, and interviewing the actors involved in the movement.

Just like in Egypt, one of the major hurdles the French movement faced was that the police systematically denied any wrongdoing—and most of the time, got away with it. Not only did police officers routinely deny wrongdoing when accused of misconduct in individual instances, the whole institution was also notoriously opaque, making it difficult for victims and activists to be heard and believed when they denounced discriminatory patterns of practice. When advocates claimed that the police engaged in racial profiling, police leaders and government representatives denied it and said there was no evidence of racial inequalities. Yet, in the absence of any published statistics on stop and search, the data simply did not exist. When families of victims argued that officers were granted de facto impunity for police killings, the government dismissed the claims and said that all complaints were thoroughly and independently investigated. Without comprehensive data on police-involved deaths, or on the judicial or disciplinary outcomes of investigations into police violence, activists and victims couldn't substantiate their claims.

While I initially conceptualized this obstacle as a problem of "police opacity," I came to realize that the police do not just have the ability to dissimulate contentious practices; they can also produce knowledge that portrays them in a positive light. Police forces often control the production and dissemination of official data on crime, public safety, and policing practices, which allows them to determine what gets measured and how. They control which statistics are disseminated, which allows them to select data that portray them as essential to combating crime and insecurity. Police officers are also deemed more credible than their targets and they have greater access to the media.

This capacity of the police to shape what others hear, believe, and know about policing practices, and what remains unknown, and sometimes, unknowable, is what I call the *epistemic power* of the police. This is the first insight of the book: it is extremely difficult to challenge abusive, racist, and violent policing practices, not only because the police have coercive power (the right to use force), but also because they have substantial epistemic power. To build effective movements against racialized policing, activists must challenge the police's control over the production of knowledge and ignorance around policing and inequality.

The three coalitions that I studied worked to generate their own evidence to substantiate their claims about police discrimination and brutality. While all three groups invested in knowledge production, they used different approaches to do so, what I call *modes of knowledge production*. One group made alliances with scholars to produce statistical data, the second worked with local communities to document the recurring practices of patrol units in one neighborhood, and the third drew on victims' experiences to produce situated analyses of the policing and justice systems. Comparing these three modes of knowledge production led me to the second insight of this book: how activist groups produce knowledge matters for the discourses that they build, and for their influence on policy, judicial, and media debates. Each coalition's mode of knowledge production shaped how they constructed their discourse—who was deemed legitimate to speak, and what they stood for. It also influenced how journalists, politicians, and courts received their claims.

The book's third contribution is to intervene in scholarly and political debates about antiracist activism in "race-blind" societies. In France, the dominant ideology, Republicanism, considers that overcoming racism requires eliminating racial categories, which are viewed as essentializing and racist. French law bans the collection of data on people's race, ethnicity, or religion, which limits the ability of researchers and activists to measure racial inequalities. Many scholars have argued that antiracialism prevents the emergence of an effective antiracist movement, because it takes away the terms with which people can measure racial inequalities and make racism visible. I found that the antiracialist ideology certainly represented a hurdle for the movement, because of the legal restrictions on collecting racial statistics and because the political culture is dominated by a strong rejection of discourses about structural or systemic racism, especially when they are made by racialized people. Nevertheless, movement actors found creative ways to overcome these restrictions and to produce evidence about how race and racism shapes policing practices. My analysis suggests that the most common way to measure racial inequalities—statistical data about racial disparities—is essential to establish the existence of racial inequalities in policing. However, on its own, it is insufficient to capture the institutional and structural dimensions of racialized policing. Activists also developed other modes of knowledge production that allowed them to show how policing practices are embedded in historically constructed social and institutional structures that maintain the oppression of racialized minorities. This book examines how they did this, and how they contributed to transforming the political debate about policing, justice, and inequality in France from the mid-2000s to the early 2020s.

Introduction

It's His Word Against Mine

In France, encounters with the police are a routine part of everyday life for young men from working-class families who are racialized as Black or Arab.[1] Joseph,[2] a teenager whose parents migrated from North Africa and moved into a social housing unit in the twelfth arrondissement of Paris, told me that he started getting stopped by the police at the age of eleven. In his early teens, he was often stopped several times a week for identity checks—the French equivalent of stop and search—along with his neighborhood friends, most of them sons of sub-Saharan and North African immigrants. "Every time, the police would come, and they would check us, check us, check us; they did nothing else." Around the age of fifteen, the identity checks became more violent; "it got real tense," he recalled. Officers sometimes slapped, punched, or beat up the boys; they took them into custody for a few hours before releasing them to their parents; and they often used racist slurs.

During my interview with him, Joseph recounted a particularly memorable incident. One day, he was on his way to the local fair with other neighborhood boys after a game of soccer. He recalled, "We see a police car stop and officers come toward us with tear gas [shouting] 'Stop! If you don't stop, you're dead!' We were super scared, we ran and ran and ran." The officers soon caught up with them:

Then, an officer grabbed me, it was Jacques.[3] He knocked me to the ground, dragged me, pulled me up and then slapped me. And then another policeman, he was Indian,[4] I don't remember his name, he was mad because I had run away from him. He saw me, pulled me up and punched me in the face. With the adrenaline I didn't feel the pain, and I didn't want to play the rebel, so I pretended as if nothing was happening. They knocked me to the ground and dragged me again, they kicked my head to the ground several times with their boots. I will remember it my whole life.[5]

After the beating, the officers searched Joseph and took him to the police station before releasing him without charge. When his father picked him up, officers warned him, "by the end of the year, we promise you, both your sons will be in prison, we'll make sure of it."

Joseph's encounters with the police are typical of the experiences of racialized young men from low-income families in France. Studies show that police use identity checks extensively, not only for investigating suspicious behavior but also to affirm police authority, to gather intelligence, or to dispense a form of "justice in the street" against groups they perceive as hostile.[6] During these stops, officers routinely use humiliating and racist insults, physical violence, arbitrary detention, and abusive fining.[7] Some of these encounters lead to serious injuries or even death. In the 2010s, on average, twenty-one people died during police interventions every year, most of them while unarmed,[8] a number that has risen sharply since.[9] In a country with relatively low rates of gun violence, this represents a significant proportion of all homicides.[10] In line with other scholars, I refer to these violent and abusive policing practices that disproportionately target racial minorities with the term *racialized policing*.

During my fieldwork, I met dozens of people like Joseph who routinely experienced racialized policing. All considered that these practices were wrong, but the vast majority saw no avenue for contesting them. Despite describing it as the worst identity check of his life, Joseph did not consider filing a complaint or taking any sort of action. This was not because of political apathy or because he normalized these abuses, as is sometimes believed. Rather, in my conversations with him and other racialized young men, I found them to be acutely aware of the power differential between them and the police. One of the most common sentences I heard was "there's nothing I can do, it's his word against mine."

The authorities, they reasoned, would not believe a poor Black or Arab teen over a police officer. Most of the time, their complaints were not even recorded. Even when they were, victims had few means of producing evidence of the abuses they suffer. They don't have access to surveillance footage, they have no way to prove that their injuries were caused by police officers, and in most cases, they can't identify the officers they encounter. Many also feared that speaking up could backfire—a fear that was justified. When Joseph and other local teens started filing legal complaints against police officers and speaking to elected leaders and police commanders, things only got worse. Many complaints were dismissed without investigation; the political leaders deemed the teens' claims to be untrustworthy and took no further action; but patrol officers retaliated with intensified harassment, threatening them with more violence if they complained again.

This example illustrates a major obstacle people face when they try to contest policing practices: there is a huge power imbalance between the police and their most common targets, regarding which voices are heard and believed, and which are silenced and discredited. In most Western countries, the police are widely assumed to be reliable and credible, while the populations they target are stigmatized as criminal and untrustworthy.[11] Police forces are also notoriously opaque,[12] releasing only a carefully selected set of data on their actions, which makes it difficult to prove that incidents of abuse are part of broader patterns of practice.

In France, victims face another obstacle. The country's *antiracialist* ideology, which deems the concept of "race" essentializing and racist, makes it difficult to demonstrate the racial dimension of policing practices. Antiracialism is posited on a universalist ethos of "indifference to difference," according to which the best defense against racist oppression is to eliminate racial categories. In line with this understanding, the law bans the collection of data on people's race, ethnicity, or religion, and the state is not allowed to take these factors into account in policymaking.[13] In the twelfth arrondissement, virtually all the youth targeted by the police were sons of immigrants from former French colonies. But given the absence of data broken down by race or ethnicity, it was difficult for them to prove that these practices were racially biased.

In this context, when people try to organize collectively against racialized policing, they must produce their own evidence of the practices they denounce. They must mobilize data that can disrupt the assumed trust-worthiness of the police, bolster the credibility of victims, and substantiate their claims. These knowledge-making efforts are at the heart of this book.

The Police, Activists, and Knowledge examines the contemporary movement against racialized policing in France, and asks: How do activists shed light on abusive policing practices that remain largely hidden from public view? How do they make visible, and articulate, the role of race in policing, in a "race-blind" context? What are the implications of their knowledge-making practices for how activists frame the problems with policing and inequality, and for their influence on political debates and judicial decisions?

Drawing on an ethnographic study of three activist coalitions that were organizing against racial profiling, police violence, and impunity throughout the 2010s, I make three interlinked arguments.

First, I argue that, to understand what it takes to resist policing practices, we must pay attention to the capacity of the police to control what we know, and what remains unknown (and sometimes, unknowable) about policing and inequalities. Existing scholarship has emphasized the police's coercive power (the ability to use force or coercion) and their symbolic power (the ability to produce meanings that become taken-for-granted about crime, safety, and policing).[14] I highlight a third dimension of police power: the ability to influence what others know and don't know about policing and inequalities, which I call the *epistemic power* of the police.[15] When collective actors contest policing practices, they must not only protect themselves from coercion and challenge the cultural ideas promoted by the police; they must also confront the power of the police to construct truth and manufacture ignorance.

As a result, knowledge production is often a central strategy for movements organizing against racialized policing. The second argument of the book is that the way activist groups produce knowledge—their *modes of knowledge production*—matters for the discourses they build about who they are and what they stand for, and shapes their influence on policy, judicial, and media debates. This study compares three coalitions, which adopted different modes of knowledge production. In one, NGOs collaborated with scholars to produce statistics on racial disparities in identity checks; in another, community leaders documented local youths' experiences to produce a grounded account of routine policing practices; in the third, families of victims of police killings drew on their own experiences to develop an analysis of what they called the "manufacturing of police impunity." These differences were important because they determined the truth claims that activists could substantiate, which contributed to shaping how each group conceptualized racialized policing—as a problem of bad cops, unfair institutional policies, or structural oppression. It also shaped their ability to push the boundaries of what is knowable and sayable in the media, policy, and judicial fields, and to challenge which voices are heard and legitimated.

My third contribution is to add nuance to the argument that race-blind ideologies are an obstacle to antiracist activism. I show that, while antiracialism makes it difficult to produce data on racial inequalities, it does not make race and racism "unmeasurable and unspeakable," as some scholars have argued.[16] The three groups I studied produced knowledge on the role of race in policing by quantifying racial disparities in police stops, uncovering internal policies and practices that exclude racial minority youth from certain urban spaces, and highlighting the colonial legacies at play in contemporary practices of the police and judiciary. Each mode of knowledge production had important consequences for how activists defined racialized policing. It shaped their ability to push against the dominant perception of racism as isolated, individual attitudes and toward a theorization of institutional, systemic, or state racism.[17] It also influenced how they articulated the intersection of racial inequality with other forms of inequality, based on class, gender, place, and age.

While this study focuses on France, the questions it investigates have broader relevance. Across the world, the 2010s were marked by growing movements against abusive, violent, and racist policing, from the Arab revolutions in Tunisia or Egypt, to the Black Lives Matter movement in the United States, to protest actions in Brazil, Hong Kong, Nigeria, and other countries.[18] These movements faced similar challenges regarding how to produce evidence of abusive policing practices, and how to make visible the role of law enforcement in (re)producing systems of oppression. *The Police, Activists, and Knowledge* uses France as a case study to analyze why social movements struggle to contest oppressive policing practices, and what it takes for them to transform what we know, what we believe, and how we understand issues of policing, equality, and justice.

Contesting Racialized Policing

The contemporary movement against racialized policing has its roots in the 1970s. As migrant workers from former French colonies started settling in the metropole, they were faced with high levels of racist violence, including by police officers. In the early 1970s, the Arab Workers Movement (Mouvement des travailleurs arabes) organized protests and strikes against what they called "racist and securitarian violence," demanding justice for victims.[19] Toward the end of the decade, a series of urban revolts erupted following incidents of police brutality targeting immigrants' children in impoverished housing projects. The second generation revolted against what they denounced as a violent and racist police force, and a complicit judiciary, which is quick to convict racialized youth for minor crimes but reluctant to indict police officers who kill.[20]

At the time, the French state was formulating its policy to combat racism and discrimination. Under the influence of nongovernmental organizations concerned about racist violence and resurging anti-Semitism, legislators passed the country's first law against racism in 1972. The law criminalized incitement to racist hatred or violence and banned discrimination in employment and services. In parallel, lawmakers revived a strict understanding of antiracialism, all but banning the collection of data on people's race, ethnicity, or religion and prohibiting the government from considering these criteria in public policies.[21] The goal was to prevent a repetition of what happened during France's occupation by the Nazis, when police forces rounded up over 13,000 Jews and sent them to death camps, using police databases.

While France's antiracist policies were influenced by the memory of the Holocaust, there was limited consideration for the country's colonial past.[22] Yet, this history has enduring effects on state practices in general, and policing in particular. During the French empire, the colonial police was deployed to repress labor dissent and anticolonial resistance, using surveillance, counterinsurgency tactics, and brute force.[23] Law enforcement played a central role during France's bloodiest decolonization war, the Algerian war of independence, with both colonial and metropolitan police forces participating in the repression of anticolonial militancy, arresting, brutalizing, and killing peaceful protesters en masse. After decolonization in the 1960s, the strategies and tactics developed by the colonial police were imported to the metropole and deployed against postcolonial migrants, who replaced anticolonial militants as the new "internal enemy."[24]

This legacy is neither acknowledged nor addressed in state policies. Since the 1970s, antiracist policies have been founded on the idea that racism in postwar Europe has been fundamentally transformed, from a state-sponsored project to an issue of individual attitudes and isolated practices.[25] In line with this view, mainstream antiracist organizations such as SOS Racisme have focused on promoting cultural understanding and tolerance, without addressing the role of the state in perpetuating racial inequalities.

Within this context, activism against racialized policing took two competing approaches. On one hand, nongovernmental organizations close to the political left drew on liberal principles of democracy and human rights to call for accountability in individual cases of police misconduct, and to offer legal aid to victims.[26] They released statements opposing the expansion of police powers without adequate judicial review. These organizations, which are largely funded by the state, endorsed the antiracialist ideology, framing police actions as racist only when there was evidence of an officer's racist prejudice. On the other hand, autonomous organizations in marginalized neighborhoods (*militants des quartiers populaires*) developed a more radical discourse, framing the state and capital as the main drivers of racist oppression. They denounced police violence and judicial complicity as symptoms of the "postcolonial management" of poor racialized communities.[27]

The 1980s witnessed a short-lived attempt at building coalition across these divisions. Some grassroots organizers in the Lyon suburbs formed an alliance with Christian left, proimmigration groups. This coalition led to France's first national antiracist protest, the 1983 March for Equality and Against Racism, which went from Marseilles to Paris.[28] But while issues of police violence and equal justice were at the heart of this unprecedented national mobilization, by the time the march reached Paris, left-wing organizers and their governmental allies downplayed issues of police violence and instead emphasized reforming immigration laws to expand migrant workers' residency rights.[29] Within a year, the fragile coalition collapsed, and the movement against racialized policing remained divided between reformist NGOs and grassroots *quartiers populaires* organizers.

The mid-2000s were a turning point for activism against racialized policing, with the emergence of new actors and new strategies of action. The Open Society Foundation, the second-largest philanthropic foundation in the world, launched large-scale programs against racial profiling in Europe. Their goal was to encourage mainstream NGOs to challenge the country's race-blind culture. In parallel, among autonomous groups, new "political antiracist" groups emerged, which mobilized around racial identities such as "Black," "Indigenous," or "racialized" (*racisés*) and promoted a decolonial discourse condemning institutional or state racism.[30] Through their savvy use of social media and their networks within academia, they quickly became a visible—and highly controversial—new voice in the movement.

With the arrival of these new actors, in the 2010s, there were two main axes of division within the broader movement against racialized policing. Activist groups differed in their degree of radicality, with some adopting a reformist perspective that advocates for incremental policy changes and others taking a more radical approach built on direct action to empower the oppressed. There were also disagreements on how to talk about the inequalities policing generates. Within both the reformist and the radical camps, some groups promoted a race-centered discourse that framed race as the most important factor of inequality in policing, while others preferred to talk about inequalities in terms of social class, place of residence, age, and origin. The former framed the targets of policing in racial terms (as Black, Arab, Travelers, or *racisés*); the latter preferred referring to their class and place-based marginalization, as residents of working-class neighborhoods (*habitants des quartiers populaires*), sometimes, but not always, adding an attention to their migration backgrounds. Figure 0.1 illustrates these divisions, naming some of the groups that were active in each approach in the 2010s.[31]

The Police, Activists, and Knowledge examines the organizing efforts of these groups from the mid-2000s to the early 2020s, a time when the movement made significant headway in the public and political debate. While organizers had struggled for decades to place the issue on the agenda, by the early 2020s, multiple political parties included police reform in their electoral platforms, and lawmakers regularly introduced and discussed law bills aiming to reduce racial profiling and police-involved deaths. Mainstream media covered issues of police violence, racism, and accountability more extensively than ever before and gave voice to leading figures of the

FIGURE 0.1 **Lines of division in the movement against racialized policing, 2010s.**

Race-centered

International NGOs (e.g., Open Society Justice Initiative)
National NGOs (e.g., Conseil Représentatif des Association Noires)

Political antiracist groups (e.g., Parti des Indigènes de la République)

Reformist ←————————————————————→ Radical

National NGOs (e.g. Ligue des droits de l'Homme)
Unions (e.g., Syndicat des Avocats de France, Syndicat de la Magistrature)
Local NGOs

Quartiers populaires organizers (e.g., Mouvement de l'Immigration et des Banlieues)

Class, space, age, origins

Source: Magda Boutros.

movement. After decades of political denial, both the socialist government during François Hollande's presidency (2012–17) and the center right government under President Emmanuel Macron (2017–) admitted that there was a problem with policing and racial inequalities in France.

These changes were remarkable, because they took place in an unfavorable political context. While a small window of opportunity opened when the socialists came to power in 2012, it quickly closed. Following the deadly terrorist attacks of 2015, a bipartisan consensus emerged to expand police powers significantly, and to strengthen the preventive and punitive arsenal to combat "Islamic radicalization." In this context, criticizing the police and organizing against racial inequalities became increasingly difficult. Legislators and governments on the right and on the left intensified their actions to combat *communautarisme*, an accusation typically levied at Muslims and other minorities, denounced for promoting ethnic "separatism" and refusing to integrate into French society. Islamophobic rhetoric surged and was increasingly normalized, including in the political left. Politicians launched campaigns against activists, scholars, and political leaders working on racial and gender oppression, who were accused of promoting "woke culture" and "Islamo-leftism," a term used to suggest that some on the political left are in bed with Islamists.[32]

The late 2010s and early 2020s saw a stark shift to the right in the political arena, with the growing popularity of Marine Le Pen's Rassemblement National party, and with Macron's government increasingly endorsing far-right rhetoric on immigration and the need for "order and authority." Mainstream media outlets gave more airtime to far-right politicians and commentators than ever before, as billionaire Vincent Bolloré bought TV channels, radio stations, and written press, and transformed their editorial stance. Police brutality increased, with higher numbers of police-involved deaths and an expansion of the groups targeted to include antigovernment protesters.[33] At the same time, police unions, which hold significant political weight, portrayed law enforcement as the last bastion against terrorism and framed any criticism of the police as dangerously anti-Republican. They demanded stronger protections for officers and a "presumption of self-defense" that would shield them from legal accountability in cases of alleged misconduct.[34]

This book examines how, in this unfavorable context, movement actors succeeded at placing the issues of police violence, racism, and impunity on the political agenda. The central contention is that their efforts to produce and mobilize knowledge about policing and inequalities were key.

Using ethnographic and qualitative methods, I zoom in on three coalitions that were active in contesting racialized policing in the late 2000s and throughout the 2010s. Each group exemplifies a distinct model of activism and approach to knowledge production.

The campaign against racial profiling, which was led and funded by a large transnational organization (Open Society Justice Initiative) working in cooperation with national NGOs and lawyers. The campaign leaders lobbied politicians for reforms, filed strategic lawsuits, and launched media campaigns against discriminatory stops. They produced knowledge by making alliances with scholars to conduct France's first study quantifying racial disparities in identity checks.

The neighborhood mobilization against police harassment targeting racialized young people in the twelfth arrondissement of Paris. This organizing effort was initiated by teenagers (including Joseph) and their youth counselors, who sought the support of activists, lawyers, and Open Society to build community organizing efforts and launch litigation against one police unit. This work involved documenting the experiences of local youth with the police over an extended period of time, by collecting testimonies, medical certificates, photo and video evidence.

The Truth and Justice movement led by families of victims of police killings who, with the help of *quartiers populaires* organizers and antiracist activists, organize protests and commemorations to raise public awareness of police violence and impunity. They aim to pressure the judiciary to indict police officers who kill, and to introduce the issue of police violence and accountability in political debates. This movement adopted a bottom-up approach to knowledge production, led by families of victims who drew on their personal experiences to develop an analysis of the "manufacturing of police impunity."

As table 0.1 illustrates, the campaign against racial profiling took a top-down approach; its principal leaders were lawyers and NGO workers who sought to use their professional expertise and proximity to elite networks to promote social change. The neighborhood organizing effort

TABLE 0.1   **Characteristics of the coalitions studied.**

	Racial profiling campaign	Neighborhood mobilization	Truth and Justice movement
Leading actors	International and national NGOs, lawyers	Local residents and professionals, NGOs, activists, lawyers	Families of victims of police killings, activists
Focus	Discrimination in identity checks	Police harassment and violence	Police killings and impunity
Main tactics	Political lobbying, public campaigns, litigation	Community organizing, litigation	Protest, community organizing, litigation
Resources	Substantial financial resources; legal and advocacy expertise	Limited financial resources; legal and social work expertise	No financial resources; experiential and organizing expertise
Knowledge production	Expert-led, quantitative	Community-led, grounded	Victim-led, liberation

Source: Magda Boutros.

was initiated by local actors directly affected by racialized policing; when they sought help from Open Society and lawyers, these experts intervened in a support role to address locally identified needs. And the Truth and Justice movement was a bottom-up movement, led by those most directly affected by racialized policing (*les premiers concernés*). The study's comparative design allows me to examine the implications of their distinct models of activism and approaches to knowledge production.

A Knowledge-Centered Analysis

To analyze why movements contesting policing practices have struggled to obtain meaningful change, and under what conditions they can transform the public and political debate around policing and inequality, scholars have developed three sets of explanation.

First, social movement scholars have analyzed how activists mobilize constituents, frame their cause, generate funding, and build alliances.[35] Studies of the movement against racialized policing in France point to internal divisions among activist groups and to the difficulties of creating political alliances on this issue.[36] Since the 1980s, the activist field has been fragmented and divided, with conflicts over how to frame the cause and which strategies of action to privilege. Mainstream human rights organizations, which are primarily funded by the state, have sought to maintain a moderate discourse, calling for accountability in individual cases of misconduct and opposing laws that expand police powers.[37] In parallel, autonomous groups in *quartiers populaires* have developed a structural analysis of police violence and impunity as postcolonial domination,[38] but they have remained chronically underresourced and struggled to sustain their actions. Within each of those groups, there were ongoing debates about whether to center the analysis on race or on class and place and about whether to invest in local organizing or in national-level political lobbying. Moreover, movement actors have struggled to build alliances with the mainstream left, which tends to downplay and sideline the grievances of racialized people[39] and to address the issue of police violence more forcefully when it affects middle-class White, protesters.[40]

In a second scholarship, policing and sociolegal scholars show that the police benefit from structural advantages in the judicial, political, and media fields, which allow them to counteract political challenges.[41]

In judicial and disciplinary proceedings, allegations of police misconduct are investigated by internal inspection services. Studies show that these agencies, which are part of the same organizations they oversee, rarely discipline police officers for excessive use of force or discriminatory treatment, and when they do, the sentences are less serious than for other types of infractions such as loss of police equipment.[42] Police officers are rarely charged with criminal offenses, especially when their victims are poor and racialized.[43] When they do go to trial,[44] officers get their legal expenses fully paid for by the state, and convictions to prison terms are extremely rare.[45] In addition, the police have strong lobbies in the political sphere. In France, police unions have significant political weight, which they routinely use to oppose reforms that might restrict police powers or strengthen monitoring and accountability mechanisms.[46] Police forces also have privileged access to mainstream media, thanks to well-resourced communications teams and the ability to leverage access to crime news in exchange for favorable coverage of policing practices.[47]

A third field of research has focused on the difficulties of contesting racialized state practices in a "race-blind" context. Critical race scholars have argued that France's antiracialist ideology represents an obstacle for organizing effectively against racism.[48] By delegitimizing racial categories as essentializing, they note, antiracialism takes away the terms of reference through which activists can measure racial inequality and name racial oppression, rendering race and its effects invisible and unspeakable. It "suggests forgetting, getting over, moving on" from the racial horrors of the past, undermining the possibility to understand the continued legacy of colonization and slavery.[49] Scholarship shows that antiracialism has been an important hurdle for movements organizing against racialized policing. When activists called for laws against racist violence, legislators rejected these proposals on the grounds that they went against the country's universalist ethos, instead promoting a narrow understanding of racism as the behavior of overtly bigoted individuals.[50] Moreover, activists who talk explicitly about "race" or identify in racial terms are viewed with deep suspicion and regularly accused of being *communautaristes* or Islamo-leftists.

Taken together, these three scholarships point to the vast power imbalance between the police and the communities they target. To put it in the simplest terms, they show that, in France, the movement against racialized policing is too weak, the police are too strong, and the context unfavorable. This helps explain why, despite sustained organizing since the 1970s, there have been few meaningful changes in policing practices. However, this research is less helpful to understand how movement actors address or overcome these obstacles, or to explain how they managed to place the issues of racial profiling and police violence on the political agenda in the 2010s. Political scientist Anthony Pregnolato has shown how, in the second half of the 2010s, activists organizing against racialized policing have built alliances with other social movements that faced unprecedented levels of police repression, including antifascist, environmentalist, and labor rights activists.[51] But we know less about how they managed to influence the mainstream public debate, beyond far-left movements, despite a political culture that remains opposed to race-based analyses.

My study suggests that an essential, but understudied, part of the explanation is movement actors' efforts to produce their own knowledge about policing and racial inequalities. The three coalitions I examined invested significant time and resources in collecting, analyzing, and disseminating data to substantiate their claims. These knowledge-making projects allowed them to disrupt the credibility of the police, promote alternative narratives about what the police are and do, and highlight the racialized nature of policing practices. This helped movement leaders gain enough legitimacy and credibility to be able to build durable alliances and to impose their analyses of racialized policing in the political and media debate.

Conceptual Tool Kit and Key Arguments

While existing research tends to focus either on the movements (and their weaknesses), or on the police (and their strengths), *The Police, Activists, and Knowledge* investigates the unequal power relation between the police and the people organizing collectively to challenge them. The book examines how this power relation is produced and consolidated, and under what conditions it can be challenged and disrupted. I take a relational conception of power, which sees power not as something that one possesses or lacks, but as the property of a social relationship between actors in an unequal social structure.[52] As such, the police do not have intrinsic power; rather, in their interactions with others, they hold power over socially dominated groups in a specific sociohistorical context.

To analyze this power relation, I draw on recent insights from the sociology of knowledge, which are brought to bear on scholarship in social movements, policing studies, and critical race theory. I propose three key concepts in order to examine how the police maintain control over what we know and what remains unknown about policing and inequalities (epistemic power), how social movements challenge this control by producing and mobilizing their own data (modes of knowledge production), and the ways in which they translate and transpose this data in legal and political arenas (epistemic work).

EPISTEMIC POWER

Existing scholarship has emphasized two dimensions of police power.[53] Classical studies underscored the police's *coercive power*, which is the capacity to use force or coercion to get others to do things that they would not otherwise do.[54] This power derives from the legal authorization they have to use force, and from their substantial material resources, such as weapons, equipment, surveillance technologies, and personnel. As sociologist Egon Bittner argues, the capacity to use force is the defining feature of the police.[55] Although most officers only use force occasionally, the fact that they *can* is why most of us follow a policeman's instructions when asked to stop or pull over, show an ID, or move along, and why we let officers search, handcuff, or take us into custody.

Coercive power is the bedrock of racialized policing. Using coercion and force, the police can impose a social order that reproduces hierarchies of class, race, and gender. Coercive power allows police officers to repeatedly stop Joseph and other racialized teenagers, to beat them up, take them into custody, and threaten to find a way to send them to prison. To be sure, there are legal limits to police use of force—it must be necessary to protect themselves or others from an immediate threat and be proportionate to the threat—but studies have consistently shown that, in practice, the police largely get to determine what is considered legitimate force.[56]

Some scholars have criticized the classical conception for overlooking a second dimension of police power: *symbolic power*, which is the ability to shape what people feel and believe about crime, public safety, and the police.[57] Criminologists Ian Loader and Aogán Mulcahy argue that the police derive their power not only from the capacity to use physical violence, but also from the ability to produce cultural meanings, which portray the police as the obvious, natural solution to crime and disorder—a force for good protecting us from (often racialized) dangerous individuals. The police, they suggest, have acquired "the right of legitimate pronouncement: a power to diagnose, classify, authorize, and represent both individuals and the world, and to have that power of 'legitimate naming' not just taken seriously, but taken for granted."[58]

Of course, the groups most targeted by law enforcement rarely buy into these narratives. Studies show that negative experiences with the police lead marginalized groups to distrust the police and to develop a political consciousness of inequalities.[59] Still, the symbolic influence of the police remains important across many sections of the population. In France, a solid majority of the population reports high levels of trust in the police, a proportion that increases sharply following terrorist attacks.[60]

Taken together, the coercive and symbolic dimensions of police power represent important obstacles for movements against racialized policing. Police officers can use force, or the threat of force, to intimidate protesters, prevent people from filming police interventions, or to retaliate against those who file complaints. They can delegitimize victims by promoting narratives that portray the police as a force for good fighting dangerous criminals.

However, these two dimensions are insufficient to explain why many people suffering police abuses are reluctant to organize. When Joseph and others say, "there's nothing I can do, it's his word against mine," they are emphasizing another key consideration: whether their claims will be heard and believed. Underscoring their reluctance to take action is an understanding that the police have significant control over what we know—and what remains concealed—about policing practices, whereas victims have few means to produce evidence of the abuses they suffer. They know that police narratives tend to be deemed truthful while those of their targets are perceived as untrustworthy.

This points to a third dimension of police power, what I call the *epistemic power* of the police, which is the ability to control what people know and don't know about policing and inequalities.[61] I borrow the term from sociologists and philosophers who have shown that the capacity to determine what counts as legitimate and credible knowledge and who can produce it, is unequally distributed.[62] Epistemic power is the ability to influence what others believe and know, and to give credence or discredit others as knowers.[63] It operates not only through controlling what knowledge gets produced and disseminated but also through shaping what remains unknown, and sometimes, unknowable. As sociologist Linsey McGoey writes, we must pay attention not only to the politics of knowledge but also "to the politics of ignorance, to the mobilization of ambiguity, the denial of unsettling facts."[64] We must examine how powerful actors strategically maintain ignorance as a tool for exonerating themselves from blame. As such, epistemic power is the ability to generate truth and manufacture ignorance.

While symbolic power is the capacity to shape *normative* beliefs about good and evil, epistemic power is the ability to control people's *empirical* knowledge about what is true. When police officers beat up racialized teenagers like Joseph and then deny it, when they refuse to let watchdog institutions investigate allegations of misconduct, or when they fail to publish data on their use of force, they are drawing on their epistemic power to shape what we know—and what remains hidden—about policing.[65]

In France as in other imperial states, the police's epistemic power is a central mechanism sustaining racial oppression. Black studies scholar Simone Browne shows how the data law enforcement collect through surveillance reify boundaries, borders, and bodies along racial lines, thus allowing the police to exercise a power to define "who is in or out of place."[66] When law enforcement agencies use stops, arrests, surveillance technology, and social media monitoring to build databases of "gang members," "terrorists," or "illegal immigrants," they transform racialized discourses about crime, terror, and belonging into "facts." As sociologist Andy Clarno and his colleagues argue, this "generates an air of mathematical objectivity that allows police to weaponize data while disavowing their reliance on racialized archetypes."[67] In France, this disavowal is further facilitated by the dominant race-blind ideology, which makes it difficult to use police-generated data to capture the disparate outcomes policing practices have on racialized minorities.

Part I of the book examines the epistemic power relation between the police and the communities they target. I show that there are three main mechanisms that provide the police with significant epistemic power. First, law enforcement agencies control the production and circulation of data on crime, safety, and policing practices. They determine what gets measured and how it is measured, and they select which data to publish and disseminate.[68] Second, the police benefit from a presumption of credibility; in law, an officer's word is deemed to be truthful, and officers' testimonies are given more credence than those of the people they target.[69] Third, as a state institution with significant organizational resources, and as the main source of crime news, the police enjoy a privileged relationship with the media.[70]

MODES OF KNOWLEDGE PRODUCTION

To challenge the epistemic power of the police, social movements often seek to produce their own data about policing practices and the inequalities they generate. Producing knowledge raises a series of dilemmas. Should activists rely on dominant ways of knowing, at the risk of reproducing existing blind spots, or develop alternative epistemologies, and risk remaining inaudible in the policy and media fields? Is it better to rely on those who already enjoy high credibility such as scholars, or to try and elevate the voices and analyses of policing victims who are discredited? Given limited resources, which aspect of policing should their knowledge projects focus on, the most common practices like identity checks, or the most serious like police killings? How should they measure racial inequalities in a context where "races don't exist"?

As feminist and critical race scholars have shown, how knowledge is made matters.[71] Assumptions about the nature of social problems influence the questions asked, the actors and dynamics investigated, and those that remain out of the scope of inquiry.[72] Knowledge claims are always partial and situated understandings of the world; they convey the interests and values of their producers, the methodological and conceptual tools available to them, and the knowledge cultures of their time.[73]

Yet, while existing studies show that social movements use a wide range of approaches to produce knowledge—from making alliances with scholars, or becoming "lay experts," to developing counterhegemonic forms of knowledge production rooted in experiences of oppression[74]—less attention has been paid to comparing the potential and limitations of different approaches. One exception is Marcelo Hoffman's *Militant Acts*, which studies activist investigations in Marxist struggles, and compares questionnaires, interviews, fact-finding missions, and the solicitations of individual narratives from workers.[75] The author suggests that these research projects, which were initiated by political leaders, struggled to produce useful informational content, but that they contributed to the formation political subjectivity among workers.

Building on and expanding this work, *The Police, Activists, and Knowledge* examines how activist groups' approaches to knowledge production matter, not only for the formation of political subjectivity among the oppressed, but also for how movement actors construct a shared understanding of who they are and what they stand for, and for their influence on the political, media, and judicial conversations. I include the full range of research practices social movements engage in, from experiential and place-based knowledge produced by the oppressed, to fact-finding missions and NGO reports, to scientific studies conducted in alliance with scholars, as long as the research is generated through the collection and analysis of empirical data with the goal of promoting social change.[76] Rather than assuming a clear dichotomy between academic and activist research, I examine the degree to which knowledge produced within movements endorses or challenges the dominant paradigms of academic knowledge.[77]

To compare different approaches and examine their implications, I propose the concept of *modes of knowledge production*. Each mode of knowledge production has four features: (1) the identities of knowers: who is deemed legitimate to produce knowledge; (2) the research questions: what issues do knowledge projects seek to investigate; (3) the knowledge practices: what data is collected, where and how; (4) the analytical lenses: how knowers interpret and make sense of their empirical findings.[78]

Part II of the book shows that the mode of knowledge production differed significantly between the three coalitions studied, from data produced by scholars using quantitative methods, to community-led fact-finding projects based on victim testimonies, to victims analyzing their own experiences to build collective, situated knowledge. These differences mattered for how coalitions negotiated a shared discourse about who they are, what they stand for, and how to achieve it. The profile of knowers, the research questions they asked, the type of data collected, where, when, and how it was collected, and how it was interpreted, all contributed to shaping the scope of the empirical claims produced. They determined the actors, dynamics, and practices that were highlighted, and those that remained out of the scope of inquiry.

The truth claims generated, in turn, changed the power dynamics between movement actors. I found that the way activists work through conflicts over framing (how the problem is defined), representation (who can speak in the name of the movement), and tactics (what should be done)[79] is not just a function of their political orientations and strategic preferences.[80] It is also inextricably enmeshed with their modes of knowledge production. Decisions about who can produce knowledge, what questions they should investigate, and how they will collect and analyze data, map onto broader debates about who should speak in the name of the movement, what they can credibly say, and how they should say it. The data produced can provide those whose preferred frames were substantiated with additional leverage in framing negotiations. It can also change how movement actors strategically adapt to the context in which they operate. When research projects uncover new facts, activists and lawyers may reevaluate which claims might resonate in specific contexts and feel emboldened to endorse more radical claims. Thus, knowledge production is an important site where questions about framing, representation, and tactics are worked through. Table 0.2 summarizes these findings.

EPISTEMIC WORK

Once they have produced evidence, movement actors work to disseminate, leverage, and mobilize it in the media, policy, and judicial arenas. As sociologist Michael Rodríguez-Muñiz argues, data does not speak for itself, it must be made to speak. To turn empirical claims into political claims, movements must curate data through a work of emphasis and selection of the data collected, qualify it through interpreting the data and charging it with meaning, and narrate it by inscribing it into broader narratives about the past, present, and future.[81]

My analysis suggests that, in addition to the work of selection, qualification, and curation, activists must translate and transpose the knowledge they produce to make it legible to court actors, politicians, and journalists. Advocating for policy and judicial change requires not only engaging in the political work of mobilizing constituents and enrolling allies, and in the legal work of developing new legal arguments and garnering media attention around lawsuits. It also involves *epistemic work* to introduce activists' knowledge claims in the legal and political fields, bolster their cred-

TABLE 0.2 Three coalitions, three modes of knowledge production.

	Racial profiling campaign	Neighborhood mobilization	Truth and Justice movement
Mode of knowledge production	*Quantitative*	*Grounded*	*Liberation*
Knowers	Scholars	Youth professionals, lawyers	Families of victims
Research questions	Do officers disproportionately target certain groups?	What happens during interactions between the police and local youth?	What happened in the lethal police encounter? Why is it difficult to hold officers accountable?
Knowledge practices	Observations of police stops; quantitative analysis	Collect victim and witness testimonies and material evidence	Personal experiences compiled and compared across families
Analytical lens(es)	Legal	Legal and social work	Historical and structural
Truth claim	Police officers disproportionately target Blacks and Arabs	Officers routinely harass and assault racialized youth, based on institutional policies	The police kill and the judiciary protects them from accountability

Source: Magda Boutros.

ibility, and make an argument for their relevance to legal and political debates.

In part III of the book, I show that the type of data the coalitions introduced in legal proceedings, and the strategies they developed to translate them into legal evidence, shaped the legal questions they could raise, the narratives they were able to promote around these cases, and the way their claims were received by court actors and the media. Similarly, the pathways to credibility[82] that each group took to gain access to the political arena shaped how their discourse was translated and transposed in policy debates, the counterarguments that opponents developed, and, ultimately, the way in which they transformed the terms of the political debate about policing and inequality.

Antiracialism and Antiracism

One of the goals of this book is to examine how activist groups conceptualize and articulate the role of race and racism in policing, in a country where racial categories are deemed illegitimate and dangerous. France's antiracialist ideology is founded on the idea that, to achieve equality, the state must eradicate racial categorization by restricting the collection of data and prohibiting the use of racial categories.

In this context, there are ongoing debates over whether, and how, we should measure racial inequalities. Since the 1990s, there has been a controversy within the social sciences over the legitimacy of producing statistical data about race and ethnicity.[83] Some scholars argue that racial statistics reify racial categories, essentialize racial differences, and contribute to an identitarian shift that downplays what they perceive as the primary factor of inequality: social class.[84] Others insist that collecting data on race and ethnicity is a necessary part of any investigation of inequalities, and essential to produce legal evidence in discrimination cases.[85]

Among scholars invested in studying racial inequalities, there are also disagreements over how to name and define the problem, and how to measure it—debates that are echoed in the movement against racialized policing. Some endorse the legal language of *discrimination*,[86] which emphasizes differential treatment on the basis of race. Others promote concepts such as *systemic discrimination* or *institutional racism*[87] to point to institutional policies and practices that lead to unequal outcomes, regardless of individual attitudes. And others still promote the term *state racism*,[88] arguing that the French state produces structural inequalities by constructing the figure of the racialized "internal enemy." Each of these racial conceptualizations[89] requires different methodologies to study and measure racism.

Throughout the book, I examine how movement actors carved ways of measuring, capturing, and analyzing how policing reproduces racial inequalities, in a "race-blind" context. My analysis shows that, while antiracialism certainly makes it difficult to make race and its effects visible, it does not make it impossible. Each of the three coalitions I studied found a way to produce evidence of the way race and racism shape policing practices in France. Importantly, I find that their modes of knowledge production mattered for how they negotiated a shared understanding of police racism. It shaped their ability to push beyond the "bad apples" narrative (some cops are racist) and toward an analysis of the institutional, systemic, and structural dimensions of police racism.

While the book focuses on how movement actors conceptualize and articulate what racism is, I must also clarify my own use of the term. Building on critical scholarship on both sides of the Atlantic,[90] I use *racism* to refer to a power structure in which some groups are deemed unwelcome, undeserving, or inherently troublesome on the basis of their phenotype, ancestry, or country of origin, and in which these processes of racialization produce social hierarchies and spatial inequalities. Racism operates through multiple overlapping mechanisms, including individual prejudice, racist ideologies, institutional racism, and historical legacies of slavery, colonialism, and genocide that continue to influence where different racialized groups live and how much wealth they can accumulate. Racism works in interaction with other systems of oppression based on class, gender, sexuality, and age, in ways that are historically contingent and changing.

In contemporary France, processes of racialization associate Frenchness with Whiteness, a category that lumps together ideas about European ancestry, Christian culture, and Western civilization. People with non-European ancestry are racialized based on their phenotype, assumed origin, or religion, and described variously as Black, African, Arab, Maghrebi, Muslim, Roma, Travelers, or as descended from immigration or diversity (*issus de l'immigration ou de la diversité*).[91] These racial categories do not refer to inherent biological or cultural distinctions between groups of humans, but they nevertheless shape people's position in the social hierarchy. Said otherwise, "race" may not be real, but it has real consequences on people's lives.

Studying and Comparing Activist Groups

When I started this research project, my goal was to understand the potential and limitations of various models of activism against abusive policing; top-down versus bottom-up movements, reformist versus radical approaches. I wanted to examine the trade-offs of various approaches, what each can achieve in terms of political and social change, their limitations, and whether the coexistence of expert-led reformist efforts and community-led radical action was an asset or a hurdle for the cause. To answer those questions, I sought to compare activist groups that adopted different approaches.

I decided to conduct an ethnography, which means that I immersed myself within the groups I wanted to study. For twenty-four months, between 2016 and 2018, I became an active member of three activist coalitions that were engaged in campaigns, political advocacy, litigation, and research on issues of racial profiling, police violence, and impunity.

I started by joining two groups: the campaign against racial profiling, which exemplified expert-led, top-down activism geared toward reformist change, and the Truth and Justice movement, which is a victim-centered, bottom-up movement built on protest action. A few months into my fieldwork, I was introduced to the coalition working against police harassment in the twelfth arrondissement of Paris, which I decided to incorporate in my study as a third model, a neighborhood-based mobilization effort bringing together local actors and outside experts in an effort to transform local policing practices.

For the two years of my fieldwork, I was embedded in the three groups. In the racial profiling campaign, I became a member of the coalition that led the campaign and an unpaid intern for one of the local NGOs that participated in it. In the neighborhood mobilization, I joined the local collective that was created to support the teenagers in their lawsuit against the police. And in the Truth and Justice movement, I was a member of a collective of families of victims that organized national-level events and meetings bringing together families from different parts of France.

Like the knowledge projects I examine in this book, my study is shaped by my epistemological approach—my identity as a knower, the questions I ask, the knowledge practices I engage in, and the analytical lenses I use to interpret findings. I am a French citizen "of immigrant origin," as we are often called—both my parents are Egyptian, and my family moved to France when I was a child. As such, I have experienced racialization from a young age. However, I was shielded from much of the violence and social exclusion that most people from North African and sub-Saharan Africa are subject to in France. My family's class privilege meant that we didn't live in working-class neighborhoods and we went to schools where most kids came from privileged backgrounds. My Christian family name protected me from the widespread Islamophobia that others face. And my Egyptian background meant that the racism I faced was mostly exoticizing rather than deprecating, in contrast to immigrants from former French colonies such as Algeria, Tunisia, or Morocco.

My social location in French society influenced how I built relationships with various actors during my fieldwork. With NGO workers and lawyers, I shared a similar class background and a familiarity with the world of NGOs, which helped me be rapidly included and trusted. With some grassroots groups, my status as a North African immigrant and my participation in the Egyptian revolution granted me legitimacy and led people to welcome my presence and my research. However, for others, my middle-class upbringing and my status as a sociologist fostered a certain distrust. Some *quartiers populaires* activists explained that they were—understandably—wary of sociologists exploiting poor racial minority lives to build their careers, without giving back to the communities that provided them with their time and expertise. To address this, I made sure to spend as much time as possible participating in the events organized by each group, and to help wherever I could. I volunteered to take meeting minutes, to do background research and write internal memos, to help draft reports to funders, or to translate material into English. I also made sure that, during closed-door meetings, I only took notes when everybody present agreed with my presence as a researcher studying the movement.

Overall, I attended over 150 meetings, events, workshops, and protests. At each of those events, I took quick notes, either on my phone or on a notepad, which I typed and completed at the end of the day. To complement my ethnographic observations, I conducted over 100 interviews with active members of these groups, including NGO workers, grassroots activists, victims of police abuses, lawyers, and researchers. I interviewed the most central actors several times over two years. After completing fieldwork in 2018, I regularly checked in with my interlocutors and did follow-up interviews with the most prominent actors until 2023.

I also observed three trial hearings in cases that were initiated by the groups I studied: the civil law case against the state for racial profiling, the trial of the police unit accused of discriminatory and violent harassment against teenagers in the twelfth arrondissement of Paris, and the trial of the policeman who shot and killed Amine Bentounsi in 2012. These observations, along with interviews of lawyers and plaintiffs in these cases, and an analysis of the case files, provide the foundation for my analysis of the legal mobilization efforts discussed in chapter 5. In addition, I conducted a systematic analysis of several types of documents, including research reports published by the coalitions, political debates (in the Senate and General Assembly), and media coverage of policing issues in mainstream outlets. These data provide the basis of my analysis of the movement's influence on the political and public debate, in chapter 6.

This project did not start with an interest in activist knowledge production; it is a theme that emerged inductively from my ethnography. As I spent time with each group, I realized that, while police opacity and antiracialism represented obstacles for all three coalitions, people addressed these obstacles differently. The ways in which each group went about producing evidence seemed to matter for how they negotiated a shared understanding of who they are, what they stand for, and how to achieve it, and for their influence in the media, courts, and political arena.

The method of comparative ethnography was particularly well-suited for analyzing the implications and trade-offs of various modes of knowledge production. Ethnographic fieldwork, with its capacity to produce nuanced and textured data, allowed me to understand the complex logics, relations, and negotiations that led each activist coalition to settle on a mode of knowledge production and to negotiate shared frames. Added to this deep dive into each group, the comparative design helped me uncover the mechanisms through which modes of knowledge production shaped activists' discourse, strategies, and outcomes. While existing studies tend to focus on different approaches separately—either bottom-up initiatives to reverse the surveillance gaze and watch the police, or top-down research led by professionalized NGOs and scholars—my comparative design allows me to examine the coexistence, within the same movement, of various knowledge practices, and to analyze how their cumulative effect shapes the terms of the debate about policing and inequalities.

In the book, I quote interlocutors who are renowned public figures with their real names; for everybody else, I use pseudonyms (whenever I do, I say so in an endnote). When I describe my interlocutors, I often mention their national origin, skin color, or ethnicity, but I should note that I didn't ask interviewees how they identify in racial terms, since some people might find this question offensive in France. Sometimes, people spontaneously talked about their racial identity, sometimes they implicitly did, and some explicitly refused to self-categorize in any given racial or ethnic group. When I write that someone is White, Black, or Arab, it is based on how they are perceived based on their phenotype, name, or country of origin. I use the term *racialized people* to describe groups that are assigned a nonwhite racial identity, as this term best describes the process through which some groups are otherized based on their ascribed race.

Chapters Overview

Part I, "Police Power, Knowledge, and Ignorance," argues that, to understand why it's so difficult to contest racialized policing, and what it takes to do so, we must pay attention to the epistemic power relation between law enforcement and their most common targets. Chapter 1, "The Epistemic Power of the Police," starts with the uprising that followed the deaths of teenagers Zyed Benna and Bouna Traoré during a police intervention in 2005, to illustrate how, until the mid-2000s, the police used their epistemic power to maintain the issue of racialized police violence out of the public debate. I discuss three mechanisms that provide the police with significant epistemic power: their control of the production and nonproduction of official data on crime, safety, and policing practices; the presumption of credibility they enjoy; and their privileged access to the media.

Part II, "Producing Knowledge," examines each of the three activist coalitions in turn, analyzing how they produced knowledge, and the implications of different methods for how they grappled with conflicts over framing, representation, and tactics.

Chapter 2, "Discriminatory Stops and Racist Cops," focuses on the campaign against racial profiling, which was led by a coalition of NGOs and lawyers. To produce evidence of racial profiling, NGOs made alliances with scholars to conduct research quantifying racial disparities in police stops (quantitative epistemology). As they planned the study's design, actors debated how to conceptualize racial inequality and its intersection with class and place-based inequalities, questions that reflected broader debates among campaign actors about how to talk about race in the French context. I show that the way they addressed these questions, and the strengths and limitations of the data they produced, led campaign leaders to develop a public discourse about police discrimination, which was defined primarily as the behavior of biased officers.

Chapter 3, "Police Harassment and the Making of Undesirables," turns to the neighborhood mobilization in the twelfth arrondissement of Paris, which was led by local community actors, with the support of lawyers and NGOs. Coalition actors produced knowledge by documenting the lived experiences of police targets in the neighborhood, while making space for a variety of situated analyses of these experiences (grounded epistemology). This allowed them to shed light on a broad range of abusive policing practices, from discriminatory stops to physical and sexual violence, and to emphasize their routine, repeated nature. It also helped them develop an analysis of police harassment that went beyond a focus on police and highlighted how local conflicts over the use of public space undergirded the police's abusive practices.

Chapter 4, "Police Assassinate, Judges Exonerate," examines the Truth and Justice movement led by families of victims of police killings. This movement adopted an approach to knowledge production in which those who are usually seen as objects of research to be examined by social scientists come to analyze their own situation as knowing subjects (liberation epistemology). This provided the foundation for families of victims to develop a political consciousness rooted in their lived experiences, and to move away from their initial preference for an "apolitical" discourse and toward a structural analysis of their personal tragedies as embedded in systems of state violence and state racism. It also led them to broaden their investigations beyond policing practices to emphasize the role of the judiciary in maintaining police impunity.

Part III, "Mobilizing Knowledge," examines how the three coalitions worked to disseminate, leverage, and mobilize the knowledge they produced in the media, policy, and judicial arenas, and with what impacts.

Chapter 5, "Constructing Legal Evidence," examines how activist groups turn their knowledge claims into legal evidence. I analyze the epistemic work they engaged in to carve avenues to introduce their data in legal proceedings, bolster its credibility, and make an argument for its relevance. The analysis shows that the coalitions' litigation efforts had a limited effect on expanding legal opportunities for policing victims, but they were instrumental in promoting the movement's claims in the media, including claims about institutional and systemic discrimination, and about the structural factors maintaining de facto impunity for the police.

Chapter 6, "Transforming the Political Debate," traces the way each coalition's discourse was translated and transposed in policy debates, and the counterarguments that opponents developed. I show that the pathways to credibility that actors took to gain access to the political arena shaped the political outcomes of the movement as a whole. The racial profiling campaign, which partnered with credentialed scholars to produce statistics, helped the movement quickly gain access to the political field, but it also contributed to a public debate that framed the issue as a problem of biased officers, which can be solved through measures to identify and discipline individual misconduct. In contrast, the Truth and Justice movement worked to elevate the voices of victims of racialized policing and turn them into unavoidable political interlocutors, a pathway that helped them introduce a structural analysis of racialized police violence in the political arena, but also resulted in a fierce backlash and a highly polarized debate.

The conclusion summarizes the book's key arguments through an analysis of the public debate that surrounded the nationwide uprising triggered by the killing of Nahel Merzouk in 2023. While the core chapters compare the strengths and trade-offs of different modes of knowledge production, the conclusion discusses how the adoption of different epistemologies mattered for the movement as a whole. I show that the combination of quantitative, grounded, and liberation epistemologies led to significant changes in the epistemic power dynamic between the police and their targets. By the early 2020s, the movement was able to draw on independently produced statistics about policing and inequalities, thus challenging the police's quasi-monopoly over the production of data on law enforcement practices. It had bolstered its ability to document policing practices, including through citizen footage (the strengths and limitations of which I discuss briefly). And it had amplified the voices of victims and turned them into unavoidable political interlocutors. This allowed movement actors to place the question of racial inequality and oppression on the agenda, a success that was met with a racist backlash. Drawing on examples from other contexts, the conclusion also highlights the main lessons advocates and policy makers should keep in mind when formulating strategies of action or reform proposals that involve generating data.

Part I

POLICE POWER, KNOWLEDGE, AND IGNORANCE

ONE

The Epistemic Power of the Police

On October 27, 2005, teenagers Zyed Benna, Bouna Traoré, and Muhittin Altun, were walking home with friends after a game of soccer when they saw five police cars approach. The boys lived in the working-class Parisian suburb Clichy-sous-Bois, and all three were from immigrant families, respectively from Tunisia, Mauritania, and Turkey. When the group realized the officers were after them, they started running away. This was Ramadan, the holy month in Islam, and there was little time left before the children's families expected them at home to break the fast. "We didn't want to be stopped for an identity check," Muhittin later explained, "I've been stopped before and it didn't go well. We wanted to go home, after all, we had done nothing wrong!"[1] With the police on their heels, the three friends climbed over a wall and hid inside an electric substation. From there, they could hear sirens and police dogs nearby, so they waited. A few minutes later, an electric discharge hit them, killing Zyed and Bouna on the spot, and seriously injuring Muhittin.

That night, urban rebellions erupted in Clichy-sous-Bois with young people burning cars and damaging property to express their anger at Zyed and Bouna's death. The anger intensified after Interior Minister Nicolas Sarkozy made public statements. The right-wing politician, known for his tough-on-crime rhetoric, announced a zero-tolerance policy against urban violence and claimed that no investigation was needed into the teenagers' death since the police had done nothing wrong. Three days later, as the revolt carried on, riot police fired a tear-gas grenade that landed by the entrance of a mosque during prayer time, leading to the emergency evacuation of dozens of people. Sarkozy once again defended the police, causing the rebellion to expand to other neighborhoods. Within days, it became the largest and longest urban uprising in France's recent history, lasting for three weeks and expanding to nearly three hundred cities.

During this time, mainstream media coverage and politicians' statements focused exclusively on the violence of the uprising, without discussing the police actions that triggered it. Politicians on the right and on the left were unanimous in condemning "urban violence" and in calling for a strong police response to quell it.[2] When the causes of the revolt were discussed, two main explanations were offered. On one hand, right-wing politicians used racialized tropes to blame immigrant cultures, which were deemed incompatible with French Republican values. They denounced polygamous families from sub-Saharan Africa unable to discipline their children and the growing influence of radical Islam in housing projects. This view was summarized by Sarkozy when he said "there are more problems for the son of Black Africans or North Africans than for the son of a Swede or Dane or Hungarian, because the culture, because polygamy, because the social origins, mean there are more difficulties."[3] On the other hand, a few voices on the left criticized this discourse, arguing that while the rioters' violence was "unacceptable, inadmissible, intolerable," it illustrated the government's policy failures. They criticized the abandonment of community policing and insufficient public investment in low-income neighborhoods, which, they argued, led to increased levels of crime and violence.[4] Despite the differences between the two discourses, both framed the event primarily as a problem of urban violence and criminality in the *banlieues* (low-income suburbs).

Absent from the mainstream conversation were the voices and analyses of the participants in the uprising. The few journalists and sociologists who interviewed them found that the trigger was not only Zyed and Bouna's death, but also the authorities' denial of any wrongdoing. At a deeper level, people revolted against their daily experiences of humiliation, racism, and discrimination, first and foremost at the hands of the police, but also in schools and in the job market.[5] These grievances were not new. Both mainstream human rights organizations and more radical activists had been organizing against racism, police brutality, and unequal justice since the 1970s.

How, then, can we explain that despite these long-standing mobilizations, and even as France witnessed the largest uprising in its modern history, the issue of racialized policing continued to be ignored in the public and political debate? Existing studies point to weaknesses in the movement against police brutality and racism, such as internal divisions, dearth of resources, dependence on state funding, and an ambivalent support from the political left.[6] While these factors undoubtedly played a role, explanations that focus only on the movement's weaknesses miss a crucial piece of the story: the police's strengths.

I argue that, to understand why it's so difficult for people contesting racialized policing to make their grievances heard, we must pay attention to the ability of law enforcement agencies to control what we know, and what remains unknown, about policing practices. During the 2005 uprising, the Interior Ministry released daily statistics on the damage caused by the "riots" and the police actions taken in response. For two weeks, every day, TV, radio, and written news reported how many cars were burned and buildings vandalized the previous night, how many officers were deployed, and the number of arrests the police made. On the other hand, no data were available about police violence during or before the rebellion. At the time, the police released no systematic data on police use of force or firearms, on police-caused injuries or deaths, or on the number of complaints filed against police officers. Thus, while journalists were provided with day-by-day statistics about the rioters' violence, no information was available on police violence. This helped the government portray participants as irrationally violent rioters, while concealing the fact that police brutality triggered the revolt.

The police's ability to control what is known and what remains hidden is what philosophers and sociologists have called *epistemic power*. In a social structure where the capacity to produce knowledge is unequally distributed, epistemic power refers to the ability to influence what others know, and what they don't—or can't—know.[7] In the relation of power between the police and ordinary citizens, the police hold significant epistemic power: they are better able to generate truth claims that are widely believed, and to cultivate strategic ignorance to escape blame and accountability.[8]

This chapter starts by describing the three mechanisms that undergird the epistemic power of the police: their control over the production and nonproduction of data on crime and policing practices, the assumption of credibility that is granted to police officers, and their privileged access to the media.[9] Then I show how, in France, police forces and government representatives have relied on this power from the 1970s to the mid-2000s to deny, dismiss, and discredit activist claims about racial profiling, police brutality, and impunity.

Control Over the Production and Nonproduction of Data

The police are the primary agency producing and disseminating official statistics about crime and disorder. This provides them with significant control over how these issues are understood and debated. As sociologist Andy Clarno and his colleagues argue, "policing in the twenty-first century operates through the collection and circulation of data about individuals, networks, neighborhoods and more."[10] Law enforcement agencies use stops, arrests, and surveillance technology to compile databases and maps that help determine targets for deployment, heightened surveillance, and aggressive policing. Because these databases rely on racialized and classed policing practices, they "transform racialized discourses about crime, terror, and belonging into 'facts' that take the form of a permanent record."[11] By tagging people with labels like "gang member" or "terrorist," they reify the association between some racialized groups and criminality.

At the same time, law enforcement agencies control the collection and publication of data about policing practices. They get to determine what is measured, how it is measured, and what is made publicly available. This allows them to disseminate a carefully selected set of data, which helps portray the police as active and efficient in combating crime, while maintaining potentially contentious practices out of public view. In France, there are few legal obligations of transparency for law enforcement, and in practice, police forces maintain a high degree of opacity. For example, although identity checks are primary policing tools,[12] the police publish no systematic data on them, and it remains unknown how many stops they conduct, where, against whom, for what motives, and with what outcomes. Similarly, until 2018, no systematic counts were published of officers' use of firearms, or of the number of people injured or killed during police interventions, making it difficult to assess the nature and scope of police use of force. In contrast, the monthly crime statistics bulletin includes a specific category of reported "violence against a police agent." Interior ministers regularly draw on these numbers to argue that police officers need more weapons and stronger legal protections.

In addition to their control over the production of official statistics, the two national police forces are notoriously resistant to external scrutiny, even by governmental watchdog organizations.[13] The National Commission for Police Ethics, CNDS, regularly complained "about the persistence and recurrence of practices aiming to limit or obstruct investigations or monitoring of police actions," deploring "a tendency to deal with all problems exclusively internally."[14] In its 2010 annual report, the state agency noted, for the tenth consecutive year, the recurrence of instances in which officers refused to record complaints against their peers, failed to grant people injured during arrest with access to medical care, and refused to register their allegations of police violence in official records. The commission also noted a worrying trend whereby pieces of evidence it needed for its investigations, such as surveillance camera footage, tended to disappear.

Police opacity is further maintained by an institutional culture of secrecy.[15] Officers are subject to a rule according to which they must remain loyal to the institution in their public statements (*devoir de réserve*).[16] In practice, whistleblowers who speak up about the abuses of power, racism, and sexism they experience or witness within the institution routinely face harassment and threats by colleagues and supervisors. Many are disciplined, demoted, or pressured to quit.[17]

Academic researchers too, face restrictions when they seek to study policing practices. Research on policing is heavily dependent on state funding, and by extension, on governmental priorities.[18] Until the early 1980s, while the discipline of policing studies was blooming across the Atlantic, French law enforcement "remained closed to public research: no researcher obtained authorization to conduct observations or systematic interviews in a police service."[19] The centralization of French police forces played a key role in stifling research, as scholars must obtain permission from the central administration of the Interior Ministry, which keeps tight control over which researchers are given access, and which spaces they are granted access to. In the early 1980s, when the left came to power, some research institutes on crime and criminal justice gained a measure of autonomy from the government and launched a small but active scholarship on policing, which took off in the 1990s. However, this research field remained, in large part, dependent on state commissions and funding.[20]

Hence, while a fledgling field of policing studies emerged in France, key questions of interest to activists remained unexamined. Most notably, until the mid-2000s, academic research on police use of force was extremely limited. Researchers rarely gained access to internal police statistics on the use of force or firearms, and only under public pressure following particularly mediatized cases of police brutality.[21] When Fabien Jobard published his book on the topic in 2002, he noted, "nothing is known about the situations in which force is used: we don't know when it occurs, or what happens when it occurs."[22] His study relied on interviews with formerly incarcerated men, some police records he managed to gain access to, and an analysis of press coverage and case law regarding police brutality cases. While it shed light on the sociolegal conditions that fostered police violence, the lack of systematic records made it impossible to estimate the prevalence, distribution, and circumstances of police use of force, or to study the factors driving it.

It was also difficult for scholars to study racial disparities in policing. The country's antiracialist ideology, which deems racial categories essentializing and dangerous, limited the possibilities of measuring racial inequalities in policing. While studies can measure the prevalence of racist *beliefs* among police officers (those studies that do find high rates of racist stereotypes[23]), measuring whether police *actions* are racially discriminatory is more difficult. Until the twenty-first century, René Lévy's 1987 book *Du suspect au coupable* (From Suspect to Guilty) was the only empirical study that examined this question. Lévy had obtained access to over five hundred records of arrests in Paris between 1979 and 1981. Despite the legal ban on the collection of racial data, these records included informal racial classifications used by the police, who categorized people into three "types": European type, North African type, and African type. Lévy's analysis showed that police disproportionately target people labeled North African, and once arrested, disproportionately refer them to prosecutors, even after controlling for the type of offense, criminal record, employment status, and family situation. He concluded, "The cause of these disparities resides in selective policing practices that take place when the police take on cases, as well as during crucial decisions they make afterwards."[24] Some scholars criticized René Lévy's statistical measurements,[25] but the difficulties researchers encountered in accessing police records meant that, for thirty years, no other scholar produced a quantitative analysis that could confirm or disprove his findings.

The 2005 uprising triggered renewed academic interest in the question of racialized policing. One group of scholars relied on interviews with marginalized youth to argue that policing practices are racially biased. They noted that Black and Arab young men in low-income neighborhoods perceive brutal policing practices as racist, and that a disproportionate number of people who complain of police misconduct have immigrant origins.[26] Others countered that existing data were insufficient to establish racial bias. In the absence of quantitative data that could adjudicate whether the police target people based on their perceived race, or on other factors (behavior, social class, place of residence), they considered that racial discrimination in policing was not empirically established.[27] The question continued to divide the academic field.

PRESUMPTION OF CREDIBILITY

The second mechanism of epistemic power is the presumed credibility of police testimonies and records.[28] In France as in other Western countries, the police are at the top of the hierarchy of credibility, the "established status order in which knowledge of truth and the right to be heard are not equally distributed."[29] They are widely assumed to be reliable and trustworthy, whereas the groups most targeted by the police—marginalized and racialized youth—are at the bottom, routinely stigmatized as criminal and untrustworthy.[30] To borrow the terms of philosopher Miranda Fricker, the police benefit from *credibility excess*, they are granted more credibility than the average citizen, whereas the groups most targeted by the police suffer from *credibility deficit*, in that they are given less credibility than others due to race and class prejudice.[31] This imbalance in the perceived credibility of the police and their targets means that, when law enforcement actions are contested, police narratives are more likely to be heard and believed.

In November 2005, as the uprising intensified and spread across the country, police and government representatives persistently denied the officers' responsibility in the deaths of Zyed Benna and Bouna Traoré.

Nicolas Sarkozy insisted on national television that the police were not pursuing the youth and had been back at the station a long time before they entered the electric substation.[32] While left-wing politicians criticized Sarkozy's zero-tolerance rhetoric against the rioters, none challenged the official narrative about what happened, and it quickly became the taken-for-granted account of the teenagers' death in the mainstream media. Journalists did not seek to talk to witnesses.

It was only after sustained pressure by the uprising that the surviving victim, Muhittin, was interviewed by the local paper, *Le Parisien*, eighteen days after the incident. His account contradicted the official narrative. He remembered that, after his friend Bouna said that the police were running after them, "I looked back and I saw an officer come out of a police car with a Flash-ball. Before leaving the park, I turned back again and saw the officers running after us. They were less than 15 meters away." The three friends ran toward the electric substation and went in. "We stayed there for about thirty minutes. I wanted to get out, to go home. After all, we had done nothing wrong! But we heard voices and [police] dogs. And then, the electricity hit us."[33] Despite this testimony, politicians and mainstream media continued to rely on the police's narrative of events, considered more credible than that of the victim.

The assumption that police officers are credible is not just a social convention, it is also a legal rule. In French law, sworn police officers are assumed to tell the truth. Police records are assumed to be truthful (*le procès-verbal fait foi*), and courts have ruled that, in general, "the testimony of a police officer . . . is more credible than that of a drug trafficker," including in police misconduct cases.[34]

The legal assumption of credibility represents a formidable obstacle to police accountability. In practice, police violence is only considered illegitimate when a narrow set of conditions are met.[35] The victim must be deemed credible, which in practice means have no prior contact with the criminal justice system. The police abuse must be of remarkable magnitude. There must be external evidence, such as scientific evidence or credible witnesses who, like the victim, have no prior contacts with the police or courts. And it must be established beyond a doubt that the police acted without facing any danger whatsoever. The last condition can easily be manipulated by police officers who can file a complaint against the victim for offending and rebelling against a police officer. Because the social spaces where the police are more likely to abuse their powers are also the spaces where victims and witnesses are less likely to be deemed credible, the vast majority of police abuses escape accountability. Existing data suggest that over two-thirds of cases of police-involved deaths never go to trial, and among those that do, only one in seven ends with a police officer being incarcerated.[36]

The rule about officers' presumed credibility allowed the policemen involved in Zyed and Bouna's deaths to escape accountability. Ten years after the tragedy, two of the seventeen officers involved in the intervention faced trial for failing to assist persons in danger. Contradicting Sarkozy's account, the investigation revealed that the officers had seen the teens run toward the electric site. In radio calls, one of the officers informed his colleagues, "two individuals are located. They are climbing over the wall to go on the EDF [electric] site. We should surround the area." He added "if they enter the EDF site, they'll be dead meat."[37] Nevertheless, the officers were acquitted, based on their claim that they did not know for certain that the victims had entered the electric site.

PRIVILEGED ACCESS TO THE MEDIA

To be sure, police accounts are not universally believed, and many people—especially in marginalized communities—understand that officers can lie to escape accountability. But even then, the police maintain an epistemic advantage in that they have privileged access to the media, especially in comparison to the groups they target the most. During the uprising, Interior Minister Nicolas Sarkozy, who called himself "France's first cop," was omnipresent in the media. At the same time, the voices of the uprising participants, and of youth living in *quartiers populaires* more generally, were conspicuously absent.

As Alfred Archer and his colleagues argue, the ability to capture public attention is an important source of epistemic power:

> While attention may not boost the speaker's credibility, it does provide a platform for one's testimony to be heard. This is crucial, as it does not matter how credible someone would be perceived if he or she does not have a means of being heard in the first place. Having a platform provides new opportunities to influence what people think, believe, and know.[38]

Police agencies have professional, well-resourced communication teams, who work with journalists on a daily basis to promote news stories that portray law enforcement in a positive light.[39] The dependence of journalists on the police for crime news provides the police with leverage vis-à-vis the media. As media scholars have shown, police forces often promise access to their sources and exclusive stories in exchange for positive coverage, and conversely, they can "blacklist" some media platforms if they publish articles critical of the institution.[40]

Political scientist Paul Le Derff studied the media coverage of lethal police interventions in France between 1990 and 2016.[41] He found that only a quarter of all reported cases become salient in the news media (that is, have more than thirteen dispatches from the French Press Association). Among those, most "died out" in the media within four days. When mainstream news outlets did cover cases, they focused on politicians' statements, most of which were about condemning the revolts triggered by police-involved death, or, to a lesser extent, on the judicial investigations into the death. In the media, the voices of families of victims were largely absent.

Le Derff explains this absence through several factors. Families of victims are overwhelmingly poor, racialized people that have limited resources to access the media. It takes most families time to decide to speak publicly about their loss, and by the time they reach out to journalists, the vast majority of cases are no longer in the news cycle. Le Derff's interviews with journalists further reveal that very few of them specialize in covering cases of police violence, and among those that have written multiple pieces, most are satisfied with relying exclusively on institutional sources. The handful of journalists who sought out the testimonies of victims' loved ones faced strong resistance from their editors in chief, who perceived the families to be biased and preferred maintaining good working relationships with their police sources.

The police's privileged access to the media, combined with their control over the production of official data and their presumed credibility, grant the institution significant epistemic power in their relations with racialized and marginalized populations. The next sections examine how, until the late 2000s, the police have relied on this power to deny, dismiss, and discredit activists' claims about racial profiling, police brutality, and impunity.

No Data, No Problem

In France, the police have expansive powers to stop and search individuals, even in the absence of any suspicion. Identity checks were first formalized in a 1981 law, which provided the police with authorization to stop an individual if they have reasons to suspect that he or she committed or is about to commit a crime. Since then, governments on the right and on the left have continuously expanded police powers to stop and search. In 1983, the socialist-dominated Parliament allowed identity checks to prevent a breach of public order, regardless of a person's behavior. In 1993, the right wing added a provision stipulating that police can stop any individuals at the time and place specified in a prosecutor's requisition—a tool that has been used to provide officers with a quasi-permanent authorization to stop any person in *quartiers populaires* and urban centers. In 2001, the socialist government gave the police a blanket authorization to check any person within ten kilometers of state borders.

This continuous expansion of police powers has been criticized by many organizations warning that it increased the risk of abuse and discrimination. One of the groups that voiced its opposition to these legislative reforms was the left-leaning judges' union, Syndicat de la Magistrature. In 2001, as the socialist government was once again extending police powers, the union published a booklet titled "Your Papers! What to do when faced with the police?" (Vos Papiers! Que faire face à la police?).[42] The booklet gave information about people's rights during identity checks, identity verifications, and searches and provided tips about how to contest abusive or discriminatory stops.

The publication immediately drew the ire of two police unions, which took to the press to slam it as an "anti-cop pamphlet." They announced that one hundred police officers had filed a defamation complaint against the author for promoting "serious accusations evidently inspired by hatred and an intention to harm."[43] The unions condemned one sentence in particular, which read "although illegal, discriminatory stops (*contrôles d'identité au faciès*) are common and they are increasing." They called on the Interior minister to take action to protect the reputation of the police, and some police officers protested in front of the Justice Ministry. Right-wing parliamentarians soon echoed the unions' call and asked the government to sue the booklet's authors.[44] Within one week, the Interior minister announced that he, too, was suing the author and publisher of the booklet for defamation against the police.[45]

When the first instance court acquitted them, the government appealed. Reversing the acquittal, the Court of Appeal convicted the author and editor, arguing that they had failed to provide evidence substantiating their claim that racial profiling was widespread and increasing. The defendants had presented several human rights reports detailing multiple instances of racial discrimination in identity checks, but the judges ruled that these studies, which were based on the testimonies of people stopped by the police, "establish neither an increase in discriminatory practices, nor the very significant proportion they allegedly represent."[46] The court required that the defendants provide statistical data demonstrating that a large and increasing proportion of all identity checks are based on discriminatory criteria. Given the restrictions on accessing police data, and the ban on racial statistics, such data did not exist.

The conviction of the author and publisher were eventually quashed by the Court of Cassation in 2008, but by then, the government had reached its political goals. It had appeased police unions, maintained public support for policies expanding police powers, and effectively shut down any political debate about racial profiling.

This episode was not isolated. For decades, governments on the right and the left successfully kept the issue of racial profiling out of the political debate by arguing that there was no evidence to support allegations of racial disparities. Between 1980 and 2005, racial profiling—commonly referred to as *contrôles au faciès* (appearance-based stops)—was raised in Parliament only four times, always in the context of bills that broadened police powers to conduct identity checks. Every time, members of the far-left opposition raised concerns that expanding powers would lead to racial profiling. Interior ministers always gave the same response: "there is no *contrôles au faciès*, police officers respect the law, and if mistakes were made, they would be firmly disciplined."[47] In the absence of any data on identity checks, and given the restrictions on collecting racial data for research, opposition voices had no evidence to substantiate their claims and push against governmental denial. The debate ended there. Thus, until the late 2000s, the police and government relied on the manufactured ignorance around racial disparities in police stops to deny any institutional practice of racial profiling and shut down attempts to bring up this issue in the political arena.

Dismissing Reports of Police Brutality

In the 1990s and in the first decade of the twenty-first century, several reports documenting cases of excessive use of force and racist abuse by the police were published by human rights organizations and watchdog institutions. For example, Amnesty International published three reports on police violence and accountability in France, in 1994, 2005, and 2009.[48] Based on investigations into dozens of judicial cases of police misconduct, they found evidence of human rights violations, including unlawful killings, excessive use of force, and torture. They argued that the police enjoy "*de facto* impunity," produced and maintained by "gaps or flaws in legislation; reluctance or failure of police, prosecutors and courts to thoroughly investigate and prosecute human rights violations involving law enforcement officials; and sentences which were not commensurate with the gravity of the crime."[49] The reports suggested that racism played an important role in police violence. The victims in nearly all the cases they investigated were of North African or sub-Saharan origin, and many reported explicit racist abuse by officers. In parallel, the National Commission for Police Ethics, CNDS, released annual reports detailing the findings of their investigations into police misconduct complaints. The commission reported receiving increasing numbers of complaints of police violence and warned that they were disproportionately from people of color.[50]

While these reports were generally covered in the media, none led to a political debate about the issue. Only a handful of left-wing politicians brought them up during parliamentary questions to the government, and when they did, government representatives quickly shut down their questions. Every time, Interior ministers on the right and on the left dismissed the reports' findings and argued that, far from being perpetrators of violence, the police were, in fact, facing increasing levels of violence and hatred. They argued that the data that human rights reports relied on—testimonies of police targets and case files—were incomplete and untrustworthy. Instead, they drew on police-produced statistics to make claims about the "truth" of police relations with racialized residents of *quartiers populaires*.

Nicolas Sarkozy's response to a parliamentarian's question in May 2005, a few months before Zyed and Bouna's deaths, is illustrative of this rhetorical strategy. After the watchdog institution CNDS published its annual report for the previous year, a socialist parliamentarian filed the following question to the Interior minister:

> This annual report is marked by an increase in the number of cases examined by the CNDS. In 2004, 97 cases were referred to the commission, compared to 70 in 2003, a 38% increase. The primary victims are youth with immigrant backgrounds in Maghreb or Africa, who are French citizens for 64% of them. Moreover, the feeling of impunity is also an important cause of misconduct, according to the CNDS. . . . In its conclusion, the CNDS study notes, among other things, that "a fracture is occurring, which can lead citizens to doubt that they live in a country operating under the rule of law if they are not treated as such."[51]

The elected official ended by asking the minister what urgent measures he planned on taking to address these issues. In response, Interior Minister Nicolas Sarkozy drew on police statistics to suggest that the police were "on the frontlines, facing multiple forms of violence." The previous year, he stated, "there were 21,723 incidents of violence against police officers (which is a 90.2% increase compared to 1996) and 3,852 officers were injured in the course of their duties."[52] The minister then contrasted these police-produced data to the CNDS data, arguing that, when one compares the number of complaints received by the CNDS to the total number of police interventions, allegations of unlawful violence affected only 0.03% of police interventions.

The minister's argument was flawed in several respects. For one, the claim of a 90% increase was misleading; it hinged on the choice of 1996 as the comparative point, yet available data show that between 2000 and 2004, there was no significant increase of the number of recorded incidents of violence targeting officers.[53] The increase in the late 1990s could signal shifts in the way incidents of violence against police were defined or counted, rather than an actual increase in rates of violence, but parliamentarians had no way of knowing how these statistics were constructed.

In addition, Sarkozy contrasted police-produced data about violence against the police, which represented a comprehensive count of all reported cases, with CNDS-produced data about police violence, which did not capture all the reported cases: victims of police brutality were much more likely to file complaints for police brutality through police stations or prosecutors' offices, as the CNDS was still relatively new and not well known to the public. Yet, the police never released any data on reported cases of police violence, nor did they publish comprehensive statistics on police use of force and firearms, or on the number of people injured or killed during police interventions. Thus, the government drew on police-produced knowledge and police-manufactured ignorance to dismiss the CNDS's claims. Lawmakers, who could only access the data police forces selectively chose to release, had no way to effectively challenge the argument that officers are overwhelmingly victims, not perpetrators, of violence.

What's more, Sarkozy's response relied on the credibility deficit that the police's most common victims suffer, to suggest that nearly all the complaints received by the CNDS were unreliable. He said, "although judicial review of police activities is permanent and diligent, 98% of complaints filed for illegitimate use of force are dismissed by the prosecution."[54] Of course, this statistic could be interpreted as a sign that the police fail to investigate allegations, or that prosecutors are reluctant to charge officers, which would confirm the CNDS' allegations of impunity, but the Interior minister used it to suggest that nearly all allegations of police violence were unfounded, a claim that aligned with the widely held perception that Black and Arab youth are untrustworthy.

The minister also brushed aside claims of racial bias by reminding parliamentarians that the law prohibits the collection of data on race or ethnicity, thus suggesting that claims of racial bias are impossible to prove. Given that parliamentarians had no access to data about the disciplinary judicial proceedings in police misconduct cases, or on racial disparities in police stops, they had no way to counter the minister's interpretation. Once again, the debate ended there.

While Sarkozy was notorious for embracing a tough-on-crime discourse, socialists used the same rhetorical moves when they were in power—drawing on partial and misleading police statistics, and on the credibility deficit of racialized groups—to discredit claims of police brutality and shut down any political debate on the issue. In this way, successive governments could rely on the police's control over the production of

data on crime and public safety, and their opacity around policing practices, to dismiss reports of police violence and prevent the emergence of a
political debate on the issue.

Discrediting Activists

In parallel to the work of human rights organizations and watchdog institutions, grassroots activists from *quartiers populaires* organized against
racialized policing. One of the most active organizations in the 1990s and
early 2000s was the Mouvement de l'immigration et des Banlieues (MIB),
an autonomous group, which developed and disseminated a repertoire
of action for residents of *quartiers populaires* to organize against police
abuses.[55] Whenever an urban revolt erupted following a case of police brutality, MIB activists met with local youth and trained them in organizing
strategies. They taught them to form local "Truth and Justice committees,"
explained how to conduct counterinvestigations to expose the flaws and
inconsistencies in the police narrative of events, how to organize peaceful
protests and sit-ins to pressure the judiciary to indict officers, and how to
garner media attention.

The MIB helped local youth in the Parisian suburb Mantes-la-Jolie
organize following the death of their friend Youssed Khaïf. On June 9,
1991, police officer Pascal Hiblot shot and killed Youssef Khaïf, a twenty-
three-year-old of Algerian origin, as he was driving away from a police
checkpoint. Immediately following the shooting, and without waiting for
the results of the investigation, the authorities claimed that the shots that
killed the young man were fired "in the context of" the death of a policewoman that same night, who was run over by a stolen car escaping the
checkpoint. The official narrative suggested that Youssef Khaïf had been
involved in the killing of the policewoman, and that, when he was shot, he
represented a threat to the officers.

With the support of the MIB, local organizers conducted a counterinvestigation, collecting evidence about the events that led to Khaïf's death.
Their work contradicted the police account. It showed that the victim had
nothing to do with the death of the policewoman, which had happened
thirty minutes before and for which a suspect had already been arrested.
The autopsy further showed that he was shot in the back of the neck and

from a distance, which suggested that Pascal Hiblot was not acting in self-defense.

The MIB struggled to get the results of their investigation covered in mainstream media. They published and disseminated leaflets and spoke about the case in independent, activist-run media, but their analyses were ignored in the mainstream press coverage of the case.

When, ten years later, officer Hiblot finally faced trial, media outlets regained interest in the case. In preparation for the trial, the MIB printed and disseminated 50,000 copies of a leaflet summarizing their investigation; they shared elements of the criminal investigation with journalists; held a sit-in in front of the courtroom; and organized a press conference in which they denounced a "colonial judiciary" granting police a "license to kill."[56] However, even as journalists covered the trial extensively, they mostly ignored the activists' voices. The trial's coverage largely endorsed the police narrative suggesting a link between the policewoman's death and Youssef Khaïf, but the actions and discourse of the activists were absent. Researcher Mogniss Abdallah noted, "the written press and television channels were there . . . [but] no paper covered the public debates around 'colonial justice' [that the MIB organized]."[57]

Not only did the media ignore activists' analyses, they also covered police unions' claims extensively, including statements portraying MIB activists as dangerous terrorists. In most media outlets, union representatives were quoted accusing the MIB of launching a campaign of "anti-police racism." The unions also claimed, without providing any evidence, that flyers were circulating in some neighborhoods calling for violent actions against the police, or even for "jihad" (armed struggle) if the officer was acquitted.[58] Their statements relied on the racist and Islamophobic stereotypes equating Muslims and Arabs with terrorists. In the context of the 9/11 terrorist attacks, mainstream media were particularly receptive to this discourse. The left-wing newspaper *Libération* published a short piece on the sit-ins, in which they mentioned "Intifada," "faces hiding behind red keffiyehs" (the scarves that symbolize solidarity with Palestine) and quoted a police union representative deploring the MIB's "constant delegitimation of Republican institutions."[59] The right-wing newspaper *Le Figaro* noted in a similar spirit, "the 'youth' demanded 'justice,' that is, a tough sentence for the officer, but they don't stop there. The affair degenerates into a pro-

Islamic protest, during which they praised Arab leaders and criticized the Americans."[60] No journalist in mainstream outlets interviewed any of the MIB activists or double-checked the unions' claims.

Despite the stigmatization and delegitimization of the activists, their work helped cast doubts on the police narrative and succeeded in introducing an alternative narrative in the media. When the court acquitted Pascal Hiblot, several TV and press pieces framed the verdict as a denial of justice. In an article titled "A 'Guilty Man' Ultimately Acquitted," *Libération* quoted Youssef Khaïf's mother, saying, "It's a license to kill, I am now certain that there is no justice."[61] An editorial in *Le Monde* titled "One-Way Justice" deplored a verdict that "provides police officers with a blank check for future police violence" and fosters a sense of injustice among youth of the banlieue.[62] One MIB activist recalled:

> We cried when we heard that officer Hiblot was acquitted. We were dismayed. But the 8pm TV news titled "A guilty man acquitted," TF1 and France 2 [TV channels] and *Libération* talked about it. We didn't realize it then, but actually, we had won. . . . It's a victory when the media picks up the writings of [MIB activists] on the basis of the counter-investigation they conducted.[63]

Even though the media had ultimately relied on the activists' counter-investigation, they continued to silence their analysis of colonial justice and to use racist stereotypes to discredit them. The left-wing magazine *Marianne* even suggested that the activists' actions were responsible for the acquittal, writing that the MIB's actions constituted "inadmissible pressure, shocking blackmail, which led to the scandalous verdict," calling it "an attempted assault on justice that led to a breakdown of justice."[64] Thus, even when the MIB's counterinvestigation ended up being picked up by the media, the activists themselves continued to be discredited and delegitimized on the basis of race and class prejudice.

Conclusion

Until the late 2000s, the police were able to counteract most attempts to challenge their discriminatory and violent practices, in large part by relying on their epistemic power. Even when the deaths of Zyed Benna and

Bouna Traoré in 2005 triggered an unprecedented urban uprising that spread across the country, activists and victims struggled to make their claims heard. The police relied on their near monopoly over the production and nonproduction of data about crime and policing; they drew on their assumed credibility; and they leveraged their privileged access to mainstream media, to dismiss and discredit the movement's claims.

Nevertheless, the year 2005 was an important turning point for activism against racialized policing. The deaths of Zyed Benna and Bouna Traoré were a defining moment for a whole generation of activists who came of age during the revolts. Many of the activists involved in the coalitions I study in this book told me that the 2005 revolts were key in building their political consciousness. As one organizer put it, "we're the Zyed and Bouna generation. There's a generation for whom May '68 was a defining moment in their political consciousness, for us it was the 2005 riots."[65] These activists were aware of the obstacle their predecessors faced, namely, the police's power to control what is known and what remains hidden about policing and inequalities. As a result, they invested significant resources in producing their own knowledge to challenge the police's epistemic power. Part II examines how they did this.

Part II

PRODUCING KNOWLEDGE

TWO

Discriminatory Stops and Racist Cops

A few months after the 2005 uprising, the Open Society Justice Initiative (OSJI), an international human rights organization, launched a European program against racial profiling. In an opinion piece published at the start of the program, OSJI's leaders wrote, "Six months after the deaths of two Muslim youths fleeing police sparked riots across France, many European leaders continue to equate security with tough policing of minority communities."[1] This ethnic profiling is a recipe for disaster, they continued, because it engenders feelings of humiliation and resentment among targeted groups and breeds violence. To them, changing these practices required monitoring the performance of law enforcement agencies, "to foster accountability and provide a foundation of knowledge on which to build policy."[2] Yet, in their analysis, the absence of racial or ethnic statistics in most European countries made such monitoring complicated and facilitated "Europe's conscious avoidance of racism."[3] Their program aimed to change that.

At the time, OSJI, a member of one of the world's largest philanthropist organizations (Open Society Foundations), had been working on promoting antidiscrimination laws and norms in Europe for years.[4] Senior staff felt that continental Europe was lagging behind in the fight against racial profiling, in comparison to the United States and the United Kingdom. One of them explained to me, "That's not to say it wasn't a known issue, it was extremely well-known in the affected communities. . . . But it was not being systematically worked on [by civil society], because the challenges of doing so are so very great."[5] In her analysis, there were two main factors preventing European civil society from addressing racial profiling. Their countries were resistant to the collection of racial and ethnic statistics, and NGOs were largely dependent on state funding, which meant that their work was channeled into service provision and away from rights advocacy. The goal of OSJI's project was to fund and empower civil society actors who would campaign against racial profiling and call for establishing mechanisms to monitor racial disparities in policing.

To Open Society, France was a particularly interesting place to develop this work. The 2005 uprising signaled that it was a country where racial profiling was a significant problem, yet the French government systematically denied it and closed off any debate on the issue. As a senior adviser explained, "France is one of the most obdurate countries in terms of discourse about ethnic statistics, in terms of cultural and constitutional construct that denies race, and given how pissed off people are, it just seems like it's an important place to do it." Plus, because of the country's centrality in the European Union, "the visibility of anything that we did in France would have much greater regional resonance."[6] As a result, France was chosen to be among the handful of countries where OSJI launched a racial profiling project.

The OSJI team believed that "given denial of the issue, and a refusal to discuss race and how it was playing out in policing, that conversation was impossible to start without having an evidence base."[7] Their first step was therefore to conduct research to prove the existence of racial disparities in identity checks. After releasing the results of their study in 2009, they started building coalitions with civil society actors—human rights and antiracist organizations, lawyers, community organizers—to develop a litigation strategy and gauge interest in forming a national coalition to advocate against racial profiling.

The litigation and advocacy work was coordinated by Sarah,[8] a senior legal officer at OSJI, and its only employee to be based on France. Sarah, a White Canadian, had recently joined Open Society after working in international and nongovernmental organizations as a legal expert on issues of antidiscrimination, minority rights, and conflict prevention. Over the years, she worked with, and coordinated, various coalitions,[9] which included international organizations like Human Rights Watch, national human rights and antiracist groups like the Ligue des droits de l'Homme or the Brigade Anti-Négrophobie, left-wing lawyers' and judges' unions, and smaller NGOs focused on community organizing.

This chapter examines the Open Society–led campaign and analyzes how coalition actors produced knowledge about racial profiling. It shows that their mode of knowledge production—*quantitative epistemology*—mattered for the way the campaign defined racial profiling and organized against it. The research produced strong evidence of disparities in police stops, which helped consolidate a discrimination frame. But its limitations sustained divisions among members of the coalitions, about how to frame the drivers of these disparities and how to conceptualize the role of race. Eventually, the campaign's public discourse framed the problem as one of officers who select whom to stop based on appearance, with persistent disagreements over how to define "appearance." The chapter then examines why, when advocates launched a local project to empower young men to contest discriminatory stops, neither the way the campaign had framed the problem, nor the solutions they proposed, resonated with victims of racialized policing.

Top-Down Activism and the Transnational Dilemma

Open Society is a transnational organization with no territorial anchoring. Therefore, launching a program in France required enrolling local organizations in their network and building coalitions.[10] To do this, they reached out to organizations that shared OSJI's commitment to progressive liberal values. Many of these actors were not directly affected by racialized policing, but they sought to use their expertise in law and political advocacy to promote principles of equality and nondiscrimination. Within the broader movement, the campaign against racial profiling exemplified a specific model of activism: it was a top-down coalition, funded by a private foundation, and staffed with professionals promoting progressive reforms (in figure 0.1 of the introduction, they are mostly on the left-hand side).

For the French organizations that joined the coalition, partnering with OSJI provided important benefits. It gave them access to Open Society's extensive networks within the international human rights field, and for some, to grants. However, it sometimes entailed trade-offs, especially for smaller organizations that also worked with more radical, autonomous groups. Samia,[11] one of the activists who joined the campaign, told me that, within the French leftist and antiracist field, many criticized her for accepting Open Society funding, because it made her participate in an elite-led, reformist agenda that aimed to prevent revolutionary social transformation. She agreed with this criticism. To her, the model of activism that Open Society promoted was problematic; it gave billionaires, who acquired their wealth in a deeply unequal capitalist system, undue power to influence democratic processes, and it provided them with "a way to avoid paying taxes while buying themselves a better image."[12]

Nevertheless, she joined the coalition because she felt that there was no other space, within the French movement, where she could work on this issue while sustaining the financial stability of her organization. Nonprofits had their state funding systematically cut as soon as they started speaking up about discrimination in policing, and there were no other large donors interested in supporting this work. "The problem is that [Open Society] have a monopoly over this work," she said, "and since they are the primary funder on issues of discrimination in policing, everybody ends up adopting their language."[13]

Yet, this language, especially around race, bothered her and other members of the campaign. While some French antiracist groups were aligned with OSJI's approach, it made others uneasy. In my interviews with them, many explained that they welcomed Open Society's focus on racial discrimination in policing, but they worried that the organization's race-conscious, race-centered discourse was not adapted to the French context. They were also uneasy with the promotion of racial statistics as the solution.

When I asked why, they expressed two main concerns. First, they worried that adopting explicit race language and calling for racial statistics would immediately delegitimize the campaign. These fears were not exaggerated. In France, references to race or racial categories are seen as incompatible with the country's antiracialist ideology, according to which combating racism requires eradicating racial categories and banning the collection of racial data. Activists and researchers who endorse race-conscious language or call for the collection of racial statistics systematically face fierce criticism, from the right and the left, for "importing American ideology" and promoting essentializing notions of biological races. The activists' second concern was that an exclusive focus on race would downplay other important factors of discrimination, including class, residence, age, and gender. One of them put it thus:

> I understand that we talk about racial discrimination, but it bothers me when we *only* talk about that. Territorial discrimination is also very important in France. And we have a problem with youth. And there is also the whole dimension of criminalization of poverty, [yet Open Society] refuse to talk about class.[14]

For these reasons, most French organizations pushed for using the term *contrôles au faciès*, which means police stops based on appearance, instead of the literal translation of racial profiling, *profilage racial*. The term *contrôles au faciès*, a commonly used term in France, denotes discrimination based on skin color, but also on other visible features, such as age, gender, or how people talk, walk, or are dressed.[15] To many coalition members, framing the campaign as combating *contrôles au faciès* was strategic. It would prevent the campaign from being delegitimized from the outset. Plus, they argued, emphasizing appearance more accurately described the intersecting forms of discrimination that the targets of policing suffered, which were based on racial appearance but also age, gender, social class, and other factors. OSJI's team members understood the difficulties of introducing explicit race language in the French context, but they worried that a reluctance to do so would water down and obscure the role of race.

This type of conundrum is common in campaigns led by transnational organizations. It reflects what political scientist Wendy Wong calls the *transnational dilemma*, the need to strike a balance between the ideas promoted by transnational organizations and the local context's specificities and culture.[16] Open Society's race-conscious approach aligned with the idea, dominant within the transnational human rights field, that measuring racial inequalities through the collection of racial statistics is essential to promoting racial equality. But it went against France's dominant ideology, according to which combating racism requires promoting universal rights, eliminating racial categories, and banning the collection of data on race or ethnicity.

As coalition actors started working together in the late 2000s, they grappled with how to adapt Open Society's race-conscious (and class-blind) frame to the French context. They discussed and debated how to strike a delicate balance between aligning with the dominant culture in order to be heard and challenging that culture in order to be influential. Their knowledge practices played an important role as they worked through these disagreements and negotiated a shared frame for the campaign.

Quantitative Epistemology

When Open Society launched their campaign in the mid-2000s, politicians and police representatives systematically denied the existence of racial profiling, arguing that there was no evidence to prove it. They dismissed the reports published by NGOs and watchdog institutions, which relied on the testimonies of people targeted by the police, deeming this evidence anecdotal and untrustworthy. The OSJI team therefore decided to start with conducting research that could measure racial disparities in identity checks.

Doing so was a significant challenge. They had to come up with a methodology that could produce statistical measures of racial disparities without access to police records, which would comply with the legal ban on the collection of racial data, and avoid critiques of "ethnicizing" French society and importing racialist rhetoric. Addressing these challenges required making careful decisions about who would conduct the study, which methodology to use, and how to analyze the findings.

Their first step was to get in touch with well-known scholars with a reputation for rigorous, nonpartisan research, to gauge their interest in collaborating on a study. As a coalition member explained, the idea was "to seek validation by sociologists because they were external actors who provided a professional expertise, a technical knowledge . . . they brought a certain neutrality."[17] They contacted Fabien Jobard, one of France's most respected policing scholars, who works at the country's main national research institute, CNRS (Centre national de la recherche scientifique). OSJI's manager told him they were looking for French scholars to collaborate on a research project that would be modeled on a study Open Society had recently conducted in Moscow.[18] The Moscow study had used a methodology developed by US researcher John Lamberth, which relies on observing police stops in public spaces, without the knowledge of the police. The research observers record the characteristics (race, gender, age) of all the people present in a specific place, to create a benchmark of the available population. Then, they record the characteristics of people stopped by the police in order to find out whether the police disproportionately stop certain groups.[19]

This research design piqued Jobard's interest. In my interview with him, he recalled, "She told me about the research design, and I was immediately sold . . . we weren't going to have undergrads fill out a survey [about their experiences with the police], it was fun, it was promising." He proposed working with another policing scholar, René Lévy. Both had previously published research on ethno-racial inequalities at various stages of the criminal justice system,[20] but the absence of records of identity checks had prevented them from measuring racial disparities in police stops. Lamberth's methodology would help overcome the obstacles they had faced so far: it did not require access to police records; it did not involve collecting racial data on identified individuals and therefore complied with French law; and the creation of a benchmark of the "available population" made up for the absence of data on the racial composition of public spaces in France. To Fabien Jobard and René Lévy, this was an opportunity not to be missed, especially since this study would be costly, and OSJI was offering to fund it.

OSJI suggested adding civil society organizations to the research team, but the French academics were strongly opposed to the idea. "It would have ruined it," Fabien Jobard told me. The scholars wanted to make sure that the study would be viewed as a serious piece of scholarship, rather than as an activist report. This was important not just for their academic reputation but also for the study's political resonance. "Be careful," he told OSJI, "the only safe label, the quality label, is the CNRS; if you mix up references and interlocutors [by involving activists], the opponent will shoot you."[21] Open Society's team heeded this advice, and the research team was limited to OSJI's staff who coordinated the study, the two French scholars who implemented the study, and John Lamberth who acted as a consultant on the methodology.

Thus, in an effort to produce knowledge that academics and politicians would perceive as credible, the research was designed and conducted by a team composed of a transnational NGO and White, middle-class scholars, with no input from local civil society or from the communities most affected by racial profiling. This meant that the research questions and scope of the study were determined on the basis of these professionals' interests and values.

As they set out to plan the research, the first question the team needed to agree on was the scope of the study. According to the researchers, at one of the meetings, the OSJI team suggested several topics, which seemed to be pressing concerns in the activist field at the time, including tensions between teenagers and police in low-income neighborhoods, police harassment of migrant children, or deportation practices. Fabien Jobard and René Lévy worried that these issues could not be examined with rigorous quantitative methods. To ensure the study's credibility in academic and political settings, they argued, it should focus on using Lamberth's methodology to produce solid statistical measures on disparities in identity checks. This meant excluding issues that could not be quantified. Addressing too many issues, or using qualitative data, ran the risk of producing one more report that would be dismissed as unreliable. "What we wanted to do was a clean study on identity checks in Paris; period period period," Fabien Jobard explained, "unaccompanied minors, deportations, everything related to immigration, no: we wanted the least possible pollution on the research project." Eventually, staff at OSJI agreed, "we knew we needed something quantitative that couldn't just be denied."[22] They were also anticipating that statistics can be required as evidence in discrimination lawsuits. Since the campaign planned on launching litigation, limiting the study to a quantitative analysis made sense.

Thus, the coalition settled on a *quantitative epistemology* in which (1) movement actors made alliances with scholars, (2) to quantify racial disparities in police stops (3) through observing hundreds of police stops in public spaces, (4) and analyzing the findings through a legal lens. This mode of knowledge production had important implications for the knowledge claims they produced.

Do Cops Target Blacks and Arabs, or Guys with Caps Worn Sideways?

As anthropologist Sally Engle Merry reminds us, while quantitative studies are widely perceived to be the most reliable and credible form of knowledge, like any epistemic approach, they produce "a particular way of dividing up and making known one reality among many possibilities."[23] Statistics emphasize the aspects of an issue that are amenable to quantitative measurement and obscure those that are not, such as the social, cultural, and political context of a social phenomenon, its historical roots, or the subjective experiences of those who live through it. It also leads to a certain way of measuring, and therefore conceptualizing, inequality. Merry noted that, to understand the specific ways in which quantitative indicators distort social phenomena, we must examine the assumptions embedded in quantitative methodologies, and the motivations and concerns of those who produce them.

The central assumption of Lamberth's methodology was that discriminatory policing can be captured by observing the appearance of all the persons present in a space and comparing it to the appearance of those who get selected for stop and search. As such, the study tested whether individual officers relied on physical characteristics when making discretionary decisions about whom to stop. This fostered an understanding of police discrimination as something that happens when on-the-ground officers select their targets (rather than, for example, when police chiefs decide where to deploy units or when governments set enforcement priorities).

This emphasis on individual bias was reinforced by the spaces in which researchers made their observations. Lamberth's methodology required selecting spaces where the crowd was racially diverse and where there was a high density of police stops. During the pilot phase of the study, Jobard and Lévy tested several sites before settling on four spaces in and around Paris's largest railway stations, Châtelet les Halles and Gare du Nord. They also tested spaces in low-income neighborhoods, where most tensions between the police and racialized people occur, but they did not include them, because it was difficult to predict when the police would conduct stops and impossible for observers to remain undetected. This meant that the study captured a specific type of identity check: investigatory stops[24] conducted in high-density, anonymous spaces, where the police are looking for potential evidence of criminal conduct or undocumented status. It did not include stops in low-income neighborhoods against young people the police know and encounter frequently, and which are often used for social control and intelligence gathering, rather than just for detecting crime.[25]

The study's design also fostered a conceptualization of race as phenotype. The methodology relied on the assumption that officers differentiate people racially based on their physical features (and not, for instance, their name or accent). Based on this assumption, the scholars had to come up with racial categories, which research observers could distinguish from a distance. After testing several possibilities, they settled on five categories: White, Black, Arab, Asian, and Indian/Pakistani. They considered adding a category for Roma/Travelers, "because we know that police officers can tell the difference," but they decided against it for two reasons. First, as René Lévy explained, the methodology entails making quick assessments of large numbers of people, so "our categories have to be rudimentary, we can't make fine-tuned categories."[26] Second, there were simply not enough Roma/Travelers in the spaces they observed, because these groups are hypersegregated in peri-urban areas. "We know that Travelers experience racial profiling," OSJI's Sarah later told me, "but it's not in mixed neighborhoods, so you would need to develop a different research protocol [to capture discrimination against this group]."[27] This meant that the study measured discrimination against what the French call "visible minorities," that is, people whose skin color is not white, which contributed to obscuring discrimination against Roma, Travelers, and Eastern Europeans.

While OSJI was primarily interested in producing evidence of racial profiling, the scholars saw this project as an opportunity to contribute to the ongoing debate within French academia about whether inequalities were primarily based on race or class. Jobard explained, "One of the goals was to figure out whether it's Blacks and Arabs who are stopped, or whether it's guys with caps worn sideways."[28] Thus, in addition to noting the apparent race, age, and gender of the people observed, the study added a measure of clothing styles, with three categories: business, casual, and "youth culture style," a reference to the sportswear typically worn by youth in low-income neighborhoods (*quartiers populaires*).[29] This transformed the project's primary focus, from examining whether the police disproportionately target racial minorities, to an attempt to adjudicate whether they target people based on their racial or class appearance.

The decisions the research team made about what to measure, how, and where, had important implications for what the study captured, and how it conceptualized race and class discrimination. By comparing how similarly situated White and racialized people are treated by the police in mixed spaces, the study tested whether individual officers rely on people's physical appearance when making decisions about whom to stop in large crowds. This approach focused on a specific, and narrow, understanding of discrimination as individual bias, something that happens when on-the-ground officers select whom to stop. It could not capture the institutional policies that may shape officers' decision-making, such as where units get deployed, what instructions they are given, or how they are incentivized. It also obscured the structural inequalities that make racialized people more vulnerable to police attention in the first place.

As legal scholar Issa Kohler-Hausmann argues, in racialized societies, all major aspects of life are structured by race, from residential patterns to quality of education, access to health care, and employment opportunities. As a result, "It is not meaningful to talk about an otherwise identical person suddenly swapping racial status at the time of a given encounter because the raced status a person has inhabited since birth has shaped so many aspects of the person relevant to the encounter that it is impossible to disentangle those factors from the person's raced status."[30] Thus, the study's design was powerful to capture one dimension of racialized policing—the biases that come into play when officers make discretionary decisions—while downplaying others. This shaped how the research team interpreted the study's findings.

Strong Evidence of a Narrow Claim

The study produced the first quantitative measure of disparities in identity checks in France, and these disparities were staggering. After seventy-five days of observations, during which researchers recorded the characteristics of almost 38,000 persons and observed 525 identity checks, they found that on average, people perceived as Black and Arab were six and eight times more likely to be stopped by the police than those perceived as White. People dressed in youth culture styles were eleven times more likely to be stopped.[31]

As OSJI staff and the French scholars jointly drafted the research report, *Profiling Minorities*, in 2009, they agreed that the findings provided strong evidence of discrimination in identity checks. The statistics clearly established that the police disproportionately target certain groups, they wrote, and in the absence of legitimate policing strategies that explain these disparities, this was evidence of unlawful discrimination.

While the report made a strong claim that there was discrimination in identity checks, it remained ambiguous about the mechanisms driving this discrimination. Without data about the cause of these disparities, *Profiling Minorities* emphasized the role of individual prejudice, noting "ethnic profiling remains persistent and pervasive precisely because it is the result of a habitual, and often subconscious, use of widely accepted negative stereotypes in making decisions about who appears suspicious or who is more prone to commit certain types of crimes." The authors added that "profiling may also result from institutional policies targeting certain types of crimes and/or specific geographic areas without consideration for the disproportionate impact such policies can have on particular ethnic groups."[32] This ambiguity over how to frame the mechanisms of discriminatory policing would later translate into the campaign's discourse.

Profiling Minorities was also ambiguous about the relative role of race in discriminatory stops. During the drafting of the report, disagreements emerged between the French scholars and OSJI's staff over how to interpret the findings. The statistical analysis could not dissociate the effect of racial appearance from that of clothing, because two-thirds of those dressed in youth culture styles were also Black or Arab. While OSJI staff wanted to emphasize ethno-racial discrimination, the French scholars preferred stressing both racial appearance and clothing style. Without a clear answer from the statistical analysis, the issue remained unresolved. The final French-language report was a compromise between OSJI's and the French scholars' positions. It used both the terms *contrôles au faciès* and *racial profiling*, noting "the police regularly engage in what we commonly call *contrôles au faciès* in France (or "racial profiling" at the European level)." In some sections, the report emphasized appearance as the basis of discrimination ("The study confirms that identity checks are conducted by police officers who rely primarily on appearance: not what people do but what they are or appear to be"). In others, it focused on racial discrimination ("the behavior of the French police documented in this study is highly consistent with ethnic profiling").

The report stated, "clothing style can be described as a racialized variable, as stops that were directed at certain styles of clothing resulted in disproportionate stops of ethnic minorities, particularly Black youth."[33] However, Fabien Jobard told me that, in hindsight, this claim made him uneasy. "With our data, we simply don't know," he said, "sometimes I think it is [a racialized variable], if I think in postcolonial terms, and how specific populations are assigned to territories, namely colonial populations. But then again, [wearing a] cap [sideways] is primarily the marker of a young man who lives, and signals that he lives, at the margins. And to the cop, this means: you belong to me."[34] The data were insufficient to conclusively answer this question. In their scholarly publications, Jobard and Lévy moved away from describing clothing as a racialized variable and argued that *contrôles au faciès* should be understood as stops based on people's "appearance," including their skin color, but also their gender, age, and type of clothing.[35]

The study's authors also disagreed on how to contextualize the findings, and specifically whether to make connections to France's colonial history and race-blind ideology. Fabien Jobard told me that the first draft of the report, written by OSJI's senior advisers, started with a discussion of France's colonial history and criticism of the government's race blindness and its refusal to collect racial statistics. "It was a disaster!" he recalled. Starting the report with a critique of a constitutional principle—that the Republic recognizes no races—risked disqualifying the whole report, especially since it was written by a foreign organization that would be perceived as "giving lessons to the French government." If they kept this version, he thought, "it's over, they won't even look at the findings." Upon receiving the first draft, Fabien Jobard and René Lévy started revising the report; "we rewrote everything, we removed it all," he told me, "zero consideration for France's [military] action in Libya, the postcolonial, nothing."[36] To the scholars, the strength of the report lay in its "magic numbers"—close to 38,000 people observed, over 500 identity checks, high odd ratios. It was essential not to pollute the "demonstrative purity" of these numbers by making politically controversial statements that might overshadow the findings. The final version of the report did not contextualize the patterns uncovered in the country's colonial history.

Ultimately, *Profiling Minorities* made a strong claim that the police disproportionately target certain groups based on their appearance, but this claim remained relatively narrow. It emphasized the (conscious or unconscious) biases officers rely on when making discretionary stops in mixed spaces, but it could not capture the routine stops racialized young men experience at the hands of officers they encounter daily, nor the institutional and structural mechanisms that foster racially disparate policing practices. Moreover, without clear adjudication from the statistical analysis, the study could not determine whether disparities were primarily based on race or class discrimination. The strengths and limitations of the report played an important role as coalition actors negotiated a shared frame.

Discrimination Is Scientifically Proven

The impact of the study on the public debate cannot be overstated. When *Profiling Minorities* was published in 2009, its public reception was unanimously positive, with mainstream media calling it the "scientific proof" of the reality of *contrôles au faciès*,[37] and politicians and police representatives recognizing the scientific validity of the study. As the scholars had hoped, the credibility of quantitative methods, their reputation as serious, nonpartisan academics, and their care to align with the dominant antiracialist culture, ensured the report's positive reception. Almost overnight, the claim that the police disproportionately target minorities went from being a contested partisan claim to being an established reality—a story I tell in more detail in chapter 6.

To OSJI, this newfound recognition of the reality of *contrôles au faciès* represented an opportunity to jump-start their campaign and push for reforms. They started building coalitions to engage in political advocacy, initiate litigation, and organize public awareness events.

As they developed these collective actions, coalition partners quickly converged around framing the issue as a problem of discrimination. Initially, some preferred to develop a broader critique of identity checks, which would condemn the vast powers granted to police officers and the abuse of power resulting from it. But the statistical data produced in *Profiling Minorities* provided unprecedented evidence proving that the police disproportionately target racialized minorities—evidence that was particularly suited to a claim of discrimination. Given decades of political denial, most actors understood that this was an opportunity not to be missed.

In every press statement, campaign tool, and political advocacy meeting, statistical claims were front and center. In a traveling photo exhibition that OSJI created to raise awareness on *contrôles au faciès*, the first poster was titled "Contrôles au faciès: The Statistical Evidence." Under the title, in a large font, visitors could read "'Blacks' and 'Arabs' are 6 to 8 times more likely to be stopped by police," followed by a graph illustrating this disparity. Other groups involved in the campaign created visual illustrations of the disparities in identity checks, with pictures of people of different skin colors, genders, and clothing styles, each holding a sign with the number of times they were stopped by police. Juxtaposing the pictures of those who are routinely stopped next to those who are never stopped conveyed the differential treatment racial minorities and youth from *quartiers populaires* experience. These visuals gave life to the statistics and allowed the campaign to convey the scale of disparities, thus bolstering their framing of identity checks as discriminatory.

Racial or Appearance-Based Discrimination?

While the data produced in *Profiling Minorities* helped consolidate a discrimination frame within the campaign, it also contributed to sustaining internal divisions about how to name and frame the problem of discriminatory stops. These divisions came to the fore when coalition members set out to find plaintiffs for a lawsuit they were preparing against the state for discriminatory stops. To find potential plaintiffs, OSJI's Sarah collaborated with Kiara,[38] a French White woman who worked in an international organization and was interested in the issue of *contrôles au faciès*.

In 2011, Kiara cofounded a community organizing collective, Stop le contrôle au faciès (hereafter Stop), which brought together half a dozen local and national organizations to coordinate grassroots work on the issue. To find potential plaintiffs, OSJI and Stop organized local meetings and street actions to encourage victims to provide their testimonies. Stop also released a YouTube series called "My first identity check," which featured French rap artists recounting their first police stops.[39] The videos ended with an encouragement to viewers to call the collective's hotline to report any abusive stop.

In this work, different organizations promoted competing conceptualizations of discriminatory stops. In their written material, Stop contended that "what characterizes a *contrôle au faciès* is not its ethnic or racial dimension: it's the fact that it is based solely on the appearance of a person, and not on their behavior."[40] To Kiara and some other members of Stop, avoiding explicit references to race and racism was necessary to garner widespread support. The goal of Stop, she told me, was to create a coalition around the issue of discriminatory stops, which would include a wide range of actors, from antiracist groups to organizations that endorsed race-blind approaches to equality. This required framing the issue in ways that would resonate widely:

At the time, the collective included neighborhood organizations and antiracist organizations. The antiracist organizations were okay with [emphasizing race], but the neighborhood organizations, they said, "we're working on citizenship, we don't want to be in a racial thing, and the youth are not into this, and we don't want them to be." So, we couldn't sell it like that anyway, and since we were looking for the common denominator . . . we didn't need to agree on the causes [of discrimination].[41]

Kiara believed that terminology that centered race would not resonate with victims of discriminatory policing.

In contrast, OSJI's campaign material emphasized racial discrimination and downplayed discrimination based on class or place. In their public statements, OSJI defined *contrôles of faciès* as identity checks "based on skin color, ethnic belonging, religion, or national origin, rather than on elements related to the behavior of individuals or on objective clues."[42] To Sarah, centering race was a conscious strategy to challenge the tendency, within French civil society, to downplay racial discrimination:

People don't always understand that for us, it was an intentional bias (*un parti pris*), it was part of the strategy. . . . In France, you always have a focus on social [class] problems, and [racial discrimination is] euphemized, socialized. . . . This was really about getting recognition that there is discrimination against Blacks and Arabs, that this is not just about social discrimination, it's not just about poor people.[43]

While this disagreement was rooted in strategic differences, it was also influenced by the knowledge that the campaign produced. Because the *Profiling Minorities* report failed to adjudicate whether race trumps class, both sides could draw on the findings to justify their position. In all their campaign material, Stop consistently cited the statistic about clothing style (people dressed in youth culture styles are eleven times more likely to be stopped) alongside the statistics about racial appearance (Blacks and Arabs are six and eight times more likely to be stopped), to promote the idea that discriminatory stops can be based on any aspect of people's appearance. For their part, Open Society's publications and statements focused on the statistics about Blacks and Arabs but did not include the finding about clothing style. When I asked Sarah about it, she said that it was not necessary to cite this statistic, because to OSJI's team, "clothing is a racialized factor."[44]

This disagreement had important implications for who the campaign deemed to be the victims of discriminatory policing. When the time came to select plaintiffs for a lawsuit, in 2011, Kiara suggested including not only racialized people, but also White people living in *quartiers populaires* who were stopped on the basis of their social class. "I had in mind this dream intersectional approach, *à la* Kim Crenshaw [the scholar who popularized the term intersectionality]: it's because they are young and/or Black or Arab, and/or from low-income neighborhoods."[45] The OSJI team and the lawyers categorically refused, arguing that the case should focus on a clear argument of racial discrimination, without getting into complicated claims about intersectional discrimination. This would only confuse the judges and lead to a loss.[46]

Eventually, a legal strategy centering racial discrimination prevailed, and the plaintiffs selected were all Black and Arab men. Still, the disagreement over how to define the victims of *contrôles au faciès*—as racialized people or as residents of low-income neighborhoods—persisted. This illustrates one of the arguments of this book: when movement actors work through disagreements over how to frame their cause, they don't only rely on their political preferences; they also draw on knowledge claims. When the movement's research fails to adjudicate a contested issue, it can contribute to sustaining frame disputes.

Racist Cops or Institutional Racism?

In the campaign's public statements, an ambiguity persisted over who, or what, is to blame for the race and class disparities in identity checks: biased officers or institutional policies. While all the campaign leaders believed that both were at play, they endeavored to develop a public discourse that would resonate widely, which required aligning with the dominant understanding of racism as the behavior of prejudiced individuals.

In public events and media interventions, campaign leaders often repeated that they were "not anti-police," that they understood the need for police stops, and that their struggle was meant to address "illegal" behaviors by some officers. For example, during a 2012 TV debate on the issue, a spokesperson for Stop said, "We are not suspicious of the whole police force. We know that there are police officers that do their jobs very well—and it's probably the majority. But the behavior of some is enough to discredit the whole institution."[47] Similarly, when the campaign launched a lawsuit against the state for discriminatory stops, spokespersons insisted that the lawsuit was not meant to question police interventions but only to contest discriminatory behaviors.[48]

Presenting *contrôles au faciès* in individualist terms—focusing on racist cops—was a strategic decision on the part of campaign actors, to increase the resonance of their discourse in public conversations and political settings. As scholars Margaret Keck and Kathryn Sikkink note,[49] problems that can be assigned to the deliberate actions of individuals are more amenable to advocacy strategies than problems that are viewed as irredeemably structural. But this strategic choice was also influenced by the evidence the campaign relied on to substantiate their arguments. *Profiling Minorities* had demonstrated widespread disparities in identity checks, but in the absence of evidence that these disparities were linked to specific institutional policies, advocates feared that placing the blame on institutional or structural factors would not resonate well politically.

The mode of knowledge production also influenced the kinds of examples coalition actors used when explaining what *contrôles au faciès* are, and why they are a problem. In March 2017, I spent a week with Adam,[50] manning the campaign's photo exhibition when it was hung on Paris's Place de la République. Adam is a French Caribbean from the island of Guadeloupe. He moved to the metropole as an adult and had been working for a decade as a community organizer on issues of police-youth relations and discrimination. He was one of the most active members of the campaign, engaged in a different advocacy coalition, En finir avec le contrôle au faciès. Every day for a week, he and I sat on portable chairs next to the exhibition posters to facilitate conversations with passers-by.

One day, a dark-skinned Black man came over to chat with us. I had noticed the well-dressed man—I'll call him Patrick—going around the exhibit while holding the hand of a toddler trailing along quietly. Patrick, who seemed to be in his thirties, asked us if there were ethnic statistics in France. Adam said no and Patrick continued, "because in certain neighborhoods, some communities are overrepresented, so if the police stop this community disproportionately, for example because they have a suspect description, it's normal for the police to stop people from that community, but the youth, they immediately dig their heels in. If we had statistics, we would know."

Without addressing Patrick's example, Adam replied, "Yes, but sometimes you're just sitting in a café, you're the only Black person, and you're the only one to be stopped, even though you've done nothing wrong." Patrick tried to return to his example, saying "of course this can happen, but what about when there's a suspect description." "In this case," Adam responded, "the police must follow legal procedure, but sometimes, the police stop you simply based on your appearance."

In this exchange, Adam steered the conversation toward a specific—and narrow—understanding of discrimination, which focused on individual officers selecting whom to stop based on phenotype. He did not engage with Patrick's examples of a neighborhood where racialized groups are overrepresented, or where the police stop Black men indiscriminately because they have a suspect description for one Black man. This was not because Adam did not understand these types of situations to constitute discrimination. In our conversations over the years, he and I often discussed how the policing of racialized groups was connected to institutional policies and incentive structures, and to the broader segregation and social exclusion of poor and racialized populations. However, in his interactions with visitors to the exhibition, Adam always started with an example that aligned with the dominant understanding of racism, as the behavior of prejudiced individuals.

This was something I noticed repeatedly. The examples that campaign actors used to illustrate what *contrôles au faciès* are, typically, aligned with the kinds of situations studied in the *Profiling Minorities* report: a Black or Arab person, in a mixed space, behaving in the same way as White people and yet being the only one targeted for an identity check. As a result, their public-facing discourse ended up unintentionally obscuring the institutional and structural dimensions of racialized policing, which include institutional policies, incentive structures, enforcement priorities, socioeconomic marginalization and spatial exclusion of racialized populations. This is not to say that campaign actors never addressed these issues. In fact, during conversations with visitors to the exhibition, Adam often discussed institutional factors, but he spoke of these issues as adjacent, rather than integral, to racial profiling. This shows that the assumptions and blind spots of a movement's mode of knowledge production can seep into activists' discourse as they become the taken-for-granted way of conceptualizing the problem.

Blacks and Arabs

During the conversation with Patrick, another member of the coalition En finir avec le contrôle au faciès, Mamadou, joined us. Mamadou was a Black man in his late twenties who headed a small nonprofit that organized sports and cultural events in his neighborhood northeast of Paris. He had gotten involved in the campaign through Adam, whom he met as a teenager when he participated in events organized by Adam's local organization. The three men started discussing their experiences of anti-Black racism in France. Patrick told us he had moved to France from Gabon for his studies, after completing two years of college. He had not experienced too much racism in his professional life, he said, because he worked in a field "dominated by Anglo-Saxons." He added, "It's not the same for those who grew up here, they don't face the same problems." Adam shared what it was like moving from the French Caribbean to the metropole as an adult: "I discovered that I am Black when I moved here, before then, I wasn't Black, I was just human." Mamadou jumped in, saying he had had the opposite experience, "I grew up here, so I grew up seeing myself as Black; it was only with time that I saw myself as human. And yet, I was top of my class!" The fact that his family was Muslim exacerbated the discrimination he faced in his daily life.

This conversation suggests that the way in which campaign actors defined *contrôles au faciès*, as something that targets "Blacks and Arabs," glossed over important differences within these groups. Emphasizing Blackness (or Arab-ness) as the main criteria for discrimination obscures the dynamics of class, place, religion, and legal status that shape people's experiences and encounters with the police. Patrick, Adam, and Mamadou all faced anti-Black racism, but this racism took different forms because they had different social statuses in metropolitan France. Adam and Patrick, who grew up outside of the metropole, did not share Mamadou's experience of being harassed by the police and criminalized from a young age. Their class status also meant that they were subjected to different forms of racialized policing. Mamadou was routinely stopped and searched, especially as a teenager. Patrick, while comfortably middle class, dealt with issues of immigration and legal status that exposed him to a different kind of vulnerability to police than Adam, a French citizen.

In the activist field in France, there is no consensus on how to describe victims of racialized policing. While some organizations promote a unified Black identity as a thin, but shared, identity around which to organize,[51] others push back against this, arguing that differences in social class, legal status, and historical experiences mean that there is no unified Black identity in France.[52] In my conversations with Adam, he often said that he did not self-identify as Black, because it was a limiting way of understanding his ancestry.

> When I speak to some antiracist activists, it's exasperating. They limit the very existence of the population of Guadeloupe to what happened after the colonizers and slaves arrived. As if there was nothing before. I am a descendant of the Caribbean; to me, it's important to take into account the Indian immigration that happened, and to not speak only of African slaves.[53]

This resistance to a unified identity as Black is widespread among Caribbean French people, whose experiences with the French state are very different from those of people who migrate from Africa to the metropole.[54] While many Caribbean organizers focus their activism on the memory of slavery and on challenging the neocolonial management of the French territories,[55] African migrants emphasize issues of papers and citizenship, residential segregation, and discrimination in the job market. Similarly, among people racialized as Arabs, there is no strong collective identity based on race or ethnicity. Studies show that young people more frequently adopt collective identities based on their neighborhood or their religion.[56]

Thus, while, for the research study, it was necessary to use phenotype as a proxy for the complex reality of racialization, the campaign's framing of victims of *contrôles au faciès* with the shorthand "Blacks and Arabs" obscured the multiple factors that come into play in the racialization process (phenotype, but also religion, ancestry, class, place), and relied on labels that were not necessarily salient for racialized people. This provides another illustration of how the assumptions and conceptualizations of research projects can seep into activist discourse.

Disconnect with Victims' Priorities

By the mid-2010s, a decade into the mobilization, the campaign had made significant inroads in the political and judicial spheres. Activists managed to introduce the issue on the political agenda and won a landmark lawsuit against the state for discriminatory stops—a story I tell in chapter 5. However, the campaign was still primarily led by NGOs and professionals, with limited involvement of the communities most affected by *contrôles au faciès*.

To make up for this, Sarah partnered with Adam to launch a pilot legal empowerment project in 2017, which aimed to boost victims' involvement and empower them to use a new legal recourse that the campaign had obtained through their litigation efforts. By that time, Adam and Sarah had been working together for seven years. Adam led the implementation of the legal empowerment project, drawing on his extensive networks in the northeastern neighborhoods of Paris, among residents and business owners, professionals working in youth centers, and administrative and elected officials at the municipal office. Sarah provided guidance and support, and I helped out as an intern.

On one of our first team meetings for the project, I sat down with Sarah and Adam in our usual café by the Saint Martin canal. Over the previous week, Adam and I had collected testimonies from several young men in the neighborhood who had been brutalized by the police in two public parks. Earlier that month, a fight had broken out between two groups of young men in one of the parks, and the mayor asked the police to take action. The precinct had sent heavily armed units in large numbers to the neighborhood parks, on a near daily basis, with instructions to evict everybody present—mothers, children, and young people living in the neighborhood—mostly low-income racialized residents. During these interventions, police officers beat up teenagers, including Black, Arab, and White boys, with batons and punches. As a result, one young man had a broken arm, another got stitches on his eyebrow, and one was charged with violence against a police officer.

After we updated Sarah about these developments, Adam suggested that we take immediate actions, including hiring lawyers to help the victims file complaints for police brutality. But Sarah was hesitant. The raid-like operations did not constitute racial profiling in the sense that the project defined it, that is, police stops based on race or ethnicity, rather than on people's behavior. In this case, the police seemed to target all the people present in the parks indiscriminately. "I have to say I'm a little troubled, I don't know what we can offer young people who are in a situation where the mayor's office decides to [send the police to] target a specific space." The police actions were clearly part of a discriminatory political decision, she continued, the fact that the groups targeted were majority Black likely played a role. But it wasn't a straightforward case where police officers selected their targets based on their racial appearance, which was how the courts defined discriminatory stops.

Adam emphasized that there was a whole range of issues: "to me there are discriminatory stops, there are abusive stops, there is police violence, and there is anti-youth control." While Sarah agreed, she reminded us that the project was meant to empower victims of racial profiling to use a new legal recourse to contest discriminatory stops in court. The youth targeted in the park raids would not be able to use this recourse, and we didn't have a budget to pay lawyers for criminal lawsuits for police brutality. Plus, we knew that such lawsuits were mostly dismissed. She didn't want us to make promises we couldn't keep. Addressing these issues required a different set of strategies.

The more we talked, the more frustrated Adam grew, "ethically, we can't collect their testimonies and then tell them we can't take further action!" He insisted that, if we wanted to mobilize people to file lawsuits for racial profiling, we must also be able to respond to the most pressing problems on the ground, including issues of police violence and harassment, and including when they targeted Whites.[57]

Over the first months of the project, we had many conversations like this one where we grappled with how to balance responding to local needs and advancing the project's objectives. As we began reaching out to the youth in the neighborhood, it quickly became apparent that there was a gap between the way the campaign had framed the problem and the priorities on the ground. The funding contract stipulated that Adam's NGO would provide local communities with information about the new judicial recourse against discriminatory stops, select relevant cases for lawyers to litigate, and support young people in developing collective responses to racial profiling practices.[58]

However, for the young people who were most frequently stopped by the police—mostly Black and Arab teenagers from low-income families—*contrôles au faciès* were not a priority. Our conversations with them revolved around two issues that came up repeatedly: the police used identity checks repeatedly, sometimes up to five times a day, to evict large groups of young people hanging out in public parks. And they were increasingly targeting some young men with repeated fines for petty offenses such as spitting or littering. Some had been fined for several thousands of euros in a matter of weeks.

During our team meetings, we struggled with gap between these realities and the project's main objectives, as defined in the funding contract: empowering victims of *contrôles au faciès* to file civil lawsuits using the new judicial recourse on discriminatory stops. To increase the chances of these lawsuits succeeding, we were looking for people who experienced "simple identity checks" that didn't lead to arrest, detention, or violence. Yet, when we tried to encourage racialized teenagers to document the simple checks they experienced, they didn't see much benefit in doing so. They didn't want to go to court to challenge a simple stop, when they were experiencing serious police brutality that led to physical injuries and psychological trauma and were flooded with fines that affected the financial stability of their families.

As we considered different options, Sarah suggested that reaching out to the most vulnerable populations might not be the most strategic approach, because they were the least likely to launch—and win—a racial-profiling lawsuit. She wondered if we shouldn't target racial minorities who were better off, like university students or people with stable jobs, who didn't routinely experience police abuse and brutality. In response, Adam argued that our broader goal was to improve police-citizen relationships, and this required supporting the groups most vulnerable to police abuses. He pushed for broadening the scope of the project to include all types of illegitimate policing practices, including police brutality and abusive fining practices. If we wanted people to use the judicial recourse on racial profiling, he reasoned, we needed to establish legitimacy in the neighborhood first. Responding to residents' most immediate needs was the only way.

Gradually, the project took on a broader agenda than initially planned. We provided victims of police violence with advice on how to collect evidence for criminal complaints—get medical certificates, take pictures, save any existing video, and so on—and we connected them, whenever possible, to lawyers willing to get paid through state-funded legal aid. We started documenting the fines that teenagers received and helped organize meetings with the local authorities to pressure them to abandon these abusive fining practices. And we worked closely with a youth-run local organization to organize public events and debates that revolved around policing issues broadly. These events generated discussions about potential avenues for organizing against *contrôles au faciès* but also against police violence and abuse of power. A year after its launch, the project had established its reputation as the main advocate for young people experiencing abusive policing in the neighborhood, but we had not filed a single case using the new legal recourse against discriminatory stops.

The legal empowerment project illustrates the trade-offs inherent in attempting to mobilize victims of racialized policing, when their voices have not been included in knowledge production, litigation planning, or advocacy work. The professionals who led this mobilization produced knowledge and constructed frames on the basis of what would resonate with mainstream media and political elites. This resulted in a campaign that successfully placed its claims on the political agenda but struggled to mobilize on the ground. Neither the way activists had framed the problem, nor the solutions they proposed, resonated with victims of racialized policing, because they didn't address their most pressing concerns.

Conclusion

The campaign against racial profiling produced knowledge through a quantitative epistemology, which relied on collaborating with scholars to produce a statistical measure of disparities in police stops. The research produced strong evidence of racial disparities, but it also sustained disagreements among coalition actors over how to frame the problem. The study proved that the police disproportionately target people perceived as Black or Arab, but it could not adjudicate whether they are targeted because of their skin color or their clothing style, and it could not determine what drove these disparities. Eventually, campaign actors converged around a public discourse promoting a narrow understanding of discrimination as a problem of officers selecting whom to stop on the basis of their appearance.

When they sought to help victims of racialized policing organize, there was an incongruence between the campaign's focus on discriminatory stops and the most pressing issues on the ground, namely, police brutality, harassment, and abusive fining. This illustrates the difficulties of mobilizing constituents when their voices have not been included in knowledge production or in developing political claims.

The involvement of NGOs and lawyers does not inevitably lead to a disconnect between activists' discourse and on-the-ground experiences, however. In the next chapter, I discuss another mobilization that involved some of the same actors, but which took a different approach that led them to develop frames that aligned more closely with the concerns of the policed.

THREE

Police Harassment and
the Making of Undesirables

In 2012, youth counselor Malik[1] started working in Reuilly-Montgallet, a neighborhood of the twelfth arrondissement of Paris, which concentrates a large share of social housing in what is otherwise a gentrified neighborhood. A French man of Arab origins, Malik had over a decade of professional experience supporting at-risk youth. He was employed by an organization that provides social and educational support to young people facing social exclusion or marginalization. There, he was part of a team of *éducateurs spécialisés*, social workers whose job is to do outreach in the spaces where teenagers hang out, identify those who are at-risk, and offer support and guidance in dealing with educational, social, or judicial problems.

As Malik and his colleagues got in touch with local youth in Reuilly-Montgallet, they started hearing recurring stories of police harassment.

> We realize that there is a recurrent thing, which is conflictual relationships with the police. . . . We hear about police harassment, even though they don't say it this way, they use their own words, they say [officers] are breathing down their necks [*ils sont sur leurs côtes*]. . . . And we hear mostly about the Tigers, the Tigers, the Tigers.[2]

The "Tigers brigade" was a public tranquility unit responsible for combating incivilities and urban disorder. It got its nickname from the shoulder badge that officers had chosen for their uniform, a tiger with its teeth and fangs out. According to local teens, the Tigers repeatedly stopped Black and Arab youths—some as young as twelve—for no apparent reason, sometimes several times a day. During these identity checks, police officers often insulted the children, including with racist slurs, and they sometimes punched them, beat them up, or sprayed them with tear gas. The stops always involved frisks and typically ended with the police asking the youth to "beat it." Sometimes, the children were taken into police custody for a few hours, before being released to their parents.

On hearing the teens' accounts, the counselors were initially skeptical, Malik told me, "because it's the police, the police are meant to represent the law, they are supposed to have a code of conduct." Another youth counselor, Paul, remembered, "we were wondering, thinking: this story of yours can't be true." However, "little by little, there was this realization that there are so many consistent facts, the kids always talk about the same officers, the frequency, the recurrence of this reality had us listening."[3] As they spent time on the streets with the teenagers, the counselors started witnessing some of these abuses firsthand.

Malik, Paul, and a couple of their colleagues decided to alert the local authorities. They talked to their bosses, hoping that the organization would inform child protective services, but the higher-ups were reluctant, perhaps fearing that accusations against the police might jeopardize their state funding. The counselors requested a meeting with the police district's outreach unit, during which teenagers shared their repeated and violent encounters with the Tigers brigade. The officers promised to raise the issue with their colleagues and chiefs, but on the ground, the abuses continued. In fact, some officers in the Tigers brigade retaliated against the youth who attended the meeting, calling them snitches and threatening to "beat them up" if they did it again.[4] The teens and their counselors also raised the issue with the local elected officials responsible for prevention, youth and sports, and security.[5] Once again, despite promises to address the issue, the Tigers' practices did not change.

Around the same time, Adam, a Caribbean French community organizer, launched a local project in the neighborhood, that aimed to raise awareness and empower marginalized youth. An active member of the racial profiling campaign discussed in the previous chapter, Adam's small nonprofit had received funding from Open Society to do local outreach projects focused on issues of policing and discrimination. He got in touch with the twelfth arrondissement youth counselors and suggested a series of workshops with the youth. While Malik expected a traditional session on rights and responsibilities, "it went further than anticipated." Adam, who was trained in Canadian community organizing methods, started meeting regularly with a group of teens to discuss their experiences of discrimination and their relationship with the police. They talked about what could be done to ease tensions, and he helped them think through strategies for collective action.

One of those meetings was a turning point. That day, a teenage boy arrived angry and agitated after experiencing yet another identity check. When the adults probed him, he complained that a police officer had touched his genitals and anus during the pat down. Upon hearing this, several other young men revealed that they too, had experienced unwanted sexual touching by the Tigers. Shocked, the adults asked the children why they hadn't shared these stories before. Most confessed that they were embarrassed, each one believing he was the only one this had happened to. After that meeting, Adam recalled, "we discussed what we can do about this; we launched a strategy to collect information about the scale of this in the neighborhood."[6] They started talking to residents from several generations and discovered that multiple other young adults had suffered unwanted sexual touching during pat downs as teenagers. They had felt ashamed and kept silent.

Alarmed by the severity of the police abuses, Adam reached out to Open Society and the lawyers they had worked with for the racial profiling campaign, Slim Ben Achour and Felix de Belloy, to ask for help in preparing a lawsuit. Open Society's leadership was initially reluctant to get involved. The abuses the teenagers suffered didn't fit within their racial profiling project; they involved police brutality and arbitrary detention, which was outside the scope of their project. However, Adam and the lawyers insisted that it was important to work on this case to advance the struggle against racialized and abusive policing more broadly. Sarah, Open Society's senior adviser in France, eventually convinced her organization to join "in a support role" and to partially fund the litigation effort.

By 2014, a coalition started taking shape, composed of local actors (the Black and Arab teenagers and their families, youth counselors, local organizers) as well as outside experts who played a support role (high-profile lawyers and a transnational organization).

This chapter examines the mobilization effort against the Tigers' brigade in the twelfth arrondissement of Paris and analyzes how actors produced evidence of the abuses, violence, and racism that local teenagers suffered at the hands of the police. It shows that the mode of knowledge production that actors adopted—a *grounded epistemology*, which aimed to document the collective experiences of racialized youth in one local space—mattered for how coalition actors negotiated a shared understanding of the problem. By documenting victims' experiences in one neighborhood, while making space for multiple grounds from which to build knowledge, the coalition managed to collect sufficient evidence to launch a lawsuit for police misconduct, while at the same time producing an analysis of how the neighborhood's ecology fostered racialized policing practices. This, in turn, shaped how the coalition defined the problem: as discriminatory police harassment that fosters social exclusion. It also influenced the strategies of action actors developed, in courts and in community organizing efforts.

Neighborhood Mobilization and Unbridgeable Gaps

The activist coalition involved a diverse set of actors. It was initiated by youth counselors employed by a state-funded organization who worked closely with the young men suffering police abuse and their families. Alongside these locally embedded actors, the coalition included community organizers, a transnational NGO, and high-profile lawyers. This configuration—a coalition between local actors and outside experts—required people who could play a mediating role between the different people involved. Malik, the youth counselor, was key in this regard.

On one of my first meetings with him, Malik took me on an impromptu tour of the neighborhood, where I witnessed the strong relationships of trust he had established with local teens and their families. The youth counselor had asked me to meet at his organization's office, which was on a small street, mere steps away from two of the area's main boulevards, Diderot and Daumesnil. The street had a very different feel from those large Parisian roads with their familiar Haussmanian architecture; it was a narrow street, lined with residential towers, many of them containing subsidized housing units. When I got there, Malik was deep in conversation with a teenage boy. He quickly wrapped up his meeting and asked me if it was okay to drop by the nearby middle school before sitting down for our interview. He had to meet an academic adviser to talk about a kid he worked with. I agreed and we walked the short distance to the middle school.

As soon as we passed through the school's large metal gate, the bell rang, and a swarm of preteens and teenagers came rushing out of the classrooms. The demographics of the children struck me; in this predominantly White and wealthy district, the students looked overwhelmingly Black and Arab, a sign of the well-documented pattern of White, middle-class flight from public schools in mixed neighborhoods.[7] Like most neighborhoods of eastern Paris, the twelfth arrondissement had undergone a process of gentrification starting in the 1980s, with housing prices growing exponentially. But, to comply with French housing laws, the district maintained about 20% public housing, which meant that the largely White, middle- and upper-class residents lived alongside a minority of low-income, mostly immigrant families. The children of these families were the youth counselors' primary focus.

In the school, Malik was immediately surrounded by dozens of children who stopped to shake his hand and say hello. He gave each one of them a moment of individualized attention, asking one boy whether his grades were getting better, telling another his mother wanted him to go home straight after school today, or reminding a girl to come by the youth counseling organization to register for the upcoming field trip. After we discovered the adviser Malik wanted to meet was absent, we made our way to a nearby café. On our short walk, Malik bumped into other children he knew well, who clearly trusted and loved him.

As we sat down for the interview, Malik told me about the organizing effort. On one hand, he said, he was proud of the work they were doing. The support of an organization like Open Society allowed them to have access to lawyers who helped build a lawsuit against the Tigers and garner media attention around the case. On the other hand, the lawsuit did little to address the multi-layered vulnerabilities some teenagers struggled with. Malik wanted to use this coalition to build a sustained infrastructure to support the youth in dealing with the complex and interlocking issues they faced, which included police harassment, but also problems at school, economic precarity, discrimination on the job market, interneighborhood violence, and for some, criminal charges and incarceration. Several times, he tried to call on the lawyers to take on new cases of police brutality or to support the youth when they were charged with misdemeanors. But the lawyers' workload was already overwhelming. They were only getting partial funding from Open Society for the main lawsuit, and did not have the resources to take on many more. Malik asked whether Open Society could use their financial resources to recruit a lawyer or paralegal to work in the neighborhood, even on a part-time basis, to help local youth with their legal complaints against the police, or to defend them when they were accused of misdemeanors. However, the organization said that this did not fit within their program priorities. Malik fumed. "I don't understand why George Soros [Open Society's billionaire funder] wouldn't invest in hiring someone to work on these issues."[8] He and other local actors were often frustrated with the outside professionals. He believed that they were well-intentioned, but that "they live in another world" and did not really understand the complexity of the issues the young men faced, and the solutions required.[9]

In my conversations with Open Society's Sarah and the lawyers, they too expressed frustration. Malik and the other local actors didn't understand that they had limited resources to devote to the twelfth arrondissement, they said. Slim Ben Achour's firm did its best to take on cases when they could, and to refer others to colleagues. But this was *pro bono* work and the needs exceeded their capacity. The lawsuit against the Tigers was sizable and complex. It required both legal work and a media campaign to put a spotlight on the recurring abuses. For this litigation to be successful, they needed to focus their resources on the case and couldn't take on every problem that came up.

These types of tensions are common in movements that bring together marginalized groups and middle-class professionals working in law firms and nonprofits. Poor and racialized communities face a complex set of problems, which require sustained, multipronged approaches to address them. Yet, lawyers and NGOs are typically constrained by limited resources and narrow programmatic priorities. Moreover, there is often a disconnect between what marginalized communities need, and what these professionals can achieve within the constraints of the legal and political system. In Jaime Amparo Alves's study of Black mothers' activism against racist police brutality in Brazil's favelas, he noted an "unbridgeable gap" between the mothers' experiences of poverty and loss and the privilege of the human rights activists and state bureaucrats who tried to help them.[10] Despite their best intentions, the professionals could not address the mothers' demands, which went beyond applying for state compensation and included finding and returning the remains of their murdered sons and getting help to pay overdue bills and rent. For the mothers, these issues were inextricably linked, but the help the professionals could provide, within existing frameworks, was more limited. In the twelfth arrondissement mobilization, like in Brazil, these gaps led to mutual frustrations and misunderstandings.

In the following sections, I show how knowledge production was a key site where these issues were worked through.

Grounded Epistemology

In contrast to the campaign against racial profiling, this mobilization's knowledge-making efforts did not focus on a predefined problem that activists sought to evidence. Rather, actors aimed to document the range of abuses that the teens suffered at the hands of the police, and on this basis to inductively identify issues and priorities for action. This approach, which I call *grounded epistemology*, is a mode of knowledge production that (1) is led by a coalition of differently situated actors, (2) who aim to document the lived experiences of policing victims, (3) by collecting testimonies and material evidence in one local space, (4) and which makes space for different situated analyses of the data.[11]

Coalition actors shared a common starting point for knowledge production: centering the experiences of local youth with the police. From there, they developed two parallel projects: one that was led by the legal professionals and aimed to produce evidence for a lawsuit against the Tigers brigade, and another that was led by the youth counselors and aimed to gain a better understanding of the local dynamics of inequality and social exclusion within which these policing practices were embedded. This grounded epistemology allowed them to work through the tensions and class distance between coalition actors, by making space for different ways of knowing, within a shared commitment to centering the experiences of victims.

Collecting Legal Evidence

Before the coalition took shape in 2013, some of the teens had attempted to file complaints for police brutality against officers in the Tigers brigade, but the police inspection services (IGPN) routinely refused to take their complaints or registered them only to dismiss them without investigation. This was a recurrent pattern across the country. Given the legal assumption of credibility granted police officers and the credibility deficit suffered by racialized young men in France, and given that police misconduct is investigated by police officers, victims of policing often struggle to get their complaints registered and taken seriously.[12] As a result, coalition actors agreed that they needed to collect as much evidence as possible before filing a lawsuit, to increase the chances that their complaint would be recorded and investigated.

For the documentation process, the lawyers needed to collect the teenagers' testimonies in a form that could be used in a legal proceeding. To do this, they secured help from the legal clinic of a Parisian university, which sent two jurists to record the testimonies from victims and witnesses. Malik and Adam helped set up meetings between the jurists and the neighborhood teens who were targeted by the Tigers brigade. They told the teens that each one of them would meet individually with legal assistants to give them details about every abusive police encounter they could recall. They would have to share what happened, where, and when; who was there, what the police did and said, and so on. They also asked them to start meticulously documenting all their future interactions with the police. After every encounter, the teens should write down the date, time, and place of the stop, the names or descriptions of the officers involved, and everything that happened in the interaction. Then, they should make an appointment with one of the adults collecting testimonies to share those details, and get friends who witnessed the stops to write a testimony about the stop and bring it to the professionals. They should also immediately get a medical certificate from the medico-legal clinic stating any injuries and take photographs of any bruises or injuries.

Implementing this plan proved to be challenging. For one, since most of the victims were minors, they needed their legal guardians' consent to file a lawsuit. Getting the families to agree was not easy, counselor Paul told me. Most were first-generation immigrants who did not feel that mobilizing the law was a legitimate avenue for them. "They're not used to interacting with the justice system, it often seems out of reach, or something that is not for them, given their circumstances."[13] More importantly, most parents were unaware of the extent of the violence their children experienced at the hands of the police. In my interview with the mother of a plaintiff, she told me that her sons did not tell her or her husband about the beatings. When they were detained at the police station and their parents were called to collect them, she assumed that her kids were at fault. "I always believed the police were right. I thought, they are teenagers, they are outside, I don't know what they do, I'm not on their back, they're boys . . . they get home at 6 p.m., sometimes 7 or 8 p.m." But after hearing about the sexual abuses her boys suffered, she agreed to move forward with the lawsuit. "My kids hadn't told me anything about the sexual touching and all of this. This is when I really got mad. I told my husband: that's it. That's when we started working on the complaints."[14]

Even with the parents' approval, it proved difficult to get the children to testify and collect evidence. The teenagers found the process tedious and time-consuming. Malik recalled that many of them missed appointments with the legal assistants. "They would tell me, 'it's a drag, we have to be there for two or three hours with them, we don't know what they want, they ask a lot of questions' . . . at some point, people forget that these are children."[15] Indeed, for thirteen-, fourteen-, or fifteen-year-olds, recording every incident with the police, when they were being stopped on a near daily basis, required a level of commitment that many could not maintain. They didn't know the legal assistants and found it difficult to talk to them without an adult they trusted being present.

There was also a disconnect between what the lawyers needed to have evidence of the abuses, and what the teenagers could realistically do. For example, the lawyers advised the teens to film police stops with their cell phones whenever possible, but most of them were reluctant to do so. "The cops don't like it, they would break our phones," one of the plaintiffs told me.[16] Asking them to get medical certificates was also complicated. The teenagers were busy with school and work, and for many, their parents didn't have the time, and sometimes the language skills, to take them to the doctor for a certificate.

To overcome the teens' reluctance, the counselors decided in some cases to accompany the youth to their meetings with the legal assistants. This helped. The plaintiffs I spoke with told me that their respect and affection for their youth counselors was one of the main reasons they agreed to take part in the documentation effort. "Initially, in our heads, we thought it wasn't going to work out," one of them explained, but they trusted the counselors enough to give it a try.[17]

Thus, the relationships of trust that the counselors had built with the youth over the years were essential to the documentation process. Without Malik and his colleagues, it would have been difficult to convince teenagers dealing with multiple issues to take the time and energy to share personal and often traumatic experiences with complete strangers. This suggests that knowledge projects that rely on testimonies from policing victims can be complicated by the social distance between victims and the professionals leading the data collection effort. In these cases, the role of mediators that are trusted by both victims and professionals is essential.

Expanding Legal Claims

After months of data collection, the coalition had compiled data about dozens of police stops that involved verbal, physical, and sexual violence, arbitrary arrest and detention, and destruction of property. This became the foundation of the criminal lawsuit that eighteen plaintiffs filed collectively in December 2015, which accused eleven officers of forty-four counts of physical assault, sexual assault, discrimination, arbitrary detention, and destruction of property.

The plaintiffs, seventeen boys and one girl ages fifteen to twenty-three, were all children or grandchildren of immigrants, the vast majority from sub-Saharan Africa and North Africa. They testified that they were repeatedly stopped for identity checks without being given a legal reason, and that they received punches, beatings with police batons, slaps, arm locks, and excessive amounts of tear gas. The complaint reported multiple instances of unlawful detention, in which the minors were taken to the police station and kept for hours without legal justification and without the appropriate paperwork being filed. The plaintiffs also reported being subjected to anti-Black and anti-Muslim slurs. Several boys claimed having their genitals and anus touched during pat-downs and being mocked with homophobic remarks when they tried to resist these practices.

Bringing together forty-four incidents targeting eighteen plaintiffs allowed the lawyers to frame these practices as routine, institutionalized patterns of practice, rather than as the action of isolated "bad apples." In their litigation on racial profiling, Slim Ben Achour and Felix de Belloy had been careful to maintain a moderate discourse that denounced instances of misconduct but did not condemn patterns of practice more broadly. Now, with evidence of the repeated, routine nature of racialized police abuses, they expanded their legal claims. In the complaint, and in the media interviews they gave when they filed it, the lawyers described the Tigers' practices as systemic violence and discrimination. They wrote, "these acts, which range from daily insults to physical violence to sexual assault, are so frequent and repeated that the victims wanted to gather them in one complaint, in order to denounce their systemic nature and profound severity."[18]

After an investigation that lasted over a year, the prosecutor referred four officers to trial for aggravated assault and dismissed the rest of the allegations for insufficient evidence. The records included in the investigation file revealed that the Tigers' practices were embedded in an institutional policy, with police chiefs giving the Tigers daily orders to "evict undesirables" from the public spaces where the teens hung out. Coalition actors found out that the term "undesirables," which was historically used to designate racialized groups deemed unwelcome on the national territory, is included in the digital software used by the national police throughout the country, in a drop-down menu about the motive of an intervention, alongside rubrics such as noise disturbance, theft, or vandalism.

These revelations allowed the lawyers to move beyond their previous conceptualization of police discrimination as resulting from officers' discretionary decisions. With evidence that the national police use the term "undesirable" to designate categories to be evicted from public spaces, the lawyers developed a more structural understanding of racialized policing. At the trial in 2018, Slim Ben Achour argued that identity checks were a "useless and dangerous practice" that were not meant to ensure public safety, but rather to keep poor young men of color in a subordinated position. The Tigers' repeated identity checks and evictions, he said, were not meant to enforce public tranquility, but to call into question the youths' belonging to the national and social community and to signal to them that "they are not quite French, that their belonging to the national identity is not deserved." He continued:

We are told that the evictions target "undesirables," a term that used to be included in French public policies but that has been removed. It used to describe Jewish people in the 1930s [during World War II] and then French Muslims from Algeria [during the Algerian war of independence]. Today, it's our kids who are labeled with this term that is linked to the most painful hours of this country's history.[19]

The lawyer's argument emphasized the role of the police, as an institution, in producing racialized groups that are deemed inherently suspicious and unwelcome in public spaces, and which must be controlled through harassment and violence. In other words, he argued that racialized policing is not just a matter of racist officers, but also of institutional policies that (re)produce categories of racial difference and then use them to justify practices that "humiliate, subjugate and dehumanize" racialized groups.

This shift in the lawyers' legal arguments illustrates one of the main arguments I make in the book, namely, that the knowledge produced within a movement can transform the strategic decisions actors make about what is sayable and hearable in specific settings. The evidence they uncovered about the institutional policies undergirding routine police harassment led them to revise their previous strategy of sticking to moderate claims, and to introduce new, more radical claims in court.

Analyzing the Social Ecology of Police Violence

On the day that the Paris criminal court was due to give its verdict, I joined the plaintiffs and others involved in the mobilization to attend the read-out of the ruling. After summarizing the case, the judge said: "The police officers denied all the allegations, but the victims provided evidence, including medical certificates that aligned with the police's records." She determined that "the evidence presented is sufficient to establish the reality of the facts" and sentenced three of the officers to a five-month suspended prison sentence, and to pay two thousand euros each to the victims, in compensation for the harm caused.

As we walked out of the courtroom, everyone broke into smiles. We hugged and kissed and congratulated each other. Even though the officers would not serve any time in prison, nor get fired from their jobs, such convictions are so rare that their symbolic weight is significant. On our way out of the courthouse, we decided to go to a nearby café to celebrate.

There, lawyer Slim Ben Achour spoke proudly about the verdict. He had just given an interview to a group of journalists covering the case, in which he described the decision as a major step forward. "The verdict marks a limit to the culture of impunity. . . . Police officers can't act like criminals and must comply with the legal rules, that's what the court reminded them of today," he said, adding, "we hope that this ruling will contribute to a change of culture."[20] At the café, he shared the next steps he and his colleagues at the law firm were preparing in the litigation strategy; they would use the investigation file of this case to file a civil lawsuit against the state for discriminatory policing patterns.

As Slim was speaking, I noticed that Malik stayed uncharacteristically silent. When Adam encouraged him to share his thoughts, he hesitated, seemingly reluctant to spoil the good mood. Then, he said, "it's good what we achieved, but what will it change on the ground? . . . Of course, we're happy, but there's a little bit of disappointment because these policing practices continue."[21] This was a concern that he had repeatedly raised over the past year. The lawsuit was drawing attention to the problem of police harassment and brutality, but it did little to change policing practices on the ground. In fact, after many of the accused officers had been moved to other districts, the officers recruited to replace them were reproducing the same behaviors, and racialized young men from low-income families continued to face intense police harassment. Moreover, the police had recently started targeting Black and Arab young men with multiple fines for minor and sometimes made-up offenses like littering or spitting. Some of the neighborhood teens had accumulated thousands of euros in fines, which exacerbated their families' already precarious economic situations.[22] Having a symbolic conviction was important, Malik suggested, but it did little to improve the lives of those who are targeted by the police on a daily basis.

While Malik was proud of the work they had done in collecting legal evidence, he felt that it had done little to amplify the voices of the youth he worked with, or to capture the complexity of their social experiences. Neither the trial nor its media coverage provided an opportunity for the young men to articulate their experiences in their own words, beyond the constraints of legal proceedings. To make up for this, the youth counselors worked with a group of local teens to create spaces of youth expression. They supported them in the production of two short movies featuring neighborhood youth.

The films shed light on the neighborhood dynamics that undergird the Tigers' abusive practices. In one eight-minute film titled *The Youth in Public Space*, a half-dozen young men, all of them Black and Arab, speak about their experiences in the twelfth arrondissement public spaces. As the camera follows the group in various spaces around the neighborhood, they explain that the municipal authorities installed surveillance cameras, removed public benches, and placed steel barriers in an effort to stop them from hanging out in public places. As a result, they didn't have any spaces where they could hang out without having to purchase something, except for the Saint-Eloi square. "They are relocating the problem," several teenagers complained on camera, "but we are young, we do nothing wrong, we just want a place to hang out."

The Saint-Eloi square, which is bordered by an L-shaped residential building and a church, quickly became the space where most of the tensions with neighbors crystallized. In the documentary, the teens described how neighbors living in the privately owned building overlooking the square regularly complained that they were too loud. "Sometimes, we're at fault, we recognize that, but sometimes, they should treat us like human beings, instead of insulting us." Rather than speaking to them and asking them to lower their voices, some neighbors got into the habit of insulting them and throwing things at them from their windows, like "onions, tomatoes, and glass bottles." These neighbors also routinely called the police, "even though they see how aggressive the cops are with us."

To the teens, the harassment they suffered at the hands of the Tigers was inextricably linked to efforts by some of the older, wealthier, White residents to stop them from using the neighborhood's public spaces. In my interview with Oscar, one of the plaintiffs, I asked why he thought he and his friends were stopped so regularly. He replied, "probably because there are several of us on the square." When I pointed out that it's not illegal to be in a public square, he replied: "it's not illegal, but to them, it's *their* square."[23] The teens analyzed their experiences with the police and the neighbors as efforts to exclude them from the public spaces of their own neighborhood.

The second short film, *Discrimination*, was meant for the youth to articulate their experiences and understanding of racism and discrimination. Holding the camera, Malik asks the teens whether they ever experienced discrimination. At first, the answers focused on overtly racist police officers. "During identity checks, I have friends who got called dirty Black, dirty Arab, *bougnoule*, things like that," one boy tells the camera. Others say that the police always suspect them of being up to no good. "One day, we were coming out of that building, we were walking, they saw us, and they immediately did a U-turn and stopped by us, and said 'what were you doing in the building, you stole something?' But we were just in the youth counseling organization."

But the conversation quickly shifted to the everyday racism they faced from White residents in the neighborhood. "I don't know how to explain it, the people, they want to belittle us," one teen said. To illustrate the differential treatment Black and Arab boys received at the hands of some residents, another boy explained, "if for example we're walking in the street and we spit, [passers-by] call us thugs (*espèce de voyou*), there's at least 10,000 persons who spit every day, but of course it's us, the youth with dark skin, who get called thugs." He added that, when children of "French people" (code for White) do the same thing, they are treated kindly by adults, "but to us, they're mean, they talk to us like we're animals."[24]

Thus, the teens' analyses highlighted a dimension of racialized policing that the legal case could not capture, namely, that policing practices responded to, and fostered, widespread societal racism. To them, police racism was embedded in a broader local context in which Black and Arab boys were routinely belittled, patronized, and deemed unwelcome in public spaces by wealthier White residents and by municipal authorities.

Analyzing these dynamics through a social work lens, the counselors developed an ecological analysis of racialized policing, which emphasized the local context within which policing is embedded. They highlighted the social, economic, and racial inequalities in the neighborhood and the role of ordinary residents, municipal authorities, and schools in producing and maintaining race and class inequalities. Malik put it thus:

> They are in precarious [economic] situations; they have problems at school, they have a bad reputation, they tend to drop out of school. It's a population that has few economic means, but that still lives—and that's the crazy part—between Bastille and Nation, which is a nice neighborhood, quite hipster-ish (*bobo*), where there's money. That's the problem with Paris, to live in Paris, you're either rich or you're poor. The kids we deal with are all poor, only the poor hang out in public spaces, really. So, of course, in relation to the residents, they have a bad reputation. The residents, the majority, are, quote unquote "White," I don't know if I

should speak like that . . . lots of Whites, and elderly, and they have their apartments, they generally rent here. So, they call the police to complain about these youths. Which means the police are responding to this demand. Except they then feel all-powerful, because they are validated by the residents who send these petitions. It's a whole context, it doesn't come from nothing these [policing] habits.[25]

Echoing this analysis, counselor Paul summed up:

We're in a neighborhood that's polarized, with populations that don't interact. . . . Some residents think of public space in terms of their own security, their own tranquility, [and say to the youth] "you have no business being here." Then, we hear the police telling them the same thing: "you have no business being here."[26]

Thus, the creation of spaces for young people to articulate their lived experiences led to highlighting how the Tigers' violent harassment was embedded in local dynamics of exclusion and marginalization sustained by privileged residents and local authorities. It shed light on persistent race and class conflicts over the use of public space, with wealthier, White residents unhappy with the visible presence of racialized youth from working-class families, and local authorities responding to these grievances with urban planning changes and police harassment.

This suggests that the mode of knowledge production—who leads knowledge projects, what questions they ask, and how they interpret the findings—shapes which actors, interactions, and dynamics of power are emphasized, and which are obscured. When the lawyers sought to collect evidence for a lawsuit, they needed data on police-citizen interactions, but the role of other actors was irrelevant to the legal case. In contrast, when the youth counselors led the knowledge project, they broadened the scope of their inquiry to examine the teens' experiences in other areas of life. This shed light on the ecology of racialized policing, which involves not only the police and the youth but also neighbors, business owners, and elected officials invested in maintaining an exclusionary spatial order. This ecological frame, which highlights the relationships of power that lead to social and spatial exclusion, had important consequences for the political practice of local activists who supported the youth.

Making Space for Youth

When the criminal lawsuit was filed in 2015, it caught the attention of an existing network of local leftist and human rights organizations that worked on issues of social justice in the twelfth arrondissement of Paris. The network included local branches of national human rights and social justice organizations (Ligue des droits de l'Homme, Amnesty International, Attac), local groups promoting social solidarity (Commune libre d'Aligre), and anticapitalist activists. It was led by primarily White, middle-class volunteers.

A few months before the teens' complaint, this group had launched an initiative to monitor policing practices during the state of emergency that the government declared following the 2015 terrorist attacks. "When we heard about the lawsuit, the topics converged," explained Victor, a retired economist who volunteered for the local branch of the Ligue des droits de l'Homme (LDH). "At a time when there was a lot of pressure on the youth, we wanted to show that the organizations were concerned about this issue and supported them in their lawsuit."[27] The activists got in touch with Malik and Adam, and they established a collective of residents and local activists to support the youth, which they called Making Space for Youth (Place aux jeunes).

As the collective Making Space for Youth started organizing events, their actions went beyond supporting the plaintiffs in their lawsuit and sought to promote the teens' social inclusion. In 2016, the collective started organizing regular meetings, which brought together the plaintiffs, their families, the youth counselors, and left-leaning residents, local activists, and local organizations. Together, they discussed ways they could support the neighborhood's marginalized youth and started planning collective action and public events.

Based on the counselors' analysis of the experiences of racialized teens, Making Space for Youth advocated for municipal policies that fostered social inclusion and promoted the well-being of marginalized youth. Using the political clout of its member organizations, the collective reached out to the mayor's office to present the youth's grievances and propose solutions.

For example, the collective wrote a letter to the twelfth arrondissement mayor in February 2017 to raise concerns about the mounting tensions in the neighborhood. In it, the organizations said they had identified two main root causes. First, poor urban planning meant that young people had no spaces to hang out in other than public squares. Urban spaces in the neighborhood, they wrote, are "poorly designed in terms of sound isolation . . . [and] the reduction in the number of businesses, cafés, etc. has contributed to the decline of traditional social ties." The lack of spaces for young people was made worse, the collective added, by the mayor's actions to remove benches, install cameras, and construct barriers. These measures, they argued, privileged the interests of home-owning residents and ignored those of the renting residents.

Second, to the collective, these problems "are exacerbated by the increasing inequalities between residents of the neighborhood and the discrimination young residents with immigration backgrounds face in the workplace." The collective deplored the dearth of opportunities for professional training and internships, which are "even less accessible to the residents with immigration backgrounds because of a lack of social network and of the reluctance of employers toward them."[28] The activists ended the letter by requesting clarifications about the mayor's urban planning projects, and by asking whether she would create more spaces for youth and how she would "improve the social integration of young residents who face difficulties in a job market that is very deficient toward them."

In these exchanges, the collective focused squarely on the discrimination and social exclusion that racialized young people face in terms of their access to public spaces and to employment opportunities. They held the mayor's office primarily responsible for finding solutions to these twin problems and enjoined her to give the same weight to the interests of these youths as to those of the wealthier residents.

Within the collective, there was no consensus about the effectiveness of this sort of advocacy toward the mayor's office. Some believed it was important for members of the collective to share their concerns with the municipality, because they had electoral weight. "It's a part of the electorate that has an important capacity to mobilize, through this network of organizations, so [to the mayor], it's important to ensure that what we say is not too critical," Victor explained, especially because they knew these organizations are well connected to the media. Others argued that these kinds of actions were useless, because the mayor's office would continue enacting their top-down policies without much consultation with residents. In practice, it's difficult to know whether these letters and meetings had any effect on municipal policies. However, they helped consolidate a group of leftist middle-class White residents invested in advocating for marginalized youths' right to public space.

Some members of this group worked to enroll more allies in the neighborhood through organizing within their buildings and blocks. Mathilde, a sixty-five-year-old self-described anticapitalist activist, lived in the building overlooking Saint-Eloi square where most of the tensions were concentrated. Having lived in the neighborhood all her life, she had noticed over the past years a dramatic escalation of police harassment and police violence targeting Black and Arab young men. "I witnessed police disrespecting the youth, using arm locks and restraining techniques against youth who were not violent, who were not running away." At the same time, in her 250-unit apartment building, some residents, whom she called "quasi-fascist," were becoming increasingly vocal about their intolerance of the youth hanging out on the Saint-Eloi square. "In the general assemblies of property owners, there were extremely violent discussions," with some residents calling for steel barriers all around the building to prevent the teenagers from hanging out in the square. Some residents' discourse, she recalled, was "full of hatred toward the youth; [they said] things like 'we will reclaim our space, we must seize the square, we will organize a 'saucisson-pinard' picnic" [a pork and wine picnic, to make Muslims feel unwelcome]. Taking advantage of the momentum created by the collective, Mathilde mobilized a group of progressive neighbors so they could attend these general assemblies in numbers and vote against the exclusionary proposals.[29]

In addition to advocating for social inclusion, members of the collective sought to help individual teens struggling with discrimination in the labor market. Victor recalled, "when we talked with the youth, of course there were these problems with the police, but they also told us, 'my concern is that I want an internship, I want an apprenticeship, but it's impossible to find.'" In response, the collective decided to make the social networks of its middle-class members available to the youth to help them find training and employment opportunities. "With our networks, it wasn't very complicated finding a job, an apprenticeship," Victor explained.

The multiclass, multiracial network that the collective fostered thus became a social support structure for racialized young people, which facilitated their access to social networks they did not otherwise have access to. Christelle, the mother of one of the plaintiffs, told me that the collective's meetings introduced her to some of the neighbors that she never knew before. As a long-term resident of a public housing apartment, she had always believed that the wealthy homeowners of the neighborhood despised her and her children. But through the collective, she met people who are "open-minded" and "take the young people's defense," which was a surprise to her. "We all live in the same neighborhood . . . before they could walk past me and I didn't know them."[30]

The Solution Is Not Calling the Cops, It's Dialogue

In parallel to their political advocacy work, Making Space for Youth developed actions to address the neighborhood conflicts that fostered violent policing practices. In the summer of 2016, the collective organized its first event: two weeks of public debates on the theme "Making Space for Youth." The debates aimed to promote dialogue about the shared use of public space. Starting from the assumption that the conflicts were exacerbated by a lack of communication and mutual understanding, they endeavored to promote dialogue across generations, social classes, and origins.

Keen to center youth's experiences in their political practice, the collective involved the neighborhood's racialized teens in planning the event. With the help of their counselors, some young people wrote a letter addressed "to residents, families, neighbors, elected officials, police officers, and strangers," inviting them to "meet, exchange, and build together" during the two-weeks' debate. The letter was distributed in the mailboxes of the Reuilly-Montgallet buildings. In it, the young people mentioned the absence of spaces for them to hang out, the constant police surveillance they experienced, and the negative stereotype other residents held against them. They wrote:

> Some residents complain about the agitation around the Saint-Eloi church: noise, noisy motorcycles, cans left on the floor, aggressiveness . . . we hear and understand these admonitions. This agitation is that of the youth of the neighborhood who don't know where to hang out. Since the installation of cameras, the construction of fences, and the removal of benches, the church [entrance] has become the only place where it

is possible for groups to sit and be sheltered [from rain]. These changes provoke anger and hurt in us, feelings that are exacerbated by the impression that we are under surveillance and under-estimated. . . . This is the source of our aggressiveness.

The letter went on to say that while the residents' responses had so far been confined to calling the police, initiating a dialogue might be a more fruitful avenue for solving these issues. The signatories called for "learning to know each other better and getting over the prejudices that confine us, [to] find collective solutions together, to stop this escalation that is generated only by a minority on both sides." They ended the letter by inviting residents to the public events organized by the collective, and by suggesting potential avenues for solving the tensions, including the creation of spaces for youth, improving acoustic isolation of buildings, organizing more neighborhood events, or having a local mediator people could call in case of conflict. "These ideas might seem incomplete, but they aim to show our eagerness to promote dialogue in this neighborhood that we share and love, each in our own way."[31]

Throughout the two weeks of public debates, some middle-class White residents placed the blame on "the youth"—code for Black and Arab teenagers—who were collectively accused of vandalism, degrading public property, and being too loud. In response, the organizers sought to shift the blame away from individuals—loud youth or intolerant neighbors—and toward structural problems of urban planning such as the poor acoustics of the building overlooking the Saint-Eloi square, or the lack of spaces for young people to hang out. One participant to the debate summarized: "it's not a problem of people who want to sleep versus youth [who are loud], it's a problem of urban planning."[32] The organizers also sought to raise the residents' awareness on the routine police violence the teenagers experienced. For instance, Adam said:

These identity checks are veritable ceremonies of degradation. Being thrown up against a wall is very humiliating. It's akin to breaking individuals, considering them second-class citizens. So, this is something that the residents who call the police should take into account before calling.[33]

Every member of the collective I spoke with recognized that some of the complaining residents had legitimate grievances. The youth groups were sometimes too loud, and there had been a couple of assaults. "But the solution is not to call the cops, the solution is dialogue," Mathilde insisted. To her, the less communication between the youth and other residents, the more fear develops, and the more likely it becomes that every minor incident will be resolved through calling the police rather than through dialogue.

One of the most important roles that the collective played was to act as a mediator when conflicts emerged around the use of public space, to try to resolve issues without involving the police. In the summer of 2016, there was an unprecedented escalation in the tensions between some of the young men hanging out in Saint-Eloi square and some of the residents. After a particularly virulent argument between a White woman living in the building overlooking the square and a group of young people hanging out, a teenager threw a Molotov cocktail at the apartment of the woman through an open window. According to his friends, this young man was going through a difficult time, as his mother was very sick. The woman "kept shouting insults about his mother, so he didn't take it well and he made a Molotov cocktail, and he threw it."

The fire was put out and there were no injuries, but the incident quickly spread and exacerbated the feeling, among many residents, that the youth were out of control. Immediately following this incident, the collective organized a meeting with the woman and the young men involved. One of the teenagers who attended recalled:

> [The collective organized] a meeting, we were all there, including Michael [who threw the Molotov cocktail]. Michael talked to the lady and everything. She didn't know about his mother and she apologized, because Michael is in a difficult situation. We talked and things worked out, we found common ground.[34]

During the two-week event Making Space for Youth, organizers raised this incident as an illustration of the dramatic escalation that can happen when neighborhood tensions go unchecked. The woman who had received a Molotov cocktail in her apartment spoke up. One night, she said, exhausted and exasperated, she had a "brutal exchange of words with one of the young men on the square, followed by an exchange of insults." She wasn't here to point fingers, she continued, but rather to "testify to how quickly things can go awry and become dramatic when we don't find the right words"; she too had failed to speak to the young men with respect and missed an opportunity for dialogue. Several young men present came forward to thank her and to apologize.[35] To Victor, this exchange "was a way of saying: can we manage to speak to each other, to get to know each other, so that when there are tensions, we can avoid shouting at each other and letting a form of hatred emerge."[36]

Of course, these mediation efforts did not resolve all conflicts, but they helped appease some tensions and, importantly, helped build bridges between the young men and some of the residents of the Saint-Eloi square. Some of them told me that the police had been using the Molotov cocktail incident to step up their harassment of the young men, but following meetings like these, "people with complaints talk to us" rather than immediately calling the police.

By creating spaces of public deliberation in which the most marginalized residents were included, and their voices centered, Making Space for Youth created connections between social groups that did not otherwise interact in the neighborhood. This helped establish channels of communication that could be used to avoid relying on the police to resolve conflicts about the shared use of public space. It also mobilized the left-leaning, progressive residents, raised their awareness on the issues facing their racialized neighbors, and gave them a space to organize collectively to promote social inclusion policies and infrastructure.

Police Retaliation

Despite the mobilization's significant achievements in terms of expanding legal claims about racialized policing, and creating networks to promote social inclusion, the abusive policing practices targeting young men from low-income immigrant families continued unabated. The lawyers made demands on the prosecution to set up preventive measures to protect the plaintiffs, but few were implemented, and they didn't stop the accused officers—and those that came after them—from continuing their abusive practices.

More worryingly, the accused officers retaliated against the plaintiffs. A few months before the trial of the Tigers brigade, several plaintiffs received a notice to appear in court on charges of false accusation (*dénonciation calomnieuse*). In their lawsuit, the accused officers relied on the fact that most of the plaintiffs' allegations had been dismissed for insufficient evidence. The young men were alarmed; no one had warned them of this possibility, and they feared it would result in a criminal record that would jeopardize their future life chances. Within two days, Malik organized a meeting with the plaintiffs, their parents, and the lawyers, to discuss how to respond to the notices.

During the meeting, the plaintiffs and families' nervousness was striking. A North African father, who spoke with a heavy accent, told us that his son was worried. He was now in college and feared that this charge would jeopardize his studies. As a teenager, he was repeatedly stopped and detained by the police for no reason; "every time I went to collect him in police custody, they told me; you'll see, as soon as he turns 18, we're sending him to prison!" Now it seemed that they were delivering on their threats. A Black mother shared that her son had just been arrested and was currently being sentenced. She kept checking her phone throughout the meeting, waiting for updates. The few plaintiffs present remained silent.

The lawyers sought to reassure everyone that the notice to appear was nothing to worry about. "It's not credible at all for [the police] to say it was all made up, we have evidence," one lawyer said; the lawsuit led to "a huge investigation by the IGPN [police inspection services]," and there had been an indictment decision against some of the officers, two developments that were exceptional in cases of police violence. Even though a large proportion of the allegations was dismissed, she insisted, the investigation uncovered solid evidence substantiating the youth's allegations. "We have too many elements against them; their false accusations charge is not credible." In fact, she added, the lawyers planned to use the false accusation suit in the upcoming trial of the indicted officers, to show that the police "feel that they're protected by the judiciary and by the state, even when they're in the wrong."[37]

The plaintiffs and parents seemed somewhat relieved, but hearing that the false accusation charge was unlikely to succeed did little to appease their broader concerns about the continued police harassment the youth experienced in the neighborhood. Counselor Malik intervened several times during the meeting to talk about the ongoing issues between the police and the youth. "Despite the lawsuit, there's a new generation of cops that reproduce the same behaviors," he said. Some of the plaintiffs were currently under arrest or incarcerated, and others continued being subjected to police brutality. He brought up the problem of repeated fines for minor incivilities, which led some teens to have thousands of euros of debt in a matter of months. At one point, interrupting the meeting, the mother who had been nervously checking her phone announced, with tears in her eyes, that her son had just been convicted and sent to jail for three months.

This illustrates a key limitation of the grounded approach to knowledge production. It allows activists to shed light on a wide range of abusive policing practices, but it relies on the willingness of already vulnerable people to testify publicly about the abuses they suffer. Yet, neither the lawyers nor the local organizers had the means or resources to protect them from continued police abuses or retaliation.

In fact, despite the significant evidence uncovered by the investigation, criminal courts ended up siding with the police, both in the police violence lawsuit and in the false accusation case. In 2020, the Court of Appeal reversed the three officers' conviction for aggravated assault and acquitted them. Then, in 2022, four plaintiffs were convicted for false accusation and sentenced to pay between 3,000 and 9,000 euros in compensation to the police officers who had harassed and assaulted them. Ultimately, in court, the police narrative had won. The media coverage of the conviction centered on a quote by the officers' lawyer, in which he said, "this ruling finally establishes the truth in this case. The police officers I represent committed no misconduct and were the victims of instrumentalization on the part of the plaintiffs." No one involved in the mobilization was interviewed, but the dispatch mentioned that, at the trial, Slim Ben Achour had called this case a gag procedure (*procédure bâillon*) intended to silence victims.[38]

When the youth were informed of the false accusation conviction in 2022, Malik called me, upset and at a loss for how to help them. I asked whether he had spoken to someone at Open Society, but he hadn't. He believed that they had moved on from this case. By that time, Open Society was undergoing a massive restructuring and their racial profiling program no longer existed. The collective Making Space for Youth continued organizing in the neighborhood on issues affecting marginalized youth, responding to new problems as they arose, including the rise in abusive fines and interneighborhood violence. But without financial support or legal expertise, they did so with limited resources.

Soon, Malik and the plaintiffs (now defendants) connected with Sarah and the lawyers, and they worked together to appeal the decision. In 2025, the Court of Appeal confirmed these convictions and they appealed again to the Court of Cassation. At the time of writing, they are awaiting the court's decision.

In a context where the police use their epistemic power to discredit, delegitimize, and even obtain convictions against those who speak out against racialized police abuses, activists struggle to protect victims. The strength of this mobilization was that it brought together local actors who had intimate knowledge of the dynamics of the neighborhood, and outside experts who brought campaigning skills and legal expertise in support of local needs. But to the experts, their involvement was a temporary project, not a long-term investment. Without sustainable resources to continue documenting policing practices and their evolutions, and without the financial capacity to maintain public attention, the local organizers were left with few means to safeguard the neighborhood's Black and Arab youth.

Conclusion

The neighborhood mobilization produced knowledge through centering the experiences of those most frequently targeted by the police in one local space. Over an extended period of time, community organizers documented the youth's routine interactions with the police as well as their broader experiences in the neighborhood's public space. This grounded epistemology shed light on a wide range of abusive policing practices and on their routine, repeated nature—from unjustified stops, to arbitrary detention, to physical and sexual violence.

Drawing on this knowledge, coalition actors launched a lawsuit against eleven police officers, and through this case, uncovered institutional policies to "evict undesirables." This allowed the lawyers to expand their legal claims, from denouncing misconduct by individual officers, to condemning institutional policies that use racialized terminology to justify the harassment of Black and Arab youth in public spaces. Moreover, community organizers drew on the youth's testimonies to highlight how race and class tensions about the use of public space undergirded the police's abusive practices. As a result, local activists focused their organizing not only on policing issues but also on fostering social and spatial inclusion.

Centering the experiences of the policed was instrumental in allowing activists to shed light on the institutional and societal mechanisms fostering racialized policing practices. But it also came at a high cost for the victims, who suffered retaliation in the form of continued police brutality, abusive fines, and a conviction for false accusation. The NGOs and lawyers could not fully protect them. In the next chapter, I examine a movement in which victims were centered in knowledge practices, not just as the source of data but also as the main knowers, capable of drawing on their personal and collective experiences to develop a political analysis of their own oppression.

FOUR

Police Assassinate, Judges Exonerate

On June 18, 2007, Ramata Dieng was at work when she got a message from her sister that said, "this is not a joke: Lamine is dead." Lamine, their younger brother, was twenty-five at the time. The siblings had grown up in the twentieth arrondissement of Paris, a working-class neighborhood with a large immigrant community, where their parents had settled in the early 1980s after moving from Senegal. When a police officer called the family home to say that Lamine had died "on the street," the Diengs assumed he had a motorcycle accident. But when they went to the police for more information, they were told he had died during a police intervention. There, officers gave them two contradictory accounts. The police chief said that Lamine was arrested inside a hotel room where he had allegedly assaulted his girlfriend, that officers had struggled to arrest him, but eventually managed to take him outside of the hotel, where he suddenly "went limp" and lost consciousness. The police commander gave them a different story. He said the officers had found Lamine in the street hiding between two cars; that his arrest had been violent, and that he had lost consciousness when he was inside the police van. The commander added that Lamine was under the influence of drugs and alcohol. These contradictory accounts raised alarm bells for the family, Ramata recalled. "First, because why two different stories? And also, because the person they described didn't fit with what we knew about Lamine."[1] The siblings remembered how shocking it was to realize the police may be lying. "We are all socialized into believing that the police are there to protect us, that what they say is the truth, but for us, all of this was quickly swept away."[2]

Four years later, the El Yamni family went through a similar shock. On New Year's Eve of 2012, Wissam El Yamni was arrested as he was partying with friends in the parking lot of a housing project on the outskirts of Clermont Ferrand. This was where the thirty-year-old had lived with his family after they moved from their native Morocco. Shortly after his arrest, he was taken to a hospital unconscious. He remained in a coma and passed away nine days later. The police released a statement claiming that Wissam's arrest had been difficult. The man, they said, was under the influence of alcohol, cannabis, and cocaine, and was "very agitated." After a foot chase, the police caught him, pushed him to the ground, handcuffed him, and took him in a police vehicle, where he suffered a cardiac arrest. Wissam's family and friends were immediately doubtful of this narrative. Several neighborhood residents had witnessed a large group of police officers beat Wissam brutally while he was on the ground handcuffed. They told investigators and journalists that, after officers arrested Wissam, placed him face down on the ground, and handcuffed him, a dozen police cars arrived; "the officers got out of their cars, blasted funk music, and unmuzzled the dogs. They were excited, they did a countdown, 'three-two-one-go' and they beat him up."[3] This account was corroborated by multiple signs of violence on the victims' body. When his brother Farid visited him in the hospital, with his sister and parents, he noticed multiple broken bones, bruises all over his body, and red marks around his neck. Yet, the autopsy report concluded that there had been no physical violence against the deceased. Confused and grieving, Farid and the rest of his family wanted to understand what had really happened.

When she learned of her brother's death, Assa Traoré, too, found the police's story implausible. Adama Traoré was arrested on July 19, 2016, on the day of his twenty-fourth birthday. Born into a large Malian family, he lived in Beaumont-sur-Oise, a small, low-income city on the outskirts of Paris. It was on the streets of his hometown that, on the afternoon of his birthday, three police officers[4] approached his brother and him. Adama tried to run away, most probably because he did not have his ID on him, and he wanted to avoid being taken to the station for identity verification. Officers caught up with him and brought him to the police station. Shortly after, a rumor started spreading in the neighborhood that he had lost consciousness. His siblings went looking for him in nearby hospitals, and when they were redirected to the police station, Adama's mother went asking after him at the precinct. There, officers confirmed that Adama was in their custody and assured her that he was fine. She returned several times over the next few hours, and every time, officers told her that he was fine. The police station even agreed to take a sandwich that she brought for her son and promised to give it to him. It wasn't until the evening, when Adama's mother and brother forced their way into the police station and demanded to see him, that officers confessed that he had been dead for three hours. They said that Adama had "a sudden heart attack" when he arrived at the station, caused by his running in hot weather while under the influence of drugs and alcohol.[5] The next day, the prosecution released a statement clearing the police of responsibility and affirming that the autopsy suggested a death by heart attack due to "a very serious infection affecting multiple organs." Neither of these accounts seemed plausible to Adama's family and friends. The young man was known for his athleticism, he was in perfect health, and he didn't drink or do drugs. As his sister Assa told me, "we immediately thought: that's a lie, what they were saying, it wasn't possible."[6]

For Ramata Dieng, Farid El Yamni, and Assa Traoré, the shock and trauma of losing their brothers was compounded by the fact that the police accounts seemed implausible and incoherent. Intent on figuring out what had really happened, they listened carefully when activists came to them with advice. A week after Lamine Dieng's death, Ramata organized a vigil in the neighborhood where he grew up and was killed. Several activists showed up. Ramata recalled, "They explained that Lamine is not the only one, that there are others, and that, in those types of situations, you should create a Truth and Justice committee, that you should organize meetings."[7] They told her that the family must file a complaint to ensure that an investigation would be opened. They should request a counterautopsy and start doing their own investigation about what happened. Following this advice, Ramata established the committee Truth and Justice for Lamine, which brought together members of the Dieng family and local activists. The committee met weekly to organize public events demanding justice. It also followed up on the judicial investigation and coordinated joint actions with other families of victims across the country. Years later, the El Yamni and Traoré families followed the same path.

By doing so, these families joined the Truth and Justice movement, a loosely structured national network composed of local committees, which have been forming since the 1980s following cases of police-caused deaths. The committees organize protests and public events calling for justice, they conduct counterinvestigations into the circumstances of the deaths, and they provide support to newly affected families. Throughout the 2010s, around two dozen local Truth and Justice committees were actively involved in the movement.

This chapter follows some of the families that were at the heart of the Truth and Justice movement from the late 2000s to the early 2020s. It examines how they investigated the circumstances of their loved ones' deaths, and what they learned through their quest for justice. I show that the mode of knowledge production that the movement adopted—*liberation epistemology*—provided families of victims with an important foundation for the development of their political consciousness. It gave them a space to learn about the structures of oppression within which their brothers' deaths are embedded and tools to articulate their personal loss within a broader analysis of state violence, racial inequality, and injustice. Amid tensions over who should lead the movement—activists or families of victims—liberation epistemology helped families establish themselves as the voice of the movement. This led to the development of a movement discourse that made space for different families' diverse political analyses, but which emphasized common themes: the role of the judiciary in perpetuating police brutality, and the indirect harms that police brutality causes to whole communities. The chapter focuses primarily on the stories of the Dieng, El Yamni, and Traoré families, but I also draw on examples from other relatives who were active in the movement in the 2010s.

Placing Families at the Center

By the time Ramata Dieng joined the movement in 2007, conflicts were emerging over the movement's ownership, with disagreements over who should lead—activists or families of victims. Throughout the 1990s and the first years of the twenty-first century, most Truth and Justice committees were led and coordinated by activists, with limited involvement of the families. These committees' composition varied, but they typically included a diversity of activist groups, including antiracist organizations, *quartiers populaires* organizers (community organizers in low-income neighborhoods), human rights groups, and sometimes far-left political parties. At the time, the movement's most important organization was the MIB (Mouvement de l'immigration et des Banlieues), a group of *quartiers populaires* organizers who worked to disseminate the movement's tactical repertoire to communities affected by police killings.

The MIB believed that to be effective, the struggle must be led by activists embedded in local communities. To them, grieving families were dealing with significant emotional shock and trauma, which meant that they could not—and should not—deal with the political aspect of the struggle. "Within the MIB, we believe that the best way to protect the family is to manage the case from A to Z, both on a human and a financial level." Building a national network capable of developing collective political grievances, they argued, required keeping the families in the background; "it's difficult to involve the families to act collectively, because instinctively they have a tendency to bring their personal case to the fore."[8]

In the late 2000s, some families of victims started challenging the movement's activist-led structure. The MIB had been dismantled because of activist fatigue and internal divisions, leaving a void in the coordination of the national network. Some families wanted to take on more leadership roles. Ramata Dieng recalled, "an idea was emerging, that we spoke about a lot in the activist field, that there was a gap, a void that we need to fill [to coordinate various families' actions]."[9]

Ramata spearheaded the efforts to recenter the movement around families of victims. Like many of the siblings who would become leading figures of the movement, Ramata grew up in an immigrant, working-class family, and had experienced some upward social mobility compared to her parents. She was born in Senegal, the second of seven children, "but the eldest girl," she often told me, to explain why she took on a mothering role toward her younger siblings. After graduating with a technical diploma and working at McDonald's for a few years, she had attended trainings in digital technology and become a webmaster. Except for attending a couple of protests when she was in high school, she had no activist experience before losing her brother, at the age of thirty-five.

Convinced that families like hers needed an organizational structure to support their work, Ramata created a national collective of families of victims of police killings in 2010. Borrowing the name from an American group she had read about online, she called it Vies Volées (Stolen Lives).

The collective's first goal was to support newly affected families at the early stages following their loss. "We realized that when people go through a traumatic event, a terrorist attack or whatnot, the state is present, they establish a psychological support cell and so on, but we didn't have any of this." The collective aimed to provide this support to newly aggrieved families and to guide them through the steps required for demanding justice. Ramata explained, "When you find yourself in this kind of situation, you have the emotional pain to deal with, but you also have to find a lawyer, and you have to know which kind of lawyer to pick. And there's also the activist aspect [to deal with] . . . it's not easy to make the right choices and not waste time." The collective helped families take the right steps and "learn from the experiences of others to avoid making the same mistakes or wasting time."[10]

Another goal of Vies Volées was for families of victims to gain more ownership over the movement. The idea, Ramata said, was "to give these families voice and visibility" in a space "that is not co-opted by anyone, where it's really us, the families." She described it as a space where "the families are at the center, and around them there are all the allies." In my conversations with her and other families over the years, many expressed frustration that some activists would spend a few months or years in the movement, and then move on to other things, abandoning their support for the families' struggle. "There's a pattern of betrayals," Farid El Yamni once told me, "some are with you and then they end up taking on government positions."[11] Families needed a structure where they would organize collectively, he explained, because only other families would never betray the cause.

In 2010, Vies Volées enrolled half a dozen families of victims, held phone meetings, and started organizing actions to raise funds and bring visibility to various struggles for justice. Starting in 2011, the collective launched an annual march of families of victims, which took place every year in March, between the International Day against Police Brutality and the International Day for the Elimination of Racial Discrimination. This became the flagship yearly event of the Truth and Justice movement.

Alongside Ramata Dieng, several other family members emerged as leading figures of the movement. Amal Bentounsi, a woman of Tunisian origin, joined the movement after her brother Amine was killed by the police in 2012. Wanting to take a more forceful approach than Vies Volées, she created another collective of families in 2013, Urgence Notre Police Assassine (Emergency Our Police Kills). Along with a half dozen other families who joined Urgence, Amal led several high-visibility direct action events that gained her public notoriety. Then, in 2016, the death of Adama Traoré garnered exceptionally high media attention, and his sister Assa became the most visible figure of the Truth and Justice movement.

By the late 2010s, families of victims had successfully imposed themselves as the lead coordinators and spokespersons of the Truth and Justice movement. Ramata Dieng, Amal Bentounsi, and Assa Traoré were the most visible leaders. Activists remained actively involved in Truth and Justice committees and in the national network, but they were rebranded allies (*soutiens*). When disagreements emerged, families insisted that they should be the ultimate decision-makers.

Who Can Speak for the Dead?

Social movement scholars have shown that organizing around a victim identity can be a double-edged sword. On one hand, victims are more likely to garner broad support when they portray themselves as innocent sufferers motivated by a desire for justice, rather than by partisan ideology. On the other hand, to construct a sustainable movement, victims must develop a collective identity and a shared political vision, which requires contextualizing their personal tragedies within broader structures of oppression.[12] There is often a tension between victims' tendency to emphasize their specific experience of suffering and the need to generalize from these experiences to develop a shared vision for political change.[13]

Once families of victims took over the leadership of the Truth and Justice movement, this tension between the personal and the political aspects of the struggle was a recurring issue. This was particularly visible in the early days of organizing following Wissam El Yamni's death. His death, nine days after his arrest on New Year's Eve of 2012, triggered a rebellion in the neighborhood where he was killed. For three nights, young people burned cars, angry over what they perceived to be authorities' blatant lies to cover up the fact that the police had beaten an Arab man to death.

Within days, seasoned activists came to the neighborhood to help the rioters turn their revolt into a sustained political movement. They advised Wissam's friends to establish a Truth and Justice committee. They told them they should plan public actions (peaceful marches, sit-ins) and follow up on the judicial investigation closely. The goal, they explained, was to "make as much noise as possible" around the case to pressure the authorities to indict the police officers.[14] Based on this advice, some of Wissam's friends established the committee Justice Truth for Wissam, which brought together neighborhood residents and local activists, including autonomous organizers and far-left political party representatives.

A few weeks after the creation of Justice Truth for Wissam, conflicts started appearing between the El Yamni family and some members of the committee. Initially, on the advice of former MIB members, the committee sought to keep the family out of their organizing. They believed that Wissam's parents and siblings were too emotionally affected to be involved in the political struggle; "we thought, they are grieving, they are hurting, a hundred times more than us. We lost a friend, but they lost a brother, a son. So, we didn't want to involve them in the struggle, we thought we will take over the struggle and the protests and leave the family out of it."[15]

But Wissam's parents and two siblings were uneasy when they realized that some of the activists that joined the committee used Wissam's death to talk about broader issues of social exclusion and discrimination facing youth in marginalized neighborhoods. The family preferred to maintain an "apolitical" discourse focused on demanding "justice for Wissam, and nothing else." The victim's younger brother, Farid, told me that, at the time, the family trusted the state and the judiciary. "We endorsed the Republican thing, we protested with the French flag, we believed in it, we believed that obtaining justice was possible." To them, some of the committee's members were exploiting the family's tragedy for the sake of their activist or political careers. "Wissam was just a step toward something else . . . Wissam was being forgotten for the sake of something that speaks about all questions of justice."[16]

Like Farid El Yamni, most aggrieved families initially preferred adopting an "apolitical" discourse that aligned with the dominant ideology: describing the fatal encounter as a blunder (*bavure*) and expressing trust in judicial institutions. They believed that steering clear of claims that could be viewed as partisan would help them be perceived as deserving victims.

This often meant avoiding discussions of race and racism, which are always contentious in France. As racialized people, families of victims understood that they were particularly vulnerable to accusations of playing the race card (*se victimiser*), or of *communautarisme*, a critique often levied at minoritized groups to suggest they refuse to integrate into French society and promote ethnic separatism. Since their most immediate goal was to get recognized as victims of injustice, both in courts and in the eyes of the public, many were initially careful to craft a discourse that fit with the dominant antiracialist ideology.

Even when family members believed that there was a racist dimension to their loved one's killing, many were initially cautious. When I interviewed Assa Traoré two months after the death of her brother in 2016, I asked her why the Malian-origin family never mentioned racism in their public statements. Assa, who was a trained youth counselor, and would later become one of the most prominent antiracist voices in France, replied:

> Today, what we're defending, it's Adama's cause: what happened on that day, on July 19, 2016, his death: we want truth and justice for this. . . . We know there are causes: discrimination, racism, but we don't talk about that in the media because we don't want to confine ourselves, we don't want for people to confine us. Maybe it will be a struggle we will lead later on . . . the people who support us, they include all colors, all religions, all cultures, I don't want us to get confined in this, and that these people get excluded from us. . . . We don't want in our cause that some people feel excluded, because for us, the only people we want excluded and judged are those police officers.[17]

Aware of the risk of being delegitimized from the outset if they explicitly talked about the role of race in Adama's death, the Traoré family intentionally avoided the topic during the first months of the mobilization and limited their public discourse to calls for the indictment of the officers who arrested him. They only started talking about racism months later, after they garnered widespread media attention.

Within Truth and Justice committees, families' reluctance to emphasize racism sometimes triggered internal conflicts. For example, the committee Justice and Truth for Babacar was created following the death of Babacar Gueye, a twenty-seven-year-old Senegalese man who was shot dead by the police in 2015 in Rennes as he was having a mental health crisis. The committee included Babacar's sister Awa and a handful of his friends as well as local antiracist activists. During the first year of the committee's work, some activists grew frustrated at the loved ones' reluctance to address the political dimensions of Babacar's killing. They wanted to highlight his Blackness and his undocumented status in press releases, to argue that his death was part of a broader pattern of state-sponsored violence against racialized populations. But Babacar's sister Awa was reluctant to emphasize what she perceived as diminishing his legitimacy as a victim of injustice. This frustrated the antiracist activists involved in the committee: "there is a strong assimilationism when you are undocumented in France, you want to be integrated, to have a job and a house, and so to not talk about race." The activists also grew impatient with one of the founders of the committee, a White woman who was Babacar's friend. One of the committee members reflected:

> She was here because Babacar was a loved one, not because he was Black, not because he was undocumented, not because he was precariously employed, not because it was police brutality. She was here because it's an injustice. And that's okay, but how do you go from the stage "injustice" to a localized injustice, to a structural injustice and a coordinated struggle with the other collectives?[18]

This was a central question for the Truth and Justice movement. With the movement structured around victims' families, who became the primary spokespersons, the development of a political discourse had to follow the pace of politicization of victims' families. The challenge was to center each family's quest for justice while also creating the conditions for them to politicize their personal losses in order to move from a series of individual demands for justice, to a coordinated movement with a shared political vision on issues of police violence, inequality, and injustice. Seasoned families and activists needed to create the conditions for newly affected families to gain consciousness of the structures of oppression within which their personal loss was embedded.

What these conditions are remains unclear, however. Some studies show that experiences of injustice contribute to raising victims' political consciousness of structures of oppression,[19] but others find that organizing around a victim identity can be depoliticizing, especially when demanding justice in courts.[20] Even when victims take ownership of the mobilization effort, reaching a shared political vision is often fraught. In her study of mothers mobilizing to free their sons caught up in California's brutal and racist criminal justice system, Ruth Gilmore shows that, while the mothers felt a strong connection to each other because of the similarity of their experiences, there were conflicts over how to frame the cause, which political alliances to foster, and what political demands to prioritize.[21]

While existing scholarship has identified these challenges, we know less about how actors within victim-centered movements work through them, why some movements result in the politicization of victims and others foster depoliticization, and how scattered victims build a collective political voice. The next sections show that the mode of knowledge production a movement adopts can play a role by providing the foundation for victims' journey of politicization and for the development of a collective political analysis for the movement.

Liberation Epistemology

In the Truth and Justice movement, the impetus for producing knowledge stemmed from families' personal, intimate need to understand "what really happened" to their loved one, and why it is so difficult to obtain an indictment of the officers responsible for his death. Unlike the other coalitions examined in this book, knowledge-making did not start with the goal of uncovering patterns of policing practice. Rather, it began by investigating specific police interactions, one case at a time. Then, as families of victims met other families and started comparing their experiences, they broadened their knowledge practices to include an analysis of the recurrent patterns of judicial practice in cases of police violence. In both phases of knowledge production—investigating individual cases and comparing experiences in the judicial process—families of victims were centered, not just as sources of data to be interpreted by others but as knowers in their own right.

I call this approach *liberation epistemology*, a mode of knowledge production in which those who are usually seen as objects of research, as "problems" to be examined by social scientists, come to analyze their own situation as knowing subjects. Building on insights from Black feminist thought,[22] standpoint theory,[23] anticolonial and critical race theory,[24] and science and technology studies,[25] I use liberation epistemology to refer to a ground-up approach in which (1) knowledge is produced by people directly affected by a social problem (*les premiers concernés*) (2) who define the issues to be investigated and (3) produce knowledge by articulating their lived experiences (4) with theoretical analyses of systems of oppression.

Like the grounded epistemology examined in the previous chapter, liberation epistemology takes the experiences of policing victims as the starting point of inquiry. But whereas the former relies on victims' experiences as data to be analyzed and interpreted by others (lawyers, social workers), the latter deems victims to be legitimate knowers, capable of analyzing their own experiences and producing knowledge claims.

Searching for Truth

For most families of victims, the shock of losing a loved one to the police is compounded when they are given an official narrative (or several) that seems implausible or incoherent. This was the case for Adama Traoré's family and friends, who did not believe he had died of a heart attack or of a "very serious infection" as the authorities claimed. Intent on uncovering what had happened inside the police station, the grieving family listened carefully when activists came knocking at their door on the day following Adama's death. As urban revolts raged in their hometown of Beaumont-sur-Oise, they received the visit of Amal Bentounsi, who founded the collective of families, Urgence, after losing her brother Amine in 2012, along with a *quartiers populaires* organizer and an antiracist activist.

The trio of visitors warned the Traoré family that, in cases of police-involved deaths, police investigators and prosecutors do everything in their power to clear officers of responsibility. If they wanted to uncover what actually happened, the activists told them, they would need to take matters into their own hands. This meant organizing politically—with marches, protests, and press conferences—but also, importantly, conducting their own investigation into the circumstances of Adama's death.

One of the main pieces of advice Truth and Justice leaders typically gave newly aggrieved families was that they should not rely on the professionals whose job it is to uncover the truth. Prosecutors, lawyers, and judicial experts had their own interests, which may conflict with the search for truth, activists explained. Prosecutors are often reluctant to conduct thorough investigations into police-involved deaths because they work closely with the police on a day-to-day basis. Judicial experts privilege the police narrative because these are the scenarios that they are asked to investigate. Even the victim's lawyer might be reluctant to aggressively defend the family's interests in order to maintain good working relationships with investigative judges and prosecutors.

Instead, families of victims were told to launch a counterinvestigation (*contre-enquête*). This tactic consists in lay actors investigating the circumstances of the fatal police interaction independently from the judicial investigation by carefully reviewing all the pieces of evidence included in the legal file, searching for witnesses, and collecting missing elements that might help shed light on the facts.[26] Counterinvestigations have a dual goal: to cast doubts on the official version of events by exposing the inconsistencies and flaws in the police narrative,[27] and to propose an alternative narrative based on the evidence collected.

Thus, veteran leaders of the Truth and Justice movement encouraged families to go beyond the role traditionally assigned to them in the criminal justice process—to provide data to investigators, who will then analyze it to uncover the "truth." Instead, the goal was for them to take on the role of the investigator, collecting data and analyzing it themselves, thereby imposing themselves as legitimate knowers. Ramata Dieng put it this way:

> [You must] read in detail each and every police officer's interrogation [transcript], the medical file, all the police reports. Everything. You must try to put the adversary in a difficult position, find the loophole, do [the lawyer's] job in a way. You have to look for contradictions and not give *carte blanche* to those who are supposed to represent you.[28]

Following this advice, Adama's loved ones established the committee Truth for Adama, which included members of the family and close friends of Adama as well as *quartiers populaires* organizers who offered their support. They hired a lawyer, filed a complaint, requested a counterautopsy, and started reading the investigation file.

In it, they discovered that the prosecutor had lied: while the first autopsy report had indeed mentioned an infection, it also concluded that the cause of death was asphyxia, an element the prosecutor had conveniently left out of his public statements. The prosecutor had also failed to mention that the officers who arrested Adama had testified that they had maintained him in a face-down hold, on the ground, with the weight of three bodies on his back for several minutes. Adama, they said, told them that he had difficulty breathing. When the police officers got off his back, handcuffed him, and placed him in the police van, Adama fainted and lost control of his bladder.

The committee Truth for Adama also noticed an important contradiction between the officers' testimonies and those of the medical professionals who were called in. The arresting officers claimed that, upon their arrival at the police station, they placed Adama in the recovery position and immediately called medical services, but the firefighters testified that, when they arrived, Adama was lying face down on the floor, handcuffed, with no one attending to him. The officers seemed unconcerned and told them that he was "faking it." When the firefighters checked, they found he had already stopped breathing.

The investigation file included one more element that cast doubt on the official narrative. When the counterautopsy was completed, it discredited the hypothesis of an infection and confirmed that the death had resulted from asphyxia, although it remained vague as to what might have caused the asphyxia.

Based on these pieces of evidence, the committee developed a counternarrative about the circumstance of Adama's death. In the media, they raised doubts about the theory of a health condition, and they suggested that Adama died of asphyxia caused by the restraining hold that the officers used against him. They leaked elements of the investigation file to the media, argued that the prosecutor had knowingly lied about the autopsy's conclusions, and requested that the case be moved to another judicial district. Within two months of Adama's death, they had successfully introduced their counternarrative in the mainstream media. The largest local newspaper, *Le Parisien*, titled its article "Adama Traoré's Death: The Hypothesis of Asphyxiation under the Weight of the Police Officers"; while the most-read daily *Le Monde* emphasized that the police narrative was being contested, titling its article "Adama Traoré's Death: A Fireman Contradicts the Policemen's Version."[29]

Like the Traoré family, other Truth and Justice committees conducted counterinvestigations and disseminated their findings. They typically leaked elements of the investigation file to the media—autopsy reports, testimonies, or forensic evidence. Some published essays and books detailing the results of their counterinvestigation or worked with documentary filmmakers to create visual narratives of the fatal incident.

These counterinvestigations are powerful tools to cast doubts on police accounts and to promote an alternative narrative about the circumstance of police-involved deaths. They allow the Truth and Justice movement to disrupt the hierarchy of credibility by discrediting police narratives and challenging the assumption that the police tell the truth.

However, this mode of knowledge production also entails huge financial and emotional costs, which many families struggled with. The legal process is costly. Families must pay lawyers' and court fees, and given the length of these investigations, the total cost of a judicial procedure often amounts to several thousands of euros, and sometimes exceeds 10,000 euros, a sum that is unaffordable for most families of victims. The committees' efforts to raise funds by selling t-shirts or through online crowdfunding campaigns are often insufficient.

Moreover, being involved in the counterinvestigation has a steep emotional cost. Reading and analyzing the investigation file can be extremely painful for grieving families. Some find it excruciating to release elements of the investigation publicly, which can limit the committee's ability to promote a counternarrative. For example, following the death of Ali Ziri, a sixty-nine-year-old Algerian man, activists in the Committee Truth and Justice for Ali Ziri wanted to make posters with a drawing of the victim's body showing the multiple bruises recorded in the autopsy report. The plan was to display them around Argenteuil, the city where he died. However, the victim's daughter said that she could not bear seeing these posters all around town. "Of course, we didn't want to pressure her, so we had to work with this," one member of the committee told me, "which in a sense gave credence to the MIB position according to which the families are too emotionally caught up and the mobilization should be led by independent organizations."[30]

Uncovering the Manufacturing of Police Impunity

While many families initially trusted the courts to hold the police accountable, their involvement in the counterinvestigation—reading the investigation file and making requests to the judge—led the families to start questioning the practices of judicial institutions. As a result, the initial focus on investigating police killings typically expanded to add an analysis of the judiciary's response in cases of police killings. The case of Wissam El

Yamni illustrates how families' experiences in criminal proceedings can lead them to broaden their knowledge-making practice to the judicial system.

When, following activists' advice, the El Yamni family read the investigation file, they found multiple pieces of evidence contradicting the official narrative. Yet, the investigative judges did little to follow these threads and relied instead on the police officers' testimonies to make determinations about the cause of death. For instance, the preliminary autopsy report concluded that there had been no physical violence against the deceased and that the death was caused by a compression of the neck's blood vessels combined with "abnormalities in his bone structure." This gave credence to the police claim that, because of Wissam's agitation, they had to maintain him in a "folding" hold in the police car, with his head pressed against his knees, a restraining technique that was authorized in France. Yet, when Wissam's family read the full report, they noticed that it hadn't mentioned, let alone explained, the victim's bruises, broken bones, and red marks around his neck. The family contested the results of the preliminary autopsy and requested a second autopsy, but the judge refused and instead ordered an expert opinion, to be written by the same medical examiner who wrote the autopsy report. Without surprise, the examiner reached the same conclusion again. The family filed another request for a counterautopsy, but by the time the judges ordered it, the court-appointed expert found that the body had not been kept refrigerated and had started rotting. He was unable to reexamine the body.

Moreover, despite multiple pieces of evidence going against the police's narrative, the investigative judges did little to explore alternative scenarios, including the possibility that Wissam had been beaten to death. The police officers' testimonies were confused and inconsistent with one another, and their version of events was contradicted by three eyewitnesses who testified that they saw Wissam get beaten up by several police officers following his arrest. Yet, investigators did not interrogate the officers on the contradictions in their accounts, or allow the witnesses to confront them.

Many other facts remained unexplained. When investigators asked the officers why Wissam had his pants down to his ankles when he was found unconscious, they replied that he was wearing a very baggy tracksuit that dropped on its own as he exited the car. But a video captured on that night showed Wissam wearing a pair of jeans tightly held by a belt. The officers had no explanation for the belt's disappearance.

When the family made requests to the investigative judges, the judges responded with significant delay. Despite repeated requests from the family, it took the court two years to request CCTV footage and radio communications from the police station for the night of the arrest, and by that time, large parts were missing. The investigation file also included photos taken of Wissam during his hospital stay, which police claimed were taken on the day of his arrest. But the family believed that the pictures were taken several days later, when the bruises and red marks around his neck had faded away. They presented their own photos of the day of the arrest, which showed clear bruises and neck marks. It took the judge two years to order an expert IT assessor to evaluate the police station computers and determine when the photos had been taken. By then, the police claimed, all the station's computers had been reformatted.[31]

For the El Yamni family, as for most of the families of victims I met, their experiences in the judicial investigation came as a shock. When they shared their stories with other families involved in the Truth and Justice movement, they started realizing that their case was not unique. During protests and public events, I often observed families conferring about their experiences in the judicial process and being struck by the similarities. Farid El Yamni told me that realizing that others were going through the same things was "a form of therapy." Mimicking a conversation he'd had several times, he said it goes like this: "The expert lied—Yes, I know for us too, the expert lied! The prosecutor said this—Yes, I know for us too! They fabricated the evidence—Yes, I know for us too!"[32] Like Farid, many families of victims spoke about the psychological and emotional relief they felt when meeting and exchanging information with others who were going through similar experiences.

These moments of exchange did more than provide them with emotional support. They were also spaces where families could compare their experiences and compile information about recurrent patterns in the judicial response in police-involved deaths. Under the leadership of the collectives of families Vies Volées and Urgence Notre Police Assassine, families of victims worked collectively to uncover the routine institutional practices that led most police officers to escape accountability—what they called "the manufacturing of police impunity" (*la fabrique de l'impunité policière*).

The families noted a number of patterns. In the first official statements after a death, victims were systematically criminalized, even when they had no criminal record, and blamed for their own deaths. Official narratives either claimed that the deceased had represented a threat to the officers or that they had preexisting medical conditions or a drug problem that led to their "sudden loss of consciousness." In several cases, the officers involved in the fatal interaction filed a criminal complaint against the victim after his death, accusing him of assault, in order to frame their use of force as self-defense.

The families also noticed that police and prosecutors often encouraged a speedy burial abroad to preclude the possibility of a second autopsy. For instance, two days after Adama Traoré's death, a police officer called the family to inform them that, out of respect for the Muslim tradition requiring a quick burial, the police had already released the authorization to bury. Everything was arranged for the family to fly the body to Mali, and the authorities had released valid passports for all family members. The same happened with other victims' families, with the French police sometimes cooperating directly with foreign embassies to arrange the burial in the victim's country of origin. Once the body is buried abroad, the families can no longer request a counterautopsy.

While many families were surprised at the slow pace of investigations, comparing their experiences with one another revealed that judicial procedures into police-caused deaths are typically extremely lengthy. Some of the delay was caused by investigators dragging their feet, but in many instances, it was also due to disappearing files or lost pieces of evidence.[33]

Collectives of families also kept track of the outcomes of investigations, the vast majority of which ended in dismissals and nonindictment decisions. They realized that prosecutors and investigative judges tend to base their investigations and indictment decisions solely on officers' accounts, while ignoring evidence contradicting it. The rare cases that went to trial typically ended in officers either getting acquitted or receiving suspended sentences, most often with no mention on the criminal record and no dismissal from their jobs. Many families found out that the officers involved in the death of a loved one were later promoted to higher-ranking positions.

Putting these patterns together, families of victims developed an analysis of the mechanisms that preclude accountability for officers who kill. This led the movement to expand the scope of knowledge production beyond an attention to policing practices, to include how the judiciary handles cases of police crimes. It helped families broaden their understanding of police violence, from something that happens within law enforcement agencies, to an outcome of a broader system of oppression involving the judiciary and other state structures.

Counting and Mapping Police Killings

In addition to investigating individual cases, the Truth and Justice movement sought to produce data on the scale of police killings in France. Until 2018, the police did not publish any systematic data on police-involved deaths, which allowed them to frame the few cases that became salient in the media as isolated incidents. In the late 2010s, the collectives of families Vies Volées and Urgence Notre Police Assassine started keeping track of all reported cases of police-involved deaths and publishing tallies on their websites. These efforts built on previous work by activist and historian Maurice Rajsfus, who kept an archival record of all reported police violence cases from 1968 to 2014.[34]

Amal Bentounsi explained that these tallies were meant to shed light on the scale of the problem in France: "before Zyed and Bouna [who died in 2005], there were deaths, and we barely talk about them. Between Zyed and Bouna and Adama [who died in 2016] there were deaths, but we barely talk about them. Our objective is to make visible—to place all these cases next to each other in order to show that there's a real problem."[35]

In 2018, the online news media *Basta* published the country's first comprehensive database of police-involved deaths in France. To create the database, journalist Ludo Simbille relied on media coverage, the collectives' tallies, and Maurice Rajsfus's work. He found 668 recorded cases of deaths caused by on-duty police officers between 1977 and 2020, an average of fifteen deaths per year. This provided the first-ever statistics on police-involved deaths in France. Simbille's work showed that the vast majority of victims were men (92%) and half were under the age of twenty-six. Most victims (60%) died of gunshots, with the rest dying of asphyxia, loss of consciousness, or traffic accidents. Among those shot to death, 57% were unarmed. Only 3% of deaths took place in the context of terrorist attacks, whereas 23% happened during an identity check.

The data also provided a map of police killings in France and showed that half of police-caused deaths happened in the metropolitan areas of

Paris, Lyon, and Marseille, even though these regions only hold a quarter of the population. While *Basta*'s database didn't include information about the victims' origin or ethnicity, political scientist Paul Le Derff used family names as a proxy for immigrant origin and found that victims overwhelmingly had names connoting an immigrant origin in North Africa, and to a lesser extent sub-Saharan Africa.[36]

The publication of this database—the most comprehensive ever published in France—represented a formidable tool for actors in the Truth and Justice movement. It provided the movement with statistics to substantiate the claim that police killings are not isolated blunders but regular occurrences and to counter the official discourse according to which only terrorists or armed criminals are likely to get killed during a police intervention.

From Personal Tragedy to Political Struggle

The liberation epistemology played an important role in families' politicization process. By providing those most affected by police killings with tools to investigate and analyze their own experiences, it created a space for them to understand and articulate their loss as part of broader structures of inequality and injustice. As families went through the counterinvestigations and compared their experiences in the judiciary, most gradually transformed their discourse from expressing trust in state institutions and demanding justice for a police blunder (*bavure*), to denouncing police killings as state-sponsored violence and a complicit judiciary maintaining police impunity.

This shift, they told me in interviews, stemmed not just from meeting political activists and learning from them, but also from their journey seeking truth and justice. Farid El Yamni's published writings throughout the years illustrate this journey of politicization and the role of knowledge production in it. In one of his earliest texts, a call for a day of mobilization published two months after Wissam's death, he wrote that the goal was "to convict the bad police":

> We don't question the necessity of a police force and we know that the illegitimate use of violence stems from a minority. However, this minority does a lot of harm, both to families of victims, and to the reputation of the police. We simply want police officers who are guardians of the peace, and a just judiciary that we can be proud of.[37]

This contrasted sharply with what he wrote two years later in an open letter to the mother of another victim, Rémi Fraisse:

> For the past 40 years, the police kill with impunity, repeatedly. For the past 40 years, we witness the same process to drown the State's murders, despite the videos, the witnesses, the obvious facts. . . . Here is how it goes: news dispatch, lies of the prosecutor, a botched and truncated investigation that leads to a ridiculous conviction, or to the absence of any conviction. The worst is that those who bury our cases will get promoted and those who killed our brothers, our sons or friends, they will be treated like champions by their colleagues. This is the reality that you will also experience. . . . The State does not respect the law that it requires us to respect. It abuses our bodies, our trust, our money and our dignity. It demands that we bow down, it's a categorical imperative.[38]

To explain this dramatic shift in his political discourse, Farid spoke about gradually discovering the true nature of the police and judiciary, through his experience as well as his conversations with other families of victims. "People had warned us, but we didn't believe them,"[39] he told me. It was essential, he explained, to give each family the space and time to go through their own journey. In the same letter, he wrote:

> [At first,] I only wanted one thing, that the judiciary uncover the truth and give my brother the dignity he deserved. . . . I thought that the police would not accept murderers in their ranks, I didn't know them well enough at the time. I was mistaken. . . . And then, we understood that our case is not unique, that so many families experienced, and still experience, the same thing. There are so many humiliations and mutilations committed consciously by the police and shielded from accountability by the judiciary, so many!

Reflecting on his journey, Farid connected it to everything he had learned through the movement's knowledge-making practices. "To resist is first, to understand the world we live in, to understand the process that starts when a police violence occurs and ends with the production of a dismissal, acquittal or suspended sentence and [to understand] what it says about the world we live in."[40]

Farid's journey of politicization is not unique. All the families I got to know through my fieldwork went through a similar process. Like Farid, they linked this transformation to the knowledge they gained, both through the activists they met and through their involvement in counterinvestigations and in uncovering patterns of judicial complicity. This journey of politicization was instrumental in shaping the movement's political discourse.

We Are Here for All of Them

Through their active involvement in knowledge production, families of victims became some of the best lay experts on the issue in France. This allowed them to maintain ownership over the movement and to ensure that they were centered as the voice of the struggle. All the protests and commemorations I attended centered and amplified the voices of families of victims.

In November 2016, four months after Adama Traoré's death, the committee Truth for Adama organized "a great march for Adama" in Paris. When I got there, I spotted several other families of victims I had met at previous Truth and Justice protests. I saw three of Adama Traoré's siblings, Assa, Lassana, and Hawa, as well as Ramata Dieng, Amal Bentounsi, and others. A dozen families were getting positioned at the head of the procession, holding a large banner that read "Truth and Justice for Adama." Adama's siblings stood in the middle, with other families of victims on each side of them. This was a strong tradition in the Truth and Justice movement; at every protest or commemoration organized by one of the committees, the other families did their best to make it, often traveling across the country to be present. The families always opened the procession, walking at the head of the protest, with everyone else instructed to walk *behind* them.

Before we started marching, I walked around among the protesters standing behind the families, around five hundred people. I noticed several political groups among them—a student union, an anarchist group, an organization representing Malians in France, a labor union. As I chatted with some of these protesters, many brought up the same conundrum: how to show their support for the families of victims without overstepping and drawing the attention toward themselves. One student union representative told me, "it's complicated for us, we want to support them, but we also want to be careful about co-optation, so we are just here as allies."[41]

I then talked with a member of the anarchist group, who was holding a flag with the logo of his organization. Interrupting our conversation, a woman asked him to take the flag down. "The family has requested that no organization raise their flags," she explained, "banners are okay as long as there's no affiliation on them." The man apologized, said he thought his group had asked for permission, and quickly took the flag down. This was a common occurrence in Truth and Justice protests. Over and over, families and members of Truth and Justice committees reminded everyone that political groups were welcome to stand in solidarity, but they should not act as leaders or spokespersons. This vigilance that political groups should not take over the movement stemmed from families' insistence that the movement should be led by those most affected by police killings (*les premiers concernés*).[42]

A little after the official start time of the protest, we began marching toward Place de la République, chanting "Justice for Adama," and "No Justice No Peace." About halfway into our itinerary, we were stopped by several police vans blocking our way. As we waited for them to let us continue the march, Assa Traoré took the mic and said, "We are here for Adama, but not only for him. There are other families here, people who died before Adama, and also people who died after him. We are here for all of them." Then, she started reading a list of names of people killed by the police over the past years. After every name, we all chanted "We don't forgive, we don't forget!"

> Zyed and Bouna—We don't forgive, we don't forget!
> Amine Bentounsi—We don't forgive, we don't forget!
> Wissam El Yamni—We don't forgive, we don't forget!
> Abdoulaye Camara—We don't forgive, we don't forget!
> Ali Ziri—We don't forgive, we don't forget!
> Lamine Dieng—We don't forgive, we don't forget!
> Mamadou Marega—We don't forgive, we don't forget!
> Lahoucine Ait Omghar—We don't forgive, we don't forget!
> Rémi Fraisse—We don't forgive, we don't forget!
> Amadou Koumé—We don't forgive, we don't forget!
> Mourad Touat—We don't forgive, we don't forget!
> Malik Oussekine—We don't forgive, we don't forget!
>
> . . .

This read-out of victims' names was a recurring ritual in Truth and Justice protests. It played an important symbolic role in centering the movement's rhetoric on the victims. By repeating their names, we were ensuring that they would not be forgotten, and we were honoring the struggles of their families.

No Justice No Peace

When the march arrived at Place de la République, it started raining lightly, but an organizer took the mic and asked us to stay, as there would now be speeches. As was the case with every protest and commemoration I attended, families of victims spoke first, and most of the speech time was reserved for them.

Out of the three activist coalitions I examined, this was the only one in which victims gained and maintained ownership over the movement, and where both their experiences and their analyses were centered. This had two important effects on the movement's discourse: it made space for the voices of families at different stages of politicization, and it emphasized common themes that affect all families of victims. One of those themes was the role of the judiciary, which was front and center at the March for Adama.

Adama's older brother Lassana was the first to take the mic. He spoke briefly, visibly holding back tears. "I am so moved, I don't know what to say, when I see all of you here, I have no words," he started. He thanked everyone for their presence and ended on a hopeful note: "the struggle [for justice] will be long, but thanks to you, we will succeed, for sure." He called for the three officers who arrested Adama to be indicted. Then, his sister Assa took the stage. In addition to the officers' conviction, she said, the French state, too, should be held accountable. "Adama died in the police station, that's a symbolic building, it's managed by the state. Our struggle is not just against the officers, it's also against the state. . . . The state must take responsibility." Whether they defined justice as the officers getting convicted, or as the state taking responsibility, the Traoré family was, at the time, hopeful that justice could be obtained.

In contrast, when Ramata Dieng took the mic, her speech was much more critical of the judiciary. She started by making parallels between her brother's death in 2007, and Adama's nine years later. "The restraining hold officers used was the same. The prosecutor's lies were the same. They also tried to say that my brother was a drug addict to exonerate themselves, but we had scientific evidence [contradicting this]." While she praised the Traoré family's courage in denouncing state crimes, she also warned that the judicial system was complicit. After a seven-year investigation into her brother's death, she told the crowd, the prosecutor had dismissed the case. The family appealed, but the Paris Court of Appeal confirmed the dismissal. They appealed again to France's highest court and were waiting for the decision. Ramata continued, "The death penalty was abolished in 1981, but since then, dozens of people have died, and judges refuse to convict the officers, not because they are innocent, but because they are police officers. . . . These people have a license to kill with total impunity."

Ramata was followed by Amal Bentounsi. She, too, analyzed her brother's death as resulting from a system that involved not just the police but also the judiciary and the state. She began her speech. "My brother was killed on the twenty-first of April 2012, shot in the back." With tears filling her eyes and a trembling voice, she said, "he was a young man among so many others that are stigmatized, thrown to the wolves. He went to prison when he was only thirteen. He didn't choose his path; it was imposed on him." At this point, she started crying, but continued, "his sad life was cut short at twenty-nine. They had no mercy." Then, in a more poised voice, she explained that her brother's case was not isolated, saying there are one or two deaths every month at the hands of the police. Amal often ended her speeches with an analysis of what she called the permission to kill granted police officers:

> They die in different circumstances, but the process is the same. The police murder, then they lie, they conceal the evidence, and the judiciary protects them. The government, whether they are right- or left-wing, supports them. The police kill Blacks and Arabs, those who come from postcolonial migration. The police are the armed wing of the state, they are given permission to kill with total impunity.

This narrative structure—telling the story of their loved ones' death, then contextualizing it in a broader pattern of police violence and lack of accountability—was typical of veteran families that had been in the movement for years. While their analyses differed from those of the newly affected families like Adama Traoré's at the time, the movement's commitment to centering victims' voices made space for a variety of discourses—from the more mainstream to the more radical.

Despite this diversity, the role of the judiciary, and of the state more broadly, was always emphasized in Truth and Justice protests. This was one of the central contributions of the movement: it developed a critical analysis of the judiciary as part and parcel of the problem of racialized policing.

At the time of writing, almost none of the families that appear in this chapter have obtained justice. Courts have rendered nonindictment decisions (*non-lieu*) in the cases of Lamine Dieng, Adama Traoré, Babacar Gueye, and Ali Ziri.[43] The investigation into Wissam El Yamni's death is still ongoing, thirteen years later. After exhausting all legal avenues in France, the Dieng family sued the French government in the European Court of Human Rights. In 2020, the government agreed to pay 145,000 euros to the family to settle the case. None of the officers involved were convicted or suspended, except for the policeman who killed Amine Bentounsi (who was convicted but not suspended).

These judicial struggles were front and center in the movement's discourse. One of the recurring chants during protests and commemorations, which often followed the famous "*tout le monde déteste la police*" (everybody hates the police), was "*la police assassine, la justice acquitte*" (the police assassinate, the judiciary exonerate). This emphasis on the justice system's complicity resulted from the victim-centered structure of the movement, and from a mode of knowledge production that centered the experiences and analyses of victims seeking justice.

They Killed the Whole Family

Another common theme that emerged in the movement's public discourse was that police violence affects not only those who are subject to officers' physical violence but also, indirectly, their families and loved ones. The speeches of families of victims often emphasized the toll that losing someone to the police took on their loved ones.

Even seasoned families who promoted radical political analyses weaved personal, emotional stories of loss and pain together with a structural analysis of police violence. The speech Amal Bentounsi gave at the March for Adama—the same speech she gave at every protest I attended—illustrates this. Amal always started by telling her brother's life story, without holding back her emotions as she recalled that he started going in and out of prison at the age of thirteen. Every time, she let her tears flow when she talked about how he was killed.

Amal's visible, raw pain helped emphasize what sociologist Monica Bell calls *vicarious marginalization*, the idea that police abuse does not only affect the direct victims of policing but also whole communities, thus contributing to their estrangement and exclusion from mainstream society.[44] In their public statements, families often recounted the immense toll that the death of one person has on the whole family— psychologically, emotionally, and also financially to pay the legal fees. In one of my conversations with her, Lamine Dieng's sister Fatou described it this way:

> We have placed our own lives on hold. We don't allow ourselves much, we don't have projects, we are only taking care of the basics. Because for us, it's not a death, it's a stolen life. They snatched him away from us, they snatched away his life, everything he had. They took us for fools, children of immigrants, children of laborers. He was dragged through the mud, and we were too. My father always says: they didn't just kill Lamine, they killed the whole family, they killed us all at the same time. When it happens, it's a whole family that gets destroyed.[45]

Like Fatou, many families explained that losing a loved one to police violence had a different, crueler, impact than other forms of loss. First, because state representatives killed their brother and son, and then because they "took them for fools" and persisted in denying them justice. This echoes the argument, developed by sociologist Rachida Brahim, that racist violence kills twice: it kills a first time when people deemed "undesirable" are the targets of physical violence, and it kills a second time when victims and their loved ones are denied justice, and their victimization goes unrecognized.[46]

Thus, by elevating the voices and analyses of families of victims, the Truth and Justice movement made space for a diversity of political analyses of police violence and inequality while also emphasizing two core themes that all families emphasized: a critical focus on the judiciary as complicit in perpetuating police brutality, and a framing of racialized policing as a form of violence that affects not only direct victims but also their families and communities.

What Scores Is France Settling with Its History?

Another theme that was highlighted at every commemoration or protest was racism. Even though some families avoided the topic, the fact that the movement made space for different temporalities and political analyses allowed some leading figures to develop and promote a structural analysis of police racism.

During the protest for Adama in 2016, no member of the Traoré family brought up the issue of racism. This was a deliberate strategy to avoid contentious issues in order to garner as much support for their cause as possible. However, a few months later, the Traoré family started incorporating an analysis of racism in their public discourse. As they did so, they were careful to push back against the dominant understanding of racism as a problem of prejudiced individuals and toward an analysis of state structures and colonial legacies. A year after Adama's death, Assa Traoré published a book titled *Lettre à Adama* (Letter to Adama) in which she wrote:

> What scores are police and power holders settling with the population of low-income neighborhoods? What scores is France settling with her own history? With her own [children], all those French from immigrant backgrounds. We must interrogate the meaning of these acts, and the postcolonial subconscious that they carry. How long will the violent domination of Whites over Blacks, over all those with the wrong skin color, continue in the country of human rights?[47]

Such a shift was common among families of victims. Most families' politicization process entailed moving away from their initial reluctance to talk about race and racism and toward endorsing a structural analysis of police violence and impunity as racialized and classed oppression.

Key in this transformation was the historical lens antiracist activists introduced to contextualize the experiences of families of victims within France's broader history of racial oppression. The family members I spoke with said they had acquired the tools to articulate the role of race in their analysis through exchanging with antiracist activists and historians of French empire. Ramata Dieng cited historian and activist Matthieu Rigouste and antiracist activist Franco Lollia as major influences, along with the books they recommended to her. These influences, she said, "helped me a lot to analyze, to see the background." It helped her realize that "the judiciary is not operating in the way we believe it is, the judiciary, and the police too, function to tell the population, its subjects, what their place in society is, and to say, 'keep your place, or else we will come and put you back in your place.'"[48]

As Ramata and others acquired knowledge and tools to connect contemporary state practices to colonialism, some started making links, in their public discourse, between their families' intimate histories and France's imperial and postcolonial history. This allowed them to interweave the personal and the political aspects of their struggle. For instance, Awa Gueye, who initially refused to talk about her brother's Blackness or his undocumented status, eventually drew on a historical lens to make connections between France's colonial history and her family's story. In 2022, in a public speech, she spoke about her brother's murder as "state racism," adding "Babacar was a descendant of *tirailleurs sénégalais* [Senegalese soldiers who worked for the French army], his grandparents fought for France." Reversing her initial reluctance to emphasize her brother's undocumented status, she went on to talk about his being *sans-papiers*, and to discuss the way Black undocumented immigrants are treated "like shit" in France, despite being those who take on the essential jobs. She said: "Why do they not respect us? What have we done? We clean up the roads, collect garbage, clean offices and hotels and restaurants." Her speech connected her family's history—grandparents who fought for the French army during France's colonial empire, their grandchildren migrating to France after independence to take on the most low-paying jobs—to France's history of colonial and postcolonial oppression. This way, Awa could remain close to her personal story while also highlighting the historical processes of exclusion and marginalization within which her brother's death is embedded.

This historical lens is what sociologist Crystal Fleming calls *racial temporality*—making connections between France's colonial and slavery past and contemporary racist oppressions.[49] Racial temporality provided families of victims with tools to articulate how racism comes into play in the policing and judicial practices they denounced. Even though they could not prove that the officers responsible for their brothers' deaths were racially biased, or produce statistical evidence of racial disparities in police use of force, leaders of the Truth and Justice movement managed to highlight the role of race by interpreting contemporary patterns of police and judicial practice through a historical lens attentive to France's colonial history. This opened an avenue to push beyond the dominant discourse around racist cops, and to articulate how historically constructed structures of racial oppression played a role in the death of their loved ones.

While racial temporality allowed the movement to develop analyses explaining why police brutality disproportionately targets people of sub-Saharan and North African descent, the movement's victim-centered structure also made space for incorporating other marginalized groups who are victimized by the police. When Angelo Garand, a Traveler, was killed by police in his home in Blois in 2017, Amal Bentounsi contacted his sister through social media and gave her tips on how to organize. Assa Traoré visited the family to express her support and share her experience; and several other families of victims joined the first march organized by the committee Justice for Angelo in Blois. Once the committee was connected to the national network, Truth and Justice leaders started incorporating an analysis of anti-Traveler racism in their public speeches. During the first march for Angelo, a member of the committee Justice Truth for Wissam said in his speech:

> I am a French man of Moroccan origin. When I go to Morocco, people make me feel like I'm not Moroccan, and here, people make me feel that I'm not French. It's the same for Black people, and it's the same for Travelers, too. People don't consider them to be French. They are told that as long as they live in caravans, they are not French.[50]

By linking his experience as a postcolonial migrant to that of Travelers, he highlighted the way colonial logics apply to other groups, who are also considered "not French" despite historical and contemporary ties to the country. The Truth and Justice movement also extended their solidarity to White victims, in the rare instances when they were killed by the police. For example, when Jérôme Laronze, a White unionized farmer, was shot dead by officers as he was fleeing a police inspection in 2017, other families reached out to his loved ones. They invited them to Truth and Justice protests and commemorations, and his name became included in the lists of names that we chanted at each protest.

In sum, racial temporality allowed leaders of the Truth and Justice movement to promote a structural analysis of racialized policing, which emphasized the colonial legacies of contemporary policing and judicial practice. This helped them explain why victims of police killings are over-whelmingly Arab and Black. At the same time, by structuring the movement around families of victims, rather than subsuming themselves into existing antiracist organizations, the Truth and Justice movement made space for incorporating other marginalized groups who are also victimized by the police but are often invisible in antiracist and leftist movements.

Conclusion

The Truth and Justice movement adopted a mode of knowledge production that challenged dominant ways of knowing, turning those directly affected by racialized policing, who are generally seen as objects of research, into knowers in their own right. Like the neighborhood mobilization, knowledge production centered the lived experiences of victims of racialized policing, but victims insisted that they are more than sources of data; they are the best situated to analyze their experiences and to construct the movement's political discourse. The families' active involvement in knowledge production contributed to their politicization, and to shifting from an initial preference for "apolitical" claims to developing structural analyses of the systems of inequality and injustice that oppress them. The movement's discourse elevated the voices of victims, highlighted the vicarious harms suffered by the communities targeted, and expanded the scope of the cause beyond an attention on police and toward analyzing the role of other institutions in perpetuating racialized policing. The next chapters examine how each coalition mobilized the knowledge they produced in the media, judicial, and political arenas, and how it was received and interpreted by journalists, court actors, and politicians.

Part III

MOBILIZING KNOWLEDGE

FIVE

Constructing Legal Evidence

At the trial of the "Tigers brigade," a police unit accused of assaulting Black and Arab teenagers in Paris's twelfth arrondissement, the court was brimming with people. Inside the fifty-seater public gallery, there were two visibly separate groups. Sitting on the right were relatives and colleagues of the officers standing trial, some of them in uniforms. On the left, were friends and family members of the plaintiffs as well as the local activists who had helped bring this case to court.[1]

Each side supported a competing understanding of the facts of this case. To the plaintiffs and their allies, this trial was about a violent, abusive, and racist police unit that had, for years, harassed teenagers from low-income immigrant families. They claimed that this police unit repeatedly targeted racialized young men for unjustified identity checks, assaulted them verbally, physically, and sometimes sexually, and often detained them with no legal cause. The defendants and their lawyers, on the other hand, described these allegations as a "web of lies" elaborated by unscrupulous organizations to create a media buzz. They argued that this case was in reality about a youth band that terrorized the neighborhood, with police intervening at the request of residents, and always within the bounds of the law. Each side hoped that the two-day trial would vindicate their narrative and convince the judges—and the journalists scattered around the courtroom—of their version of the story.

Such trials are critical for movements contesting racialized policing.

Since courts are one of the primary sites where competing truth-claims are debated publicly,[2] they provide activists with a highly visible platform to promote their claims. These cases are as much about convincing courts to expand legal opportunities for policing victims, as they are about promoting the movement's claims in the public debate.

Existing scholarship suggests that to successfully mobilize the law, movements must engage in both legal and political work. They must select the right plaintiffs and develop novel legal arguments, and also mobilize constituents and garner media attention.[3] In lawsuits against the police, this is often insufficient, however. The police's epistemic power makes it extremely difficult for victims to get their cases to court, because investigators, prosecutors, and judges typically deem a police officer's testimony to be more credible than that of police targets.

In this chapter, I show that mobilizing the law does not hinge solely on bringing the right case to court and organizing politically around it; it also requires that movement actors engage in *epistemic work*, that is, introduce evidence that supports the movement's claims in ways that conform to legal rules about how evidence is presented and assessed in law. The previous chapters examined how activist coalitions produced their own data about racialized policing practices. Here, I analyze the strategies they developed to introduce these data in legal proceedings, and to transform them into admissible, relevant, and credible legal evidence. I show that the coalitions' epistemic work shaped the legal questions they could raise, their reception in the legal arena, and the way they were reported and debated in the media coverage of these cases. While activists' litigation efforts had a limited effect on expanding legal opportunities for policing victims, they were instrumental in promoting the movement's claims in the media, including claims about institutional and systemic discrimination, and about the structural factors maintaining de facto impunity for the police.

Epistemic Work

In law, parties must follow specific rules and procedures about how evidence is produced and assessed—what scholars call *legal epistemology*.[4] When adjudicating between competing truth claims, legal actors don't seek to uncover a preexisting truth. They construct a legally sanctioned truth based on specific procedural rules about what counts as legal evidence, who can introduce it and in what way, and how the credibility and relevance of various statements of fact should be assessed.[5]

In France, legal epistemology places policing victims in a position of structural disadvantage. There are three main reasons for this.

First, plaintiffs have limited opportunities to introduce their own evidence in legal proceedings. This is particularly true in criminal cases. France's inquisitorial system means that investigations are led by a prosecutor or an investigative judge tasked with collecting evidence in favor of, and against, the defendants. Since the country has no independent agency handling police misconduct allegations, the initial investigations are conducted by the police's internal inspection services, which are staffed by police officers working within the same institution as the accused. Plaintiffs, on the other hand, play no role in the fact-finding process. As one lawyer put it, "when we have a client that was assaulted by the police, we will file a lawsuit but then, we have no role in the procedure, we are very much spectators, witnesses."[6] In practice, this means that the police can refuse to register a complaint against colleagues, or dismiss it without investigation, a pattern that human rights groups found to be common.[7] Civil law proceedings in France provide more opportunities for victims to introduce their evidence, because each party can present evidence to support their claims and there is no prosecutor leading the investigations.[8] However, given the strong institutional opacity of the French police, much of the data that would be helpful to plaintiffs and their lawyers (internal records, statistics about police actions, body-camera or surveillance camera footage) are inaccessible to them.

The second hurdle for victims of racialized policing is that the police benefit from a legal presumption of credibility. In French law, a written police record is presumed to be truthful (*le procès-verbal fait foi*), and the testimony of a police officer is considered more credible than that of an alleged criminal. This assumption of credibility can only be challenged if there is external evidence, such as medical records or the testimonies of credible witnesses corroborating the plaintiff's claims. By contrast, the populations most targeted by the police—racialized young men from low-income neighborhoods—suffer from a credibility deficit; they are often deemed less credible than the average person due to gendered, race and class prejudice.[9] In practice, unless the alleged misconduct is extremely serious and the plaintiffs' narrative is corroborated by multiple, external

witnesses or medical professionals, victims of racialized policing are unlikely to be believed over police officers.[10] In one of the rare cases where
officers were convicted by French courts (a case for which France was later
condemned by the European Court of Human Rights for torture), the
Versailles Court of Appeal clarified the narrow conditions under which
the presumption of credibility for police can be reversed:

> In absolute terms, the testimony of a policeman, and even more so that of
> a police investigator, is more credible than that of a drug trafficker. This
> presumption is weakened when the criminal's statements are supported
> by external evidence such as medical findings, . . . when the explanations
> provided by the policemen vary significantly during the course of the
> proceedings, . . . and when it is shown, as in the present case, that the
> police reports do not reflect the truth.[11]

The third reason why legal epistemology places victims of policing in
a disadvantaged position is that procedural rules privilege evidence that
directly relates to the contested interaction and is collected close in time
and space to it. Information about the broader context within which the
interaction took place is deemed less relevant.[12] For example, if someone
accuses a police officer of having punched him, evidence pertaining to
the specific encounter, such as eyewitness accounts or a medical report of
the injuries, is considered more relevant than evidence that is indirectly
related to the incident, such as a study showing that excessive use of force
is common in this police force. This is an important obstacle for movement
actors, since one of the goals of mobilizing the law is to use the public visibility of legal proceedings to highlight broader patterns of practice.

Thus, the rules of legal epistemology place policing victims in a position of structural disadvantage when it comes to evidencing their claims in
law. To overcome these obstacles, activist groups and their lawyers engage
in *epistemic work*. They come up with innovative evidentiary strategies to
use, work around, or push the boundaries of legal epistemology in order to
advance their claims in the legal and public debate. Doing so involves three
practices. They must carve avenues to introduce their knowledge claims in
legal proceedings; discredit police narratives and bolster the credibility of
their evidence; and construct arguments to broaden what counts as relevant evidence. In the rest of the chapter, I discuss how each of the three
coalitions I examine in this book did this, and with what outcomes.

Racial Profiling Campaign: Suing the State for Discrimination

The racial profiling campaign, which was led by the Open Society Justice Initiative (OSJI), produced France's first study quantifying racial disparities in police stops. The 2009 report, *Profiling Minorities*, found that people perceived as Black and Arab were six and eight times more likely to be stopped by the police than people perceived as White.[13] To the campaign leaders, these statistics provided an unprecedented opportunity to develop new litigation strategies against *contrôles au faciès* (the French term used for discriminatory stops).

OSJI recruited two French lawyers, Felix de Belloy, a criminal lawyer, and Slim Ben Achour, an employment lawyer specialized in antidiscrimination law. They worked in coordination with OSJI's senior officer in France, Sarah, to develop the campaign's litigation strategy. Their goal was to initiate strategic litigation cases that could establish a precedent and expand opportunities for victims of racial profiling. Until then, there had been few attempts to use the law to challenge racial discrimination in policing. Some criminal defense lawyers tried to get their client's arrest annulled by arguing that the initial stop was racially motivated, but these arguments generally failed because criminal law requires proving an intent to discriminate.

Slim Ben Achour and Felix de Belloy proposed an innovative strategy: to use civil law to sue the state for discriminatory stops based on a rule stipulating that the state is accountable for misconduct by public employees.[14] Mobilizing civil law, rather than criminal or administrative law, had several advantages, they argued. For one, it allowed them to sue the state rather than individual officers, which would help the campaign frame racial profiling as a general practice that the state is responsible for, rather than a problem of "bad apples." Civil law also presented more favorable provisions and evidentiary requirements for proving discrimination. Unlike criminal law, civil law does not require proving an intention to discriminate on the part of officers; evidence of differential treatment is sufficient. Moreover, plaintiffs would be able to introduce their own evidence, rather than relying on police investigators or prosecutors.

Most significantly for the lawyers, European Union laws stipulate a shared burden of proof in discrimination cases: plaintiffs alleging discrimination need only present facts from which it may be *presumed* that there has been discrimination. Once they establish a presumption of discrimination, the respondent must prove that the difference in treatment was justified by objective, nondiscriminatory factors.[15] Although French law wasn't clear about whether the shared burden of proof applies to policing practices,[16] the lawyers based their case on the argument that it should. Given the absence of records of identity checks, they reasoned, plaintiffs had no means to prove conclusively that their stop was based on discriminatory criteria. If the burden of proof was not shared, it would effectively mean that courts have no judicial review powers over identity checks. As Felix de Belloy explained, "it was essential because we could say, it's not on me to provide evidence that it's a discrimination, I only need to provide evidence that I have reasons to suspect that it's a discrimination."[17] This argument opened the way for introducing the statistics produced in *Profiling Minorities* as evidence.

Transforming Statistics into Legal Evidence

To the lawyers and campaign leaders, one of the goals of the case was to get French courts to accept statistical studies showing a general pattern of racial disparities in identity checks as evidence of discrimination. Until then, French courts had relied on data that were directly related to the plaintiffs' situation—for example, in employment discrimination cases, panel studies showing gender wage gaps in the plaintiff's workplace. No case had tested whether general statistics that are not directly related to the plaintiff would be considered admissible evidence of discrimination.

For this case, Slim Ben Achour and Felix de Belloy decided that each plaintiff would present OSJI's statistical study as evidence to establish a presumption of discrimination. They drew on case law from the European Court of Human Rights, which ruled that general statistics about racial disparities was admissible evidence in discrimination cases.[18] In doing so, they aimed to expand the scope of evidence that is deemed relevant, to include not just facts pertaining to the contested stops but also contextual information about a general pattern of racial disparities in identity checks.

In their written arguments, the lawyers emphasized the credibility and reliability of the statistical study. They noted that it was conducted by renowned scholars of France's most prestigious research center, and that a diversity of organizations and governmental bodies had recognized the "reality" of racial profiling over the past years, in large part thanks to OSJI's campaign. These included national watchdog agencies like the CNDS and the Rights Defender, international agencies like the European Commission against Racism and Intolerance, and NGOs like Human Rights Watch. They also wrote that many government officials, including the president and prime minister, had recognized racial profiling to be an issue in France and promised reforms. Thus, the campaign's continued political lobbying around the issue of racial profiling helped bolster the credibility of the evidence they presented in court.

Still, the lawyers worried that the statistics would be deemed insufficient, on their own, to establish a presumption of discrimination. To create evidence about the specific contested stops, they asked each plaintiff to provide a witness affidavit (*attestation de témoin*). The affidavit was a brief account of the identity check, written by someone who witnessed it (often a friend stopped alongside the plaintiff) who could attest that that the plaintiff was stopped for no apparent reason. As Slim Ben Achour explained, witness affidavits are one of the most common forms of evidence in civil law; "the affidavit is deemed truthful . . . the citizen is deemed to be in good faith, unless you prove that he lied."[19] Although in law the testimony of an ordinary citizen is less credible than that of a police officer, the lawyers anticipated that, given the absence of written records of identity checks, the state would be unable to produce evidence of the motives of the plaintiffs' stops. In effect, the litigation strategy used the opacity of police actions to their advantage: in the absence of written police records, it would be difficult for the police to come up with evidence of a nondiscriminatory motive for the stop.

To bolster the credibility of the affidavits, the lawyers decided to include only "clean plaintiffs" in the lawsuit—university students or employees with no criminal records, whose stop had not led to detention or arrest. While some of the activists who helped identify prospective plaintiffs wanted to include a diversity of profiles, the lawyers insisted that, given the innovative nature of their arguments, the first case had to involve flawless victims, whose testimony would be less likely to be dismissed outright. They selected thirteen plaintiffs, all of them Black or Arab men who had been stopped for an identity check while doing a mundane activity like walking, shopping, or sitting in a café.

The lawsuit argued that these two pieces of evidence should be sufficient to establish a presumption of discrimination. The statistics demonstrated that there is a general pattern of discrimination in identity checks in France, and the affidavits suggested that the contested stop had no legal motive, leading the plaintiff to suspect that it was motivated by his skin color. Under the shared burden of proof rule, they argued, it was now up to the state to prove that the stop was not discriminatory.

Leaders of the campaign against racial profiling timed the filing of their lawsuit for maximum impact, eleven days before the 2012 presidential election. The organizations had been actively lobbying politicians to take a position on the issue of *contrôles au faciès* and had obtained from the socialist candidate (and soon-to-be president) François Hollande a promise to implement reforms. The topic was therefore already garnering media attention, and the lawsuit was widely covered in mainstream outlets. Press articles called the lawsuit "historic" and emphasized that it was the first time that citizens sued the state for discriminatory police stops. Media stories presented *contrôles au faciès* as an established practice, referring to the 2009 OSJI study and to the ongoing political debate about reforms.

The State Is Accountable for Discriminatory Stops

By 2016, the case had gone all the way to France's highest court. In what was widely considered a historic decision, the Court of Cassation convicted the state for three discriminatory stops and ordered it to pay 1,500 euros in compensation to each of the victims.[20] This decision established a new legal rule: the state can be held accountable for discriminatory stops. The court defined a discriminatory stop as a one based on "physical characteristics associated with an origin, real or imagined, without any prior objective justification," and ruled that it constitutes a "grievous fault" (*faute lourde*[21]) for the state.

The ruling effectively created a new cause of action for victims of racial profiling. The court endorsed the plaintiffs' arguments that the burden of proof should be shared, arguing that this rule is essential to secure people's right to judicial review of their stops. The absence of police records of identity checks, the court noted, hinders the possibility of judicial review and deprives plaintiffs of the chance to contest an identity check: without a shared burden of proof, plaintiffs would virtually never be able to prove a discriminatory stop. This was a significant step toward expanding the possibilities of contesting discriminatory stops in court.

Another significant advance was that the court deemed general statistics to be both credible and relevant—although insufficient—to establish a presumption of discrimination. The ruling read:

> Statistics pertaining to a general pattern constitute a relevant consideration (*un élément d'appréciation*) in that they reveal that a population that is young, male, wearing clothes fashionable among the young generation of disadvantaged neighborhoods, and belonging to visible minorities, is disproportionately stopped.[22]

The court thus broadened the scope of relevant evidence, allowing consideration of facts that are not directly related to the specific incident but provide contextual knowledge about broader patterns of practice.

The media coverage of the ruling was unanimously favorable to the campaign's claims. The decision did not make front page news, as the activists and lawyers had hoped, because of its unfortunate timing: it was released on the day of Donald Trump's 2016 election in the United States. Still, the coverage from mainstream media called the ruling a "major advance for citizens' rights," and a "historic decision" that set a judicial precedent (*qui fait jurisprudence*). The press emphasized that the state can now be held accountable for discriminatory stops and suggested that the police would have to change their practices.[23] To Slim Ben Achour, the ruling significantly strengthened the public credibility of the movement's claims: "I think we won politically, in the sense that it's not a matter for debate anymore—of course in some circles, on the far right, they will find justifications for *contrôles au faciès*—but everybody now agrees that Blacks and Arabs are disproportionately stopped."[24]

A Narrow Understanding of Discrimination

Despite the significant symbolic value of the ruling, the way in which the court assessed the evidence in each of the thirteen cases suggests that the legal recourse it opened was a limited one. The judges set narrow conditions in which plaintiffs can establish a presumption of discrimination:

they must either provide evidence of verbal expressions of racism by the officers, or prove that the police stopped *exclusively* people of color in the time and space of the contested stop.

The three stops that the court deemed discriminatory had targeted Black men as they exited a shopping mall in Paris. By happenstance, on that day, an activist involved in the racial profiling campaign was sitting in a café nearby and had been watching the police for some time. He wrote a witness affidavit for the three men in which he testified that he had watched the police unit for an hour and a half in a racially mixed space, during which they stopped only young men who looked Arab or Black, none of whom were arrested. In the absence of such evidence, the court ruled that plaintiffs had failed to establish a presumption of discrimination.

This requirement to either prove explicit racist speech or demonstrate that only people of color were stopped in a racially mixed space, suggests that the court endorsed an intentionalist understanding of discrimination, implicitly requiring evidence that individual officers were biased in making discretionary decisions. Although civil antidiscrimination law prohibits indirect discrimination, that is, apparently neutral practices that lead to disparate outcomes for minorities, the court's evidentiary requirements signaled that "there is still an underlying requirement to prove intentionality," to use the words of an antidiscrimination law specialist.[25]

What's more, the court excluded whole geographic areas from the protection against discriminatory stops by endorsing the state's argument that when a stop is conducted in "sensitive" areas, this is sufficient to prove that it was based on objective, nondiscriminatory factors. For example, the stops of two young Arab men who were sitting in front of their building talking in the suburb of Lyon, and that of a Black man who was stopped as he came out of his building, were not deemed discriminatory because the state argued that they took place in a sensitive neighborhood. In this way, the court excluded whole territories, vaguely defined as "sensitive"—code for low-income neighborhoods with high proportions of immigrants— from the protection against discriminatory stops. These restrictions have meant that, since the 2016 ruling, only a handful of people succeeded in holding the state accountable for discriminatory stops.[26]

In sum, the lawsuit was a major advance for the racial profiling campaign. It opened a new cause of action for victims of discriminatory stops and provided substantial legitimacy to the campaign's claim that *contrôles au faciès* is a political problem that the state is responsible for. This victory hinged on the mobilization's work to translate the knowledge they produced into legal evidence. This epistemic work, combined with a well-resourced media and political campaign, was essential to the success of the legal mobilization strategy. However, the understanding of discrimination that the litigation fostered was a narrow one. In the court ruling, discrimination was implicitly understood as the intentional targeting of racialized people in mixed or middle-class White spaces. This obscured the ways in which institutional policies and structural inequalities contribute to disparate outcomes for racialized minorities. The next sections show how the same group of lawyers sought to expand it.

Neighborhood Mobilization: Claiming Police Harassment

The mobilization examined in chapter 3 was led by a coalition of residents, youth professionals, and local activists of the twelfth arrondissement of Paris, who worked with the support of NGOs and lawyers to document police interventions in the neighborhood. This approach revealed the abusive patterns of practice of one police unit—nicknamed the Tigers brigade—against racialized young men. The Tigers used repeated and unjustified identity checks and arbitrary detention, which were often accompanied by racial slurs, verbal, physical, and sometimes sexual violence. To the organizers, this documentation effort had the potential to move the public debate beyond discrete incidents of misconduct and toward *patterns of practice* of discriminatory and violent policing. To promote their analysis of institutional and systemic discrimination, they developed a two-step litigation strategy, which started with a criminal lawsuit against individual officers, followed by a civil lawsuit against the state.

When Slim Ben Achour and Felix de Belloy, the same lawyers who led the litigation on racial profiling, were called in to help the local organizing effort, they decided to start by filing a criminal complaint against the officers of the Tigers brigade. The lawyers explained that the primary goal was to put an end to the Tigers' practices, and a criminal case had the potential to place the brigade "under the spotlight," to garner media attention, and thereby to pressure police to change their practices. "We thought, there's little chance to get a criminal conviction, but our first goal is for [the ongoing abuses] to stop, and the best way is by filing a [criminal] complaint."[27] Yet, in the past, some of the victims had tried to file criminal complaints, but the police inspection services (Inspection générale de la police nationale, or IGPN) either refused to register them or dismissed their allegations without investigation. Officers sometimes retaliated against those who complained with increased harassment.

To overcome the IGPN's tendency to dismiss the teens' complaints, the mobilization leaders developed two strategies. First, they decided to file a collective complaint; instead of having victims try to file reports individually every time a new incident occurred, they prepared a single complaint for several victims, alleging multiple allegations of misconduct by the same police unit over an extended period of time. Second, they prepared the complaint to include as much evidence of each alleged incident as they could gather (eyewitness testimonies, medical records, photos, videos). In other words, they sought to circumvent the police and prosecutors' monopoly over the criminal investigation process by presenting investigators with an already-completed, community-led investigation. When they filed the complaint in December 2015, it had eighteen plaintiffs, alleging forty-four counts of physical assault, sexual violence, racial discrimination, and arbitrary detention, carried out by a dozen officers, over three years.

Most of the evidence they had collected was in the form of victim narratives. In only a handful of incidents did they have cell phone footage of the interaction, photographs of bruises, or medical certificates. The lawyers believed that their evidence would be insufficient to obtain indictments: "we were talking about incidents that happened over the past three years, we had a lot of imprecise dates, and [victims who] hadn't followed the procedure . . . of going to the hospital to get their injuries certified." However, they hoped that the large number of testimonies reporting serious abuses would help garner media attention, and pressure the police to implement changes. "We went ahead as political lawyers saying, we have little chances of obtaining a criminal conviction, but our primary objective is for it to stop, and the best way is to file a lawsuit."[28]

This strategy worked. The lawyers' framing of the Tigers' practices as abusive and discriminatory successfully translated into the media coverage of the lawsuit. Right before filing the complaint, the litigation team shared it with the largest national paper *Le Monde* and the left-leaning news outlet *Mediapart*. While the media typically cover lawsuits alleging police misconduct by adopting the narrative of isolated incidents, the coverage of this complaint suggested that there was a pattern of systemic police harassment. *Le Monde*'s article was subtitled "Eighteen Boys and Girls Denounce Brutal and Daily Police Harassment,"[29] and *Mediapart* published excerpts of the complaint, including sentences denouncing the "systemic nature" of the abuses, and stating, "these practices suggest a purpose of intimidation, humiliation and harassment of these youth of foreign origins living in a disadvantaged neighborhood."[30]

The media attention made it difficult for the IGPN to dismiss the complaint, especially since there were allegations of sexual assault on minors. The police inspection service launched an uncharacteristically thorough investigation, interrogating every police officer working in a patrol unit and all the police chiefs within the district, and gathering hundreds of internal records. The investigation brought the desired scrutiny on the Tigers brigade. Many officers were moved to other positions, and the unit's staff was almost entirely replaced within months.

At the end of the investigation, the prosecution charged four policemen with aggravated assault, for incidents for which the plaintiffs had provided witness statements, medical records, photos, and videos. All the other allegations were dismissed for insufficient evidence.

We Can Now Denounce What Comes after a Contrôle au faciès

When the prosecutor released the indictment decision in June 2017, the litigation team held a meeting to discuss next steps, which I attended. Once everyone arrived, we started by discussing the prosecutor's decision to dismiss most allegations. At first, Slim Ben Achour and Felix de Belloy suggested that we could use it to "denounce the impossibility of investigating the police due to institutional solidarities [between law enforcement and the prosecution]."

However, the conversation quickly shifted as Julie,[31] Slim Ben Achour's associate, started sharing the details of the investigation file. The file, she explained, contained multiple police records that substantiated the plaintiffs' claims. "There is something in this file that is profoundly shocking to me; there is clear evidence of several criminal offenses that the cops admit to, but for which they are not charged," she started. The interrogation transcripts showed that "officers admitted that they touch the butt and groin folds when they conduct pat-downs," but the prosecutor did not charge them for sexual assault. The investigation file also showed that the children were regularly detained for "identity verification." Yet, the officers admitted that they never followed the legal procedures for identity verifications. "In law, it's an arbitrary detention, but the prosecution did not charge the officers for it."[32]

More disturbing to her was the fact that the police records gathered by investigators revealed that the Tigers received daily instructions from their supervisors to conduct "evictions of undesirables" in the spaces where the teenagers hung out. The police's routine use of the term "undesirables" surprised us. Historically, *indésirables* was used to designate racialized groups deemed unwelcome or dangerous on the national territory (Travelers in the 1920s, foreign Jews in the 1930s, Algerian Muslims in the 1960s), but it had been officially removed from public policy in the postwar years.[33] Yet, dozens of intervention records showed police officers in the twelfth arrondissement stopping racialized young men they labeled "undesirables" and evicting them from public spaces, regardless of their behavior. Nothing in French law allows officers to "evict" people from public space when they have committed no offense.

There was another critical element in the investigation file: video excerpts from a body camera that was given to the Tigers brigade following the complaint. The footage provided an unprecedented peek into the Tigers' behaviors during these evictions. Even though the officers switched the camera on and off at their discretion, and refrained from engaging in physical violence on camera, the footage clearly showed the racially disparate treatment during identity checks. Out of the seventeen interventions captured in the footage, sixteen targeted groups of Black and Arab young men who were not engaged in any visible illegal behavior, whereas only one stop targeted two White boys caught drawing graffiti on a wall. During the sixteen stops against racialized young men, the officers systematically started by telling them to line up against a wall, which the young men seem used to, and mostly did without protesting. The officers asked them to take the "check position" (*position de contrôle*), that is, to place their hands on a wall and spread their legs, so they could pat down and search every individual present. The police consistently refused to give a motive for the check when asked. When a young man complained that he and his friends had done nothing wrong, an officer answered: "When we say police check, it's police check. Period. Okay? Here, there's rule of law, it's the French Republic. During a police check, you shut up and you obey. Period." The stops typically ended with an injunction to "beat it." By contrast, when stopping the White boys drawing graffiti, the officers talked to them calmly, did not ask them to get against the wall and spread their legs, did not pat them down or search them, and simply asked if they had anything illegal on them. When one of the boys showed a marijuana cigarette (which is illegal in France), the officers simply told them to go home.

Gradually, as Julie gave us more details about the case file, Slim and Felix reevaluated their initially pessimistic reaction to the prosecution's decision. "What are we going to do with these images?" Slim asked; "they're extraordinary!" "They could really create a buzz," Felix agreed. Energized and seeing new opportunities open up, they started discussing how we could use the data included in the investigation file. Felix said, "We had denounced *contrôles au faciès*, but we hadn't been able to denounce what comes after: the pat-downs, and what follows pat-downs, the detention at the police station. Now, we will do it. This is actually a victory, contrary to what we believed when we received the prosecutor's letter!"

In February 2018, one week before the four indicted officers were due to stand trial, the coalition leaked elements of the investigation file to the press, including footage of the body-worn cameras. *Le Monde* and *Mediapart* released excerpts of the footage with voice-over commentary on their YouTube channels,[34] emphasizing the "unprecedented" nature of such images and describing them as revealing the reality of "routine police harassment." In this way, right before the trial was due to begin, the mobilization obtained favorable media coverage, which described the Tigers' practices as routine discrimination and harassment. This set the stage for the lawyers to expand their arguments in court.

"Ceremonies of Degradation" Enabled by Permissive Laws

At the criminal trial in 2018, the plaintiffs' lawyers made more radical claims than they had been able to make so far. In their previous cases, they had maintained a careful, moderate discourse that denounced illegal actions by individual officers. Now, drawing on the evidence uncovered in the investigation, they used the trial to promote a political discourse that questioned the utility of identity checks as a policing tool, condemned the permissive laws regulating them, and denounced what they called the "culture of impunity" that prevailed within the police.

In his concluding arguments, Slim Ben Achour started by saying that although the Tigers brigade was a public tranquility unit, their aggressive practices amounted to targeting racialized young men with what he called "ceremonies of degradation":

> The primary objective of the Tiger is to be there; to submit the children, not to the law but to authority. Through identity checks, identity verifications, transports to custody, they move, they handle "undesirables." In truth, it's a package: identity check, pat-down, searches, violence. This ritual aims to weaken these individuals . . . to signal, we can break you, you're under our control.[35]

The officers conduct these ceremonies of degradation "with such banality," he continued, because these practices are enabled by laws granting police expansive and unchecked powers to conduct identity checks. These ceremonies of degradation "necessarily affect the dignity of children and adolescents, humiliating, subjugating, and dehumanizing them, [yet, they are happening] within the bounds of the law, in a framework of opacity."[36] Identity checks, he concluded, even when they are conducted within the bounds of the law, are "a useless and dangerous activity" that "makes no sense."

In turn, Michel Tubiana, a lawyer representing France's human rights organization Ligue des droits de l'Homme, intervened at the trial in support of the plaintiffs. In his concluding arguments, he warned that the police chiefs' instructions fostered a culture of impunity among patrol officers. "Eviction stops," he said, "is a category that doesn't exist in law, it's a misuse of the law (*dévoiement de la loi*), [yet it is practiced] with the knowledge of, and I should even say, under orders from, the hierarchy." As a result, he continued, police officers are made to feel that they will never be held accountable for abuses: "they have crafted legal and cognitive categories that provide them with a sovereign's power"; they abuse their power with the "certainty of being unaccountable because they are police officers."[37]

These oral arguments illustrate how the coalition's capacity to introduce evidence of the repeated interactions between the police and the policed, and their success in triggering a thorough investigation, allowed the lawyers to expand their legal claims in court. While they initially denounced specific police interactions as violating criminal laws, now, they were able to criticize the laws regulating police powers, question the usefulness of identity checks as a policing tool, and denounce a culture of impunity.

These arguments were not well-received by court actors. In an uncommon move, the prosecutor took fifteen minutes to push back against the plaintiffs' lawyers' analysis before recommending that the officers be convicted. In her oral argument, the prosecutor insisted that, with the exception of three isolated incidents of physical violence, the general practices of the Tigers brigade were legitimate.

> We [the prosecution] are in a strange position in which we need to clarify a number of points. I don't want this case to be misrepresented in an excessive way. To hear that this is the trial of a group of racist and violent police officers who on a daily basis stop young innocents, we cannot accept this, this is not the reality. It's not possible today to accept such statements.[38]

The prosecutor referred to the ongoing public debate about racial profiling, noting, "it's not a debate that society has avoided, it has been taken on by organizations, institutions, and the Rights Defender . . . but it is not the reality of this case." The plaintiffs, she continued, were not innocent victims, since "their names are included in numerous police records that show that they are subjected to identity checks and police detention, either because there is a noise complaint, or because of spit, graffiti, or fireworks, or because the police unit received instructions to keep an eye particularly on this area." Thus, she used the fact that the police repeatedly targeted the plaintiffs as evidence that the stops were justified and not discriminatory, without responding to the lawyers' allegations that these stops targeted racialized young men, regardless of their behavior.

Following the prosecutor's recommendation, the Court of First Instance condemned three of the officers for aggravated assault but refrained from addressing the claims of discrimination. The convictions were reversed by the Court of Appeal in 2020, and all officers were acquitted.

Despite this judicial defeat, the lawyers and organizers successfully imposed their narrative in the media coverage of the case. Mainstream media stories went beyond the details of the three alleged incidents and contextualized them within a broader pattern of violence and discrimination. Large newspapers used headings describing it as "the trial of police violence against minors"[39] and recounted that the initial complaint denounced a series of abuses, including, "*contrôles au faciès*, intrusive frisks, including on the genitals, unlawful body searches, as well as repeated blows."[40]

In sum, the strategy of filing a collective complaint supplemented with a prior community-led investigation helped the mobilization impose a rare judicial debate about identity checks and police relations with minority youth. Even though court actors refused to endorse the movement's claims about discrimination, the media amplified the plaintiffs' allegations and went beyond the usual stories about isolated incidents, portraying the Tigers' practices as "police harassment" and "police violence."

Civil Lawsuit for Systemic Discrimination

Soon after the first instance criminal trial, the lawyers started planning a civil lawsuit against the state for police discrimination in the twelfth arrondissement. While the criminal case helped shed light on abusive patterns of practice in the public debate, it had not contributed to advancing legal rights for victims of racialized policing. The lawyers wanted to build on the 2016 ruling on racial profiling, and on the records uncovered in the criminal investigation, to expand their legal claims about discrimination in policing.

The strategic innovation of this case was to repurpose records uncovered in a criminal investigation against police officers into evidence in a civil case against the state. As lawyer Julie put it, "The criminal procedure has allowed us to see the orders given by the police commanders. There are police officers whose task it is to wipe out the undesirables. . . . The prosecutors' charging decision [to indict only four officers] suggests it's about bad apples, but the file shows that this is a society-wide policy."[41]

In a civil complaint filed in 2019, the lawyers added the IGPN's criminal investigation as evidence. This included command instructions to "evict undesirables," police records of interventions, and the body-camera footage. In this way, they sought to broaden the evidence of discrimination in civil law proceedings, beyond facts pertaining to specific police interactions or general statistics, to include evidence of institutional policies and practices. This allowed the litigation team to develop new legal arguments about institutional and systemic discrimination in policing, claims that had not been made in French courts before.

To substantiate the claims of institutional discrimination, the complaint argued that the repeated abusive practices—regularly stopping racialized young people without legal motive, evicting them unlawfully, systematically frisking them, subjecting them to insults, racist slurs, physical violence, and sexual molestation, and threatening them with retaliation if they complained—did not stem solely from officers' use of discretion, but were institutionalized in internal policies, through the use of obsolete terminology (*indésirables*) that historically designated racial groups unwelcome on the French territory. The lawyers presented evidence that the term *indésirable* is included in the national police software as one of the options in a drop-down menu to select the type of intervention. This, the complaint argued, "institutionalizes and legitimates discriminatory practices."[42]

The lawyers further argued that the abusive patterns of practice constituted systemic discrimination, in that they were part of a "discriminatory continuum," which included the officers' behaviors, the supervisors' orders to evict undesirables, the institutionalization of the term "undesirables" in the police software, and the "passivity of the authorities" who had been informed multiple times but had failed to act. The complaint added that the police were acting in response to a small minority of intolerant residents, citing a police officer who testified: "I was fed up because sometimes they were doing nothing wrong, but we were required [by our chiefs] to evict them at the demand of residents who couldn't stand seeing them." The complaint concluded: these facts produced "a situation of cumulative and dynamic inequality resulting from the interaction of practices, decisions, individual or institutional behaviors, which have intentional or unintentional prejudicial effects on the group targeted."[43]

The Court of First Instance issued its decision in October 2020. It condemned the state for grievous faults (*fautes lourdes*) regarding five instances of excessive use of force, five unlawful stops, and nine instances of arbitrary detention, but it rejected the plaintiffs' claims of discrimination. The decision to exonerate the state on the charge of discrimination hinged on the court's fragmented interpretation of the evidence. Whereas the plaintiffs asked the court to assess the cumulative effect of repeated misconduct, rooted in institutional policies, and targeting the same people, the court considered each piece of evidence separately and maintained an implicit requirement to prove police officers' intention to discriminate.

The ruling started by stating that, in line with the Court of Cassation's 2016 ruling, statistics demonstrating the disproportionate targeting of visible minorities in identity checks are insufficient, on their own, to establish a presumption of discrimination. Then, it contended that the allegations that the police used racist slurs during identity checks were not sufficiently evidenced. The plaintiffs' testimonies were not credible on their own, and the body-worn camera footage often showed officers using "denigrating" language to refer to the plaintiffs, but without a "discriminatory dimension." Next, the court assessed whether the use of the term "undesirable" in written policy and electronic records was discriminatory. It argued that it wasn't:

> The evidence suggests that the category referred to with these terms is defined not by age or origin, but by behavior in public space, as part of a policy, acknowledged by the officers and their supervisors, of securitization against *"the presence of youth in the evenings and nights on pedestrian zones, where they commit diverse nuisances and incivilities, and sometimes offenses, which are particularly bothersome to the residents of these neighborhoods"* (emphasis in the original).[44]

Interestingly, the court added "the fact that the implementation of this policy leads to irregularities or unlawful behaviors by the police, does not indicate a discriminatory connotation linked to age or origin." Thus, the judges suggested that what makes a practice or policy discriminatory is its use of racist terminology, not the fact that it results in disparate impact on racial minorities. Having found every piece of evidence insufficient to establish a presumption of discrimination, the court concluded, "given that discrimination is not established for each incident taken in isolation, it cannot be established in a global manner, whether through the existence of a phenomenon of discriminatory harassment or of systemic discrimination."[45]

It is perhaps unsurprising that the Paris court refrained from recognizing systemic discrimination, a concept for which there is little precedent in higher courts in France. However, its detailed assessment of the evidence was an important step forward. It signaled that the court considered the concept of systemic discrimination to be a valid legal claim, and the evidence the plaintiffs presented to be admissible and relevant.

Once again, despite the judicial defeat, the lawyers' claims had strong public resonance. In May 2020, the state-appointed Rights Defender (*Défenseur des droits*) published an opinion in support of the plaintiffs in which he noted that the repeated abuses committed by the Tigers brigade—discriminatory stops, racist insults, abusive frisks and searches, physical and sexual violence—constituted "systemic discrimination." He wrote, "The practices of evictions demanded by police chiefs always targeted the same youth, who were labeled 'undesirable' in the electronic records, a term that is deeply stigmatizing." The opinion concluded, "taken together, the facts establish the existence of discriminatory harassment, in that this practice of 'eviction' and the daily experience it imposes on the young people creates an intimidating, hostile, degrading, humiliating, and offensive environment."[46]

The Rights Defender's decision was widely covered in the media, with articles emphasizing the watchdog's appropriation of the terms "systemic discrimination" and "discriminatory harassment." All the article titles were variations on the theme "The Rights Defender Denounces 'Systemic Discrimination' by the Police in Paris," and most articles quoted excerpts from his opinion. This decision marked a gradual but significant evolution of the public and political debate, with terms that had hitherto been used only by activists being picked up and legitimized by institutional actors.

Truth and Justice Movement: Exposing the Judiciary's Complicity

The Truth and Justice movement, the third activist group examined in this book, took a different route to introduce their claims in the legal arena. The movement, which is led by families of victims of police killings, adopted a mode of knowledge production in which victims drew on their personal experiences to develop a structural analysis of police violence and impunity as embedded in broader systems of race and class oppression. This type of knowledge—based on personal experience and promoting a structural analysis of oppression—was not easily transferable in legal proceedings. For one, families of victims play a very limited role in criminal proceedings, since they are not a party in the legal dispute (criminal cases oppose the defendant and the prosecutor, not the victim). Moreover, the structural analysis they endorsed did not fit with the law's paradigm of individual responsibility.

To carve out avenues to transfer their knowledge claims into the legal arena, the families and activists that led the Truth and Justice movement worked to introduce their own experts—expert witnesses, medical experts, forensic specialists—in the legal proceedings. This strategy, developed by activists rather than lawyers, did not aim to advance the legal opportunities for policing victims as much as it sought to expose the judiciary's complicity with police violence.

The 2017 trial of the policeman who killed Amine Bentounsi provided an opportunity for the Truth and Justice movement.[47] It gave them a rare public platform to shed light on their struggle and legitimize their claims. The defendant, Damien Saboundjian, had shot and killed Amine Bentounsi on April 21, 2012, during a foot chase where he and three of his colleagues sought to arrest the twenty-eight-year-old, because he had failed to return to prison after a furlough. The shooter claimed that he fired in self-defense, after Amine Bentounsi pointed a gun at him. However, the autopsy showed that the bullet hit Amine in the back, and six eyewitnesses, who didn't know the victim and didn't know one another, testified that Amine had been running away from the police when he was shot.

To introduce the knowledge claims promoted by the Truth and Justice movement during the trial's hearing, the victim's family placed a request for four expert witnesses to make oral statements during the hearing: two figures from the Truth and Justice movement (Farid El Yamni and Omar Slaouti) and two sociologists (Nacira Guénif-Souilamas and Michel Kokoreff). While the rest of the trial was focused on reconstructing a detailed account of the chase and the circumstances of the fatal shot, the four expert witnesses sought to expand the attention from the particulars of this case to the broader structural patterns of police violence, racial inequality, and impunity, within which it is embedded.

Farid El Yamni shared the details of the investigations into his brother's death and talked about his realization that all families of victims faced a similar denial of justice. Antiracist activist Omar Slaouti spoke about several cases of police killings dismissed without an indictment, and about the rampant racism within police forces, evidenced by their high rates of voting for the far right.[48] Then, Nacira Guenif-Souilamas, a sociologist of gender, ethnicity, and immigration, spoke about the normalization of racialized violence in France. She said that her research shows that "the police want to affirm their authority over a population that doesn't have the benefit of the law" and is considered worthless. She ended her statement by addressing the jury and telling them that their decision "largely exceeds the case of the accused officer [and] resonates with a broader situation of injustice suffered by a population stigmatized because of its origins." Last, Michel Kokoreff, an urban sociologist, spoke about the endemic nature of racial discrimination in France, noting "the experience of racial discrimination has become central in French society and in low-income neighborhoods, in relation to schools, social housing, the police, the judiciary, and the media."[49]

Taken together, these expert statements framed police killings as a routine practice of the French police. They denounced the widespread impunity granted to police officers who kill, and affirmed that police brutality is a symptom of systemic racism in France.

The strategy did not have the impact movement leaders had hoped for. Legal professionals ignored these statements and instructed the jury to do the same. The prosecutor called on the jury to find the officer guilty but added, "this trial is not a political forum or a scholarly conference, and it's not a rally or a protest; it is a meeting of jurors who must decide on the fate of Damien Saboundjian." Even the victim's lawyer told the jury that they shouldn't listen to those "who want a conviction for the cause against police brutality."[50] What's more, the presiding judge interrupted Amal Bentounsi, the victim's sister and prominent figure of the Truth and Justice movement, during her oral statement, admonishing her for talking about her brother's experiences of police brutality, insisting "this is not the trial of the police!"

In my interview with the Bentounsi family lawyer after the trial, he explained why all the court actors ignored these statements: to them, they were irrelevant to the case. In fact, he too had been uneasy with the family's request to introduce these witnesses, because they made him seem unprofessional. "I found the female sociologist to be very polarizing," he told me. To him, the historical context she introduced on structural racism and impunity was "off-topic," especially since in this particular case, the judiciary had done "a good job."[51]

In the media too, the sociologists' and activists' statements were ignored. In the twenty-three articles published about the trial in *Le Monde*, *Le Figaro*, *Libération*, and *Le Parisien*, journalists discussed the victim's criminal history,[52] the defendant's personality,[53] the contradictions between his statements and those of the witnesses, and the police protests that followed the guilty verdict. But none mentioned the sociologists' or activists' statements. *Le Monde* even used the president's reprimand as the title of one of its articles, "This Is Not the Trial of the Police."[54]

There are two factors that explain why the movement's attempts to introduce claims of structural inequalities failed to resonate in this case. Unlike in the twelfth arrondissement lawsuits, this case focused on one police interaction, which made it easier for legal actors to frame arguments about broader patterns of practice as irrelevant and "off-topic." Also, the fact that these statements were made by activists and sociologists known for their left-leaning politics made it easier for court actors to discredit them as biased, something that was more difficult to do when the same claims were made by lawyers who relied on quantitative studies and police records, and framed their claims using legal terminology and established case law. Even though Truth and Justice actors struggled to make their claims heard during trials, they found ways to introduce their claims at the criminal investigation stage.

Discrediting Expert Reports

Most cases of police-involved death never go to trial,[55] but for Truth and Justice activists, the investigation process, which often lasts for years, represents an important opportunity to intervene in the law's construction of legal truth. One of the central ways in which they do this is by working to discredit court-ordered expert reports that clear the officers of responsibility in police killing cases.

When investigating police-involved deaths, prosecutors and judges rely on expert reports written by medico-legal and forensic professionals as key pieces of evidence. Investigative judges ask them to determine the cause of death and whether the medical and physical evidence aligns with specific scenarios. In law, these experts are considered to be highly reliable and credible. As sociologist Sheila Jasanoff argues, there is a widespread belief in modern societies "that science can deliver failsafe, and therefore just, legal outcomes."[56] One reason we tend to trust science, she explains, is because scientific norms, such as peer review, guarantee a high level of accuracy. But when science is used for legal purposes, these norms don't apply. The results of expert reports are not peer reviewed, and they are not expected to have general validity. Inaccuracies and divergent opinions are common. The assumption that scientific findings are more credible than other types of evidence is particularly strong in the French legal system, where experts are appointed by the court from a list of court-certified experts (*experts judiciaires*).

To families of victims, these reports often seemed biased, because they take the police narrative as their starting point. Farid El Yamni, who lost his brother Wissam to the police in 2012, explained:

> The judges ask leading questions to the experts, they ask them whether the police narrative is possible. So, the report doesn't give all the possible causes of death, it just says, "yes, the police version is possible, it's possible that the broken bones were caused by his slipping on a banana peel." Except then, the judges interpret this as: the expert said that he slipped on a banana peel.[57]

To contest these reports, some Truth and Justice committees have commissioned independent experts. Despite their financial cost, "it's the only possibility we have to contest these [court-ordered] reports," Farid El Yamni told me. Given that a court-appointed expert is assumed to be credible because he or she is a scientist, only another scientist—preferably one with a stronger reputation in the relevant field—can credibly contest their conclusions. In other words, families and activists seek to introduce an element of peer review where the legal process usually doesn't.

The investigation into Wissam El Yamni's death is a good illustration of how some Truth and Justice committees use this strategy, and of its effects and limitations. Following his arrest during New Year's Eve of 2012, police brought an unconscious Wissam to the hospital, where he remained in a coma for nine days before passing away. Following his death, three autopsy reports written by court-appointed experts concluded that his death was unconnected to the police's action and was due to a drug overdose combined with a preexisting heart condition. Yet, his family was highly doubtful of this narrative, given that several eyewitnesses saw police officers beat Wissam brutally, and that he had multiple broken bones and bruises when he arrived at the hospital. Moreover, the autopsy reports had been written by medical professionals who were not specialized in toxicology or cardiology.

The family decided to solicit the opinion of one of France's most renowned cardiology professors. He reviewed the court-ordered report and concluded that the anomalies that the judicial expert noted in the victim's heart rate were due to the medical treatment he received during his coma and can't be deemed to have caused the death. The El Yamni family also solicited a highly respected toxicologist, who found that the level of cocaine in the victim's blood was negligible at the time of his arrest and concluded that it's "highly unlikely" that it could have caused the coma and death. The El Yamni family presented these independent expert reports to the investigative judges.

Given that the independent reports were not written by court-certified experts, the judges deemed them inadmissible. However, the scientific credibility of the specialists, and the media attention that the family managed to obtain around these reports, led the judges to dismiss the previous court-appointed expert reports, arguing that they had proceeded "more by affirmation than by scientific demonstration." To replace them, the court appointed new court-certified experts. By 2019, seven years after Wissam's death, a fourth judicial autopsy report was released. This report rejected the hypothesis of a drug overdose or heart condition and concluded that the death was caused "by a third-party intervention" combined with the victim's consumption of alcohol. The report noted multiple bruises compatible with beatings and speculated that the restraining technique used on the victim in the police van may have played a role in the death. Thus, even though the independent specialist opinions were not deemed valid legal evidence, they helped discredit the earlier autopsy reports and led to the appointment of new court-certified experts, who concluded that the police intervention played a role in Wissam El Yamni's death. Without those independent reports, judges would have been unlikely to order a fourth autopsy report.

Like the El Yamni family, several other families of victims have solicited independent medical experts to discredit court-appointed experts who cleared the officers of responsibility. In each case, the independent reports, and the media coverage around them, helped discredit the court-certified experts and pressured investigative judges to accept the families' requests to order new reports.

Beyond their impact on specific investigations, the recurrence of court-ordered reports that are debunked by independent specialists helped promote the movement's claim that judicial investigations are biased in favor of the police. The investigation into Adama Traoré's death, and the exceptionally high media attention it garnered, played an important role in this regard. Adama Traoré, a twenty-four-year-old man of Malian origin, died during his arrest by the police in 2016. Over the six following years, nine different expert reports were released regarding the cause of death, three of which were written by independent specialists commissioned by the family. Like in the case of Wissam El Yamni, the first court-appointed experts cleared the officers of responsibility and concluded that the death was caused by preexisting health conditions combined with the victim running in hot weather. By contrast, the independent specialists argued that the police intervention played a role in Adama Traoré's death, pointing to the restraining hold that officers used to maintain him face down on the ground as the primary cause of his death by asphyxia. Every time the family presented an independent report that contradicted the court experts, investigative judges appointed new experts. Eventually, a large panel of court-appointed experts blamed Adama's death on the action of the police.

Throughout the years, every time a new report was released, the media covered it, emphasizing the contradictions between the various reports. Articles noted, "for over five years, expert and counter-expert reports follow and contradict one another" (*Le Monde*),[58] calling it "a long battle of medical expertise" (*Le Figaro*)[59] and emphasizing the "diametrically opposed findings" of various opinions (*Radio France*).[60] By highlighting the uncertain and contested nature of medical reports, the media coverage helped disrupt the widespread assumption that court-ordered medical reports are foolproof, thus contributing to legitimating the movement's claims about the manufacturing of police impunity.

More recently, Truth and Justice committees have expanded their use of independent experts beyond medical professionals. In the early 2020s, nonprofits such as Disclose, Index, and GENI started proposing counter-investigations in cases of police-involved deaths, through 3D modeling or video footage analysis. For example, in 2021, Disclose and Index released a counterinvestigation into the death of Gaye Camara, a twenty-six-year-old man who was shot by the police while driving his car in 2018. Based on the medical and physical evidence included in the criminal investigation, the nonprofit used 3D modeling to retrace the car's trajectory in space and time and to demonstrate where the officer was standing when he shot the driver. Their report concluded that, when he fired his gun, "the officer was not facing Gaye Camara's car. The driver was therefore not darting towards him, as the investigation claims."[61] While this independent report did not prevent a nonindictment decision, all the major newspapers covered it, arguing that it "undermines the self-defense thesis."[62]

In sum, Truth and Justice activists have carved avenues to intervene in the criminal investigation process by soliciting independent experts to review, and often debunk, the conclusions of court-appointed experts. In this way, they use the standards of scientific credibility—peer review by specialists—to demonstrate one of their central claims: judicial investigations into police-involved deaths are unreliable at best and at worst blatantly biased in favor of the police. But while independent expert reports help the movement highlight the biases of criminal investigations into police killings, they do not seem to prevent nonindictment decisions. Like in the case of Gaye Camara, the judiciary has dismissed Adama Traoré's case after a seven-year investigation. At the time of writing, nine years after his death, the family is awaiting the highest court's ruling after they appealed the nonindictment decision. And, thirteen years after Wissam El Yamni's death, the investigation is still ongoing.

Conclusion

Mobilizing the law was a central strategy for all three activist coalitions. The lawsuits that they initiated or engaged with played an important role for advancing the legal rights of policing victims, and for promoting the movements' claims about racialized policing in the media. For each coalition, mobilizing the law required engaging in epistemic work, that is, carving avenues to transform the data they produced into admissible, credible, and relevant legal evidence. The campaign against racial profiling introduced their statistics about racial disparities in police stops by drawing on EU evidentiary rules for antidiscrimination claims in civil law. The neighborhood mobilization relied on a community-led investigation to trigger a criminal investigation into abusive patterns of practice, and then used the police records uncovered in the investigation as evidence in a civil lawsuit against the state for systemic discrimination. And the Truth and Justice movement used external experts to debunk court expert reports and expose the role of the judicial system in preventing accountability for the police.

The analysis showed that *how* movement actors intervene in the construction of legal truth—their epistemic work—mattered for the legal claims they were able to make in court, and for the way the cases were covered in the media. While their litigation efforts had limited effects on expanding legal rights for policing victims, they had a significant impact on the media coverage and political debates around racialized policing. The racial profiling lawsuit helped promote the idea that racial profiling is a problem that the state, not individual officers, is responsible for. The neighborhood mobilization obtained media coverage that emphasized racialized policing as routine patterns of practice rather than isolated incidents. Although the courts rejected their arguments about systemic discrimination, the state-appointed Rights Defender endorsed them, thus moving the political conversation beyond an individualistic understanding of police discrimination. And the Truth and Justice movement raised the issue of unreliable court experts in the media, thus exposing a central tenet of what they call the manufacturing of police impunity.

SIX

Transforming the Political Debate

In the fall of 2017, I joined members of the Truth and Justice movement for a meeting at the National Assembly with parliamentarians of the left-wing party La France insoumise (LFI). I attended the meeting as a member of the collective of families of victims, Vies Volées (Stolen Lives), alongside other members of the Truth and Justice movement. After making our way through security checks and long corridors, we arrived at the large meeting room. There, LFI representative Danièle Obono, one of the only Black women in the French Parliament at the time, welcomed us and thanked us for accepting her invitation. She explained that her party was preparing to introduce a bill that would ban the police from using lethal restraining techniques, such as chokeholds and face-down holds, a long-standing demand of the movement. She wanted to meet us, she said, "to discuss how we can move forward on this issue together," and she asked us to share our work on this topic. We provided her with the data that movement actors had gathered about circumstances of lethal police interventions that involved restraining techniques; we spoke about the experiences of families of victims and the hurdles they face when seeking justice; and, upon her request, we shared our ongoing research on other countries' legislation banning lethal restraining techniques. We also informed her that Vies Volées was preparing to launch an online campaign to call for a ban on all lethal restraining techniques, called "Let Us Breathe." She thanked us for all this information, and we left the meeting with a promise to coordinate the timing of the bill with the launch of the Let Us Breathe campaign.

A few weeks later, I returned to the same meeting room at the National Assembly but this time with leaders of the campaign against racial profiling. That meeting was initiated by another LFI representative, Mathilde Panot, who invited members of the campaign to discuss the party's legislative agenda on racial profiling. The parliamentarian explained her party's plans to introduce a bill that would require the police to keep systematic records of identity checks ("stop forms"), the campaign's key reform proposal. She asked us to share our work on racial profiling. We gave her copies of the studies that the campaign had conducted along with our written recommendations for legislative reforms. We shared our insights about why this reform had failed to pass despite being introduced several times in the past years, and we discussed possible arguments to overcome the government's resistance. The meeting ended with an agreement to coordinate the timing of the law bill with a public rally to draw media attention.

As promised, the following winter, the LFI introduced a "Law Bill to Combat *Contrôles au faciès*." A year later, they presented the "Law Bill for a Ban on Lethal Restraining Techniques," and in 2020, they started arguing for dismantling the police inspection services (IGPN and IGGN) and replacing them with an independent investigative body, another key demand of the movement.

These meetings at the National Assembly illustrate the main political outcome for the coalitions examined in this book: in the 2010s, they gained access to the policy field and successfully introduced the question of racialized policing in the political debate. The meetings show how activists' knowledge production contributed to this advance. Politicians reached out to them not just to coordinate public campaigns around law bills, but also because they considered movement leaders to be knowledgeable experts on these issues who could be relied on to provide research to support the case for reform. Although none of these bills was voted into law, the fact that activists managed to place and sustain their issues on the agenda was remarkable, given a political context that was largely unfavorable to their demands.

This chapter examines how the movement against racialized policing placed its issues on the political agenda, and how it influenced the political debate about policing, inequality, and injustice in the 2010s. Here, I do not aim to provide a comprehensive explanation for why the political debate shifted; rather, I analyze how activists contributed to this shift, focusing on two of the three activist groups I studied: the campaign against racial profiling and the Truth and Justice movement. The neighborhood mobilization did not engage in national-level advocacy work and did not attempt to introduce legal or policy reforms, so it drops out of this part of the story.

The analysis shows that the movements' knowledge production efforts were instrumental in granting them access to the political field. In the face of the police's epistemic power, which had, for decades, allowed power holders to deny, dismiss, and discredit activist claims, activists' ability to produce their own knowledge was essential to establish the credibility of their claims and their legitimacy as political interlocutors. Importantly, each coalition's mode of knowledge production set them on different *pathways to credibility* in the political arena, shaping how their claims were received and interpreted in the political field, and how much leverage they maintained over framing the issue once it was on the agenda.

Pathways to Credibility

Social movement scholars argue that activists' ability to influence politics is constrained by the *political opportunity structure*, which is the degree to which the political arena is open to a movement's claims. The political opportunity structure is typically defined in reference to two dimensions: the institutional structure of the political system (how policy decisions are made) and the configuration of power within this system (who hold positions of power).[1] In France in the 2010s, these dimensions provided few windows of opportunity for the movement. Given the state's centralized structure, the laws and policies regulating policing are determined at the national level by the government and Parliament, with local politicians playing little role. Yet, throughout the 2010s, national politics became increasingly dominated by a securitarian discourse calling for harsh law-and-order measures. Nicolas Sarkozy's presidency (2007–12) was marked by an aggressive tough-on-crime rhetoric that blamed residents of low-income neighborhoods for rising "urban violence." The 2012 election of socialist François Hollande provided a short-lived window for the movement, but one that quickly narrowed and then shut down completely following the

2015 terrorist attacks that killed 130 people. The election of Emmanuel Macron in 2017, and the continuous rise of the far right, closed off political opportunities further. Throughout this time, most police unions, which hold significant political weight,[2] organized against any reform proposals that would restrict police powers or strengthen accountability mechanisms.

Within this context, activists sought to build political alliances with the left-wing opposition. But to do this, they first needed to gain legitimacy in the political field and to bolster the credibility of their claims. As anthropologist David Hess argues, there is a third, often neglected, dimension of the political opportunity structure: the epistemic dimension. Within policy fields, there are rules and conventions about the types of knowledge deemed reliable and the kinds of actors considered credible. Just like the judicial arena examined in the previous chapter, the political field has its own conventions about the types of information that can be relied on when making policy decisions. These conventions include which actors are deemed to be reliable experts and how open the policy field is to various research methodologies, or to the participation of lay actors.[3]

In France, quantitative data produced by public authorities are perceived as the most reliable and trustworthy to base political decisions on.[4] Yet, the police hold a near monopoly over the production of statistics about crime, disorder, and policing practices. As a result, the public debate about policing is dominated by police-produced data and expertise. At the same time, nonpolice actors, such as activist groups, NGOs, or watchdog institutions, are largely dismissed and discredited, and research that relies on qualitative methodologies such as interviews is viewed as subjective and partisan.

For social movement actors who have neither access to, nor control over, police-produced data, the challenge is not only to produce their own evidence but also to find avenues to introduce it and legitimize it in the policy arena. To do this, they can take several *pathways to credibility*.[5] Activists and NGOs can partner with credentialed experts to produce knowledge that aligns with the epistemic rules of the political field, or they can challenge the political field's assumptions about who is credible and which methodologies are reliable.[6] Sociologist Steven Epstein argued that each pathway may involve trade-offs between resonating with the political field and remaining close to the movements' claims. His study of the AIDS movement suggests that when activists got involved in the production of epidemiological knowledge, it "made it harder for them to frame issues for the media or a broader public, to recruit new members, and to maintain a broad-based and socially diverse movement . . . [because] the ways of representing natural and social reality that activists develop in their role as "lay experts" may differ significantly from the representations that they elaborate in street demonstrations and other, more conventional, activist venues."[7]

Building on Epstein's insights, the rest of the chapter examines the implications and trade-offs of two pathways to credibility that coalitions took, both for how activists were able to frame racialized policing in the political arena and for how their claims were picked up by allies and responded to by opponents. The comparison allows for an analysis of how different modes of knowledge production shape the way activists influence the terms of the political debate.

Contrôles au faciès: *Establishing the "Truth"* *of a Previously Contested Claim*

Until the middle of the 2000s, there was little research on racial inequalities in policing. The research that did exist relied on testimonies by policing victims, and government officials on the right and on the left dismissed it as subjective. This allowed politicians to deny the existence of racial profiling and to close off any political debate on the issue.

When the campaign against racial profiling launched a research study about racial profiling, they sought to produce knowledge that could not be dismissed as subjective or partisan. They collaborated with established scholars to produce statistical data—the gold standard in policy research about inequalities. To ensure that the study would be perceived as credible in the political arena, the scholars were careful to maintain their reputation as nonpartisan, objective scientists. They insisted that the study should be conducted without involving activist organizations, and they revised the final report to remove mentions of politically sensitive topics such as France's colonial history.

These efforts to frame their study as scientific and nonpartisan paid off. When the report, *Profiling Minorities*, was released in 2009, mainstream media unanimously portrayed it as the "scientific proof" of the existence of *contrôles au faciès* (discriminatory stops) in France.[8] The study showed staggering disparities in identity checks. People perceived as Black or Arab were, on average, six and eight times more likely to be stopped for identity checks than those perceived as White, and people dressed in "youth culture styles" were eleven times more likely to be stopped.[9] Over the next three days, the study's authors were invited to speak on radio, TV channels, and the press over twenty times.[10] The daily *Le Monde* headline read "The Reality of *contrôles au faciès* Is Established"; right-wing *Le Figaro* wrote, "French Police Largely Practice *délit de faciès*"; and left-wing *Libération* declared, "*Contrôles au faciès*: The Police Caught Red-Handed in Paris." Media stories highlighted the substantial empirical research on which the report relied and concluded that the study "confirms and gives scientific value to what visible minorities in France have been saying for years."[11]

Significantly, no police representatives or police unions publicly contested the study's findings. The spokesperson for the Paris Police Prefecture told journalists, "This study provides us with statistical information that appears scientifically indisputable."[12] This admission was unprecedented. In the past, police representatives had systematically dismissed NGO reports and suggested that claims of racial inequalities in policing were subjective and partisan. To Fabien Jobard, one of the researchers who led the research, this time, police representatives did not contest the study because of its robust quantitative methodology, and its striking findings: "they were impressed, there were 38,000 people in the benchmark, 525 identity checks, with crazy high odd ratios," he told me.[13] Indeed, when three years later, another transnational organization, Human Rights Watch, released an interview-based study on racial profiling in France,[14] police unions criticized it as "unscientific," "not evidenced," and "partisan,"[15] thus confirming Jobard's theory that the quantitative nature of *Profiling Minorities* was key to its widespread recognition as "scientific proof."

The media's unanimously positive reception of the study made political denial increasingly untenable. In a reversal from decades-long attitude of denial, officials of Sarkozy's tough-on-crime government started publicly recognizing the reality of racial profiling. The commissary for Diversity and Equal Opportunities, Yazid Sabeg, told the *New York Times* that profiling "has been an issue for a long time," and that it "leads to tension between the youth and the police."[16] The immigration minister, Eric Besson, recognized that *contrôles au faciès* are "a reality."[17] A few months later, the state secretary for city affairs, Fadela Amara, asked the Interior minister what he planned to do about *contrôles au faciès*, arguing that people are fed up with being stopped by police on the basis of their appearance. Interior Minister Brice Hortefeux responded by saying, as his predecessors had, "there is no *contrôles au faciès*." But this attitude of denial became increasingly marginal within the political arena.[18]

Although the study made it difficult to deny the existence of disparities in identity checks, it also opened the way for conflicting interpretations about the cause of these disparities. The statistical analysis produced strong evidence of widespread disparities in police stops, but it left open the question of what is to blame: individual officers' biases or institutional policies. The spokeswoman for the Paris Police emphasized officers' biases, saying that the targeting of young Black and Arab men is based on officers' operational sense and intuition, suggesting that "preconceptions and prejudice [may] come into play."[19] In contrast, the left-leaning police union Unité Police, which was hostile to Sarkozy's government, argued that these disparities resulted from institutional policies like quantitative performance indicators (*la politique du chiffre*) and immigration enforcement priorities. The union president, Yannick Danio, said on national television, "when there are quotas to [arrest illegal migrants to] fill airplanes, yes, there is *contrôle au faciès*."[20] For its part, the right-wing police union Alliance Police Nationale blamed the targets of discriminatory stops, claiming that racial disparities are justified by the fact that Black and Arab young men dressed in youth culture styles are more likely to commit crimes.[21] This was echoed by the prominent far-right commentator Eric Zemmour, who admitted that the police disproportionately stop racial minorities but argued, "it's because the majority of drug dealers are Black and Arab, it's a fact"[22] (for this statement, Eric Zemmour was convicted of incitement to racial discrimination[23]).

The reactions from the police and politicians illustrate the strengths and limitations of the pathway to credibility that the campaign took. By enrolling well-known scholars and using statistical methods policy makers widely perceived as reliable, they established the "scientific truth" of a previously contested claim in the political field. However, the statistical analysis could only demonstrate that the police disproportionately target racialized groups, but it could not determine what drives these disparities. This opened the way for various interpretations, with some pointing to biased officers, others blaming it on institutional policies, and others justifying racial profiling by promoting stereotypes about Black and Arab criminality.

A Simple Reform That Benefits All

In the early 2010s, campaign leaders intensified their political advocacy work. Now that there was widespread recognition that *contrôles au faciès* are a reality, they worked to gain endorsements for reforms. The campaign focused its political advocacy work on the 2012 presidential and legislative elections. The goal was to get as many political endorsements as possible. The cofounder of one of the activist collectives that joined the campaign told me that, when other activists warned them that they would get co-opted (*récupéré*), she replied "yes, that's the point, [to be co-opted] by everybody."[24]

The campaign's lobbying efforts revolved around one key reform: requiring that police officers record every identity check in a "stop form" that would record the circumstances of the stop (day, time, place, motive) and the demographic characteristics of the people stopped. This measure was promoted by Open Society, the main funder and coordinator of the campaign, throughout Europe. It was inspired by the United States and the United Kingdom, where police forces use stop forms to monitor racial disparities in stop and search. As part of their broader goal to challenge France's "race blindness," Open Society initially promoted the implementation of stop forms that would include the race or ethnicity of people stopped by the police. This, they argued, was an essential monitoring tool to "foster accountability and provide a foundation of knowledge on which to build policy."[25]

However, some of the French organizations involved in the campaign warned that, given France's antiracialist laws, stop forms recording race or ethnicity would likely be illegal. Even if the campaign found a way to overcome legal restrictions, requiring that the police collect data on people's race would be politically unacceptable, given the country's history during the Holocaust, when the police kept databases on Jews and used them to raid their homes and deport them to death camps.

This did not mean that these organizations wanted to scrap the reform recommendation altogether. There was a consensus among campaign actors that requiring stop forms without recording race or ethnicity would still be beneficial. It would provide comprehensive data on identity checks, thus shedding light on a practice that remained completely opaque. It would also require police officers to log each stop in writing, which was likely to reduce the overall rate of identity checks. They agreed to recommend implementing stop forms that would not include any racial data.

To promote this measure, the campaign had to come up with arguments different from the need to monitor racial disparities. Instead, some of the groups active in the campaign framed stop forms as a measure that would benefit all—the police, the people stopped, and the public. In their meetings with politicians and journalists, they argued that stop forms were a tool to evaluate the practice of identity checks and to foster a police-population dialogue "based on facts and not feelings." Stop forms would help identify officers who have low "hit rates" and target them for additional training, thus improving police efficiency. And they would "provide those who are stopped with an objective element of proof, and at the same time provide the police with a way to justify the stop in case of false accusations of discriminatory or abusive stop."[26]

Implicit in those arguments was an understanding of *contrôles au faciès* as a problem of biased officers, and of stop forms as a tool to identify them and hold them accountable. This shifted the stated goal of the reform from Open Society's initial emphasis on collecting ethno-racial data to monitor patterns of practice that result in unequal outcomes, to an argument about monitoring individual officers and distinguishing between good cops and bad cops.

The emphasis on biased officers was exacerbated by the fact that stop forms quickly became the main, and sometimes only, focus of legal reform efforts. Initially, Open Society and their closest partners pushed for a broader package of reforms, which also included restricting police powers to stop and search, implementing antibias training, and strengthening monitoring and accountability mechanisms. "Reforming the legal framework was the cornerstone of our recommendations," the director of Human Rights Watch told me: "we have a legal framework that is extremely permissive and allows police officers to conduct stops in nearly any situation. Even when officers act within the framework, if the framework is this wide, policing practices will violate liberties."[27]

However, the politicians and police unions they spoke with were unanimously opposed to the idea of restricting police powers. As a result, one of the groups that joined the campaign, Stop le contrôle au faciès, decided to promote stop forms only, as an achievable reform goal. Eventually, although Open Society continued to push for the whole package of reforms, the public debate revolved almost exclusively around stop forms.

The campaign's advocacy work succeeded in placing the issue of *contrôles au faciès* on the political agenda. The 2012 presidential election pitted Republican incumbent Nicolas Sarkozy, the architect of France's zero-tolerance policies, against the socialist party candidate, François Hollande. Seeing an opportunity to distinguish himself from Sarkozy's tough-on-crime rhetoric, and thereby gain votes in low-income neighborhoods, Hollande made an electoral pledge to combat *contrôles au faciès* through the implementation of stop forms.[28] This was a significant victory: for the first time in France, the issue of *contrôles au faciès* made it on the electoral platform of a major political party. Smaller political parties, too, endorsed the proposal, and elected representatives from the communist (PCF), environmentalist (EELV), and centrist (UDI) parties started introducing reform bills.

Another achievement was that the campaign gained endorsements from the largest left-leaning police union. In their meetings with union leaders, the activists emphasized that the data collected through stop forms would help officers demonstrate, to their supervisors and to the public, that they do good work. This resonated with the left-leaning unions, concerned about the negative impact that aggressive, zero-tolerance policies had on their relationships with communities. The police union Unité SGP Police-FO endorsed the campaign's reform proposals, and two of its leaders agreed to be quoted in a photo exhibit OSJI created as a public campaign tool, in which they said that "repeated identity checks are counterproductive" because they give citizens the impression that the police are not at their service.[29]

The campaign's success at gaining political endorsements was predicated on activists capitalizing on the newfound recognition that "*contrôles au faciès* are a reality," and on proposing reforms that resonated in the political arena. But given the epistemic rules of the political field, and namely the restrictions on racial statistics, aligning with the political context meant modifying the nature of the measure promoted, from one that aimed to produce comprehensive data on racial disparities in police stops, to one that was framed as a tool to challenge individual instances of misconduct. This illustrates that the epistemic rules of the policy field do not only constrain how movements can gain political credibility but also the kinds of reforms they can reasonably introduce. In this case, the fact that policy makers considered quantitative data to be the most reliable, while also delegitimizing racial statistics, limited the reform proposals the campaign could make to measures focused on disciplining individual misconduct. This, in turn, influenced the counterclaims opponents developed.

An Unprecedented Injury to the Honor of Police Officers

After François Hollande's election in 2012, his cabinet announced that they were working on implementing stop forms. Immediately, right-wing police unions took to the media to voice strong opposition to the reform. They said that stop forms would "send a message of defiance to the police who are already very exposed" and would increase "suspicion of the Republican police."[30] The largest right-wing union, Alliance Police Nationale, called the government's reform plan "an unprecedented disavowal, hurtful and injurious to the honor and probity of police officers."[31] The unions also argued that stop forms would only increase paperwork while being ineffective at combating discrimination.

Opponents of the reforms framed *contrôles au faciès* squarely as a matter of individual bias, arguing that the activists' discourse was an unfair stigmatization of police officers as racists. The left-leaning unions that had spoken up against *contrôles au faciès* retreated, perhaps under pressure from the rank and file, and said that these reforms were "not a priority." The claims they had made, that some institutional policies, such as quantitative performance indicators and immigration enforcement, fostered discrimination, dropped out of the media and political debate.

Just four months after Hollande's election, his Interior minister, Manuel Valls, announced that the government would abandon the implementation of stop forms. Echoing the unions' rhetoric, he said, "this measure is not sufficiently effective, and would risk being considered by police officers as a sign of defiance."[32] Instead, the minister implemented a series of smaller changes in 2013. The police launched an experimentation of body-worn cameras, the code of ethics was modified to specify the rules of conduct during identity checks, a new online platform was created for citizens to file complaints of police misconduct, and it became compulsory for uniformed police to wear a tag with their badge number.[33]

Activists criticized these measures and called them ineffective.[34] They pointed to the fact that officers would be able to switch body-worn cameras on and off at their will, thus rendering cameras ineffective as a tool to monitor police conduct;[35] that the changes to the code of ethics failed to reduce police discretion. They also noted that the agency handling complaints for police misconduct lacked independence, and that there is little compliance with the requirement to wear the badge number tag, and no enforcement. Still, the debate around these measures further consolidated the understanding that *contrôles au faciès* is a problem of "bad apples" that can be solved by strengthening the institution's ability to identify and discipline them.

Contrôles au faciès *Becomes a Recurring Political Issue*

After François Hollande abandoned the promised reforms, the campaign shifted its attention to elected representatives in Parliament. Activists reached out to opposition parties and provided them with proposed reform bills. Members of the Green Party (EELV), the center-right party (UDI), and the French communist party (PCF), saw this as an opportunity to expose the socialists' failure to keep up their electoral promises.

During Hollande's five-year term, opposition members presented eight bills and several legal amendments to combat *contrôles au faciès*. All of these bills included the campaign's key proposal: the implementation of stop forms that would record the circumstances and motive of every stop and demographic data about the person stopped (without recording ethnicity or race). To motivate their bills, opposition members argued that the reality of discriminatory identity checks was now undeniable. Borrowing the campaign's discourse, they claimed that *contrôles au faciès* are ineffective because they increase mistrust in police and reduce citizens' cooperation, and that they are harmful to both the persons stopped and the police because they increase tensions between police and communities. Stop forms were presented as a tool to "evaluate their frequency and, when relevant, to serve as an element of proof in litigation."[36]

The socialist majority persisted in their rejection of these proposals. Every time lawmakers sought to introduce stop forms, the government argued that they would stigmatize police officers as racists, echoing the police unions' rhetoric. Hollande's Interior minister publicly deplored "the theorization of a proclivity toward discrimination on the part of the police," arguing that police officers are no different from other public servants and don't deserve to face so much suspicion around their moral character.[37]

Following the deadly terrorist attacks of 2015, the government declared a state of emergency and endorsed a securitarian discourse, vowing to provide the police with expanded powers and added resources, and to increase the penalties for insult, contempt, or violence against the police. In this context, the government doubled down on their opposition to any reforms that police officers may perceive as stigmatizing.

Nevertheless, the campaign's advocacy work led to a significant increase in the rate at which the issue was debated in Parliament (see figure 6.1). The law bills introduced by opposition members triggered two important shifts in the legislative debate. First, while the issue of *contrôles au faciès* had so far been raised rarely, and only in reaction to proposals to expand police powers, now, it was raised regularly and proactively, with representatives introducing bills to combat the practice. Second, the parliamentary discussions illustrate a noticeable shift in the terms of the political debate. Elected representatives opposed to the reforms no longer denied the existence of *contrôles au faciès*. Instead, they argued that the proposed reforms were inappropriate and ineffective. In other words, the debate shifted from one about whether *contrôles au faciès* exist, to a widespread recognition that they do, and a discussion about what, if anything, should be done about them. By the end of Hollande's presidency, the campaign had succeeded in placing, and sustaining, the issue of *contrôles au faciès* on the political agenda.

In sum, the campaign against racial profiling took a pathway to credibility that relied on aligning with the epistemic rules of the French political field. This helped them overcome political denial and establish the "scientific truth" of a previously contested claim: that the police disproportionately target Black and Arab men. Capitalizing on this newfound recognition, campaign leaders sought broad political endorsements for their reform proposals. However, uncertainty about the causes of disparate outcomes, and the way the campaign adapted their reform proposals to France's antiracialist context, contributed to fostering a political debate that focused on monitoring and disciplining biased officers. This down-

FIGURE 6.1   Number of parliamentary sessions in which "contrôles au faciès" is mentioned, 1982–2018.

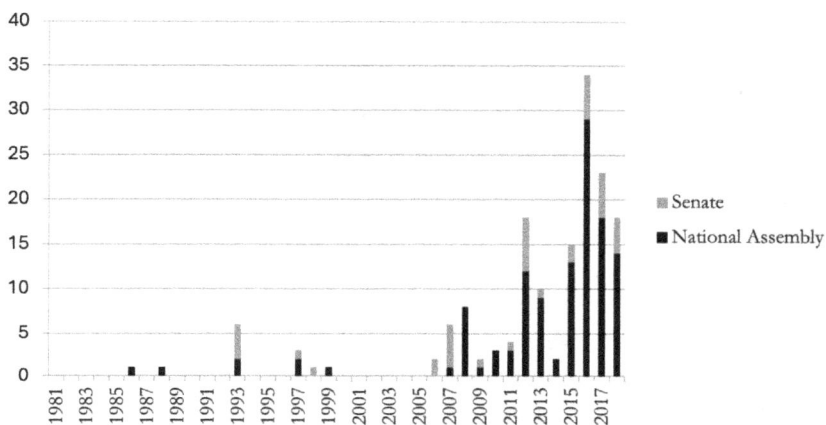

Source: Magda Boutros.

played the institutional policies and structural inequalities that underlie racial profiling. The Truth and Justice movement took a different approach.

Truth and Justice: Raising the Profile of Previously Discredited Actors

The Truth and Justice movement's approach to knowledge production aimed to legitimize and elevate the analyses of those most affected by police violence. Their liberation epistemology entailed centering the voices of families of victims, who drew on their personal and collective experiences to develop a structural analysis of police violence and impunity. In this way, victims pushed back against being used simply as sources of data and imposed themselves as knowers in their own right.

This mode of knowledge production opened a different pathway to credibility: instead of raising the credibility of a previously contested *claim*, it created an avenue to raise the credibility of previously discredited *actors*. The goal was for families of victims to establish themselves as a legitimate and credible voice in the political field that can no longer be ignored.

This was no easy feat. Until the mid-2010s, the Truth and Justice movement was largely ignored and discredited by the mainstream media and political arena. Even as politicians started endorsing calls to combat *contrôles au faciès* during the 2012 elections, the movement's grievances about police violence and impunity remained largely absent from the media and political conversation. When the police killed Amine Bentounsi in April 2012, in the middle of the presidential election campaign, the media and political coverage focused on police union's demands for a law that would grant officers a "presumption of self-defense." No activist voice was covered.

Left-wing parties, too, largely ignored the movement's claims. In fact, when some political parties started speaking up against police violence in the mid-2010s, they focused exclusively on violence targeting mostly White, middle-class protesters and sidelined the routine violence targeting young Black and Arab men living in low-income neighborhoods. In 2014, Rémi Fraisse, a twenty-one-year-old White environmental activist, was killed by the police during a protest. The Green Party EELV called the death of a protester "intolerable" and condemned the police intervention, saying it "raises extremely serious questions" about the government's action.[38] Under pressure from the left, lawmakers voted to launch a parliamentary investigation. However, the investigation focused solely on protest policing and refused to engage with questions of police use of force during routine actions in low-income neighborhoods (*quartiers populaires*).[39] Starting in 2015, with the increasing militarization of protest policing and unprecedented numbers of injuries and arrests among protesters,[40] several other left-wing parties and labor unions joined the calls for reforming protest policing. But like the environmentalists, they limited their condemnation to the policing of protest, thus reifying a distinction between police violence during demonstrations, which became an issue of political debate, and police violence during routine interventions in low-income neighborhoods, which was still largely invisible in the political field.

In this context, to make their voices heard, Truth and Justice leaders started by working to gain media attention, both in traditional media and on social media. After her brother's death, Amal Bentounsi spearheaded a new communications strategy based on high-visibility disruptive tactics. She quit her job to focus full-time on the struggle and created a new collective of families, Urgence Notre Police Assassine (Emergency Our Police Kills). She chose the name, she told me, because it was "hard-hitting" and "radical," adding, "all they can do is attack us—and if they do, then so much the better!"[41] On the collective's website, she published a parody video mimicking a recruitment ad for the national police, which said, "you want to commit violence and crimes with total impunity without ever being bothered? The police recruit, and the judiciary protects you!" The provocative ad led her to be sued by the Interior minister for defamation against the police, a lawsuit that was widely covered in mainstream media and helped established her as a public voice against police brutality. She also engaged in a series of visible direct actions, for example, interrupting a police protest to throw fake blood at their feet while shouting "murderers." She was arrested multiple times for these direct actions, arrests that she made sure to publicize as widely as possible. Soon, journalists identified her as a leading activist and started inviting her to debate with police representatives on talk shows.[42] In my interview with her, she reflected, "the media didn't come to me, I imposed myself on them."[43]

The work of Amal Bentounsi paved the way for other families of victims to gain media visibility. By 2016, when Adama Traoré died at the hands of the police, the Truth and Justice movement had gained enough experience to help the Traoré family rapidly gain—and retain—media attention around their struggle. To steer media attention away from their usual focus on the urban revolts triggered by the young man's death, and toward questioning the police's responsibility, the committee Truth for Adama worked on several parallel tracks. They established a strong social media presence, posting regular press releases, videos, and Facebook lives to disseminate the findings of their counterinvestigation, give updates on the judicial process, and inform followers of the repression facing the family. They organized regular events, including protests, sit-ins, commemorations, and press conferences, but also cultural events, sports tournaments, and concerts in the name of Adama. The committee also worked on turning Assa Traoré, Adama's sister, into an iconic figure of the movement. She traveled across the country to speak about Adama at political and cultural events, she published two books about her struggle, and she accepted invitations to televised talk shows to speak about her brother's death. In addition, the committee Truth for Adama sought out a wide diversity of celebrities to speak about Adama's case, including artists such as actor Omar Sy and rapper Booba, who are followed by millions, and public intellectuals such as Geoffroy de Lagasnerie and Edouard Louis, who used their platforms to reach educated elites. The Traoré family also recruited a high-profile lawyer, Yassine Bouzrou, who regularly appeared on TV and on the radio to discuss the legal developments of the case.

These strategies allowed the Truth and Justice movement to gain unprecedented public visibility. The Twitter and Facebook accounts of the
committee Truth for Adama were soon followed by tens of thousands of
people. The Adama Traoré case earned higher media attention than other
police violence cases, with mainstream media calling it "the case that
symbolizes the struggle against police violence."[44] Assa Traoré became
an iconic public figure, making it on the cover of several magazines and
gaining media attention comparable to other high-profile female activists,
such as antiracist activist Rokhaya Diallo or Yellow Vests leader Priscilla
Ludosky.

Once leading actors like Amal Bentounsi and Assa Traoré imposed
themselves as recognized public figures in the media, the movement could
capitalize on this visibility to gain leverage in the political arena.

Victims as Unavoidable Interlocutors

To introduce their claims in the political arena, leaders in the Truth and
Justice movement worked to turn themselves into unavoidable interlocutors in leftist spaces. Unlike the racial profiling campaign, the movement
remained wary of political co-optation, especially given the left's history
of betrayal toward racialized people from low-income neighborhoods.
Instead of providing politicians with reform proposals to endorse, they
worked to take space in leftist circles.

The movement's liberation epistemology, by centering the voices of victims, made it easier for leading figures to demand a seat at the table. Their
status as those most affected, *les premiers concernés*, provided them with
added legitimacy to speak as, and for, racialized and marginalized communities who suffer at the hands of the police.[45] At the same time, because
this mode of knowledge production fostered victims' politicization, when
they did access the political arena, they introduced a structural analysis
that framed their suffering within (post)colonial structures of oppression.

Throughout the 2010s, leading figures of the movement sought to take
space in progressive social movements. Families of victims participated in
protests against labor law reforms, they visited defended zones occupied by
environmental activists (*ZAD*), and they participated in large-scale coalitions bringing together various groups facing state repression.[46] The goal
was to tap into the left's recent interest in protest policing to push them

to address routine racialized policing in *quartiers populaires*. Relentlessly, on every occasion, victims and activists repeated that the struggle against police violence must center on the routine violence targeting racialized people, explaining: "while some people are targeted for what they do, others are targeted for who they are." The recent expansion of police violence against middle-class protesters, they argued, was made possible by decades of experimenting new weapons and policing tactics against racialized people in *quartiers populaires*.

They also called on progressive movements to join their struggle for truth and justice. In 2017, an election year, the collective of families Urgence Notre Police Assassine invited a broad range of political groups to participate in the annual march of families of victims of police killings. Until then, the march had typically gathered a few hundred protesters, most of them active members of local Truth and Justice committees. That year, organizers worked to convince leftist parties and labor unions to endorse the call for the march. Dozens of organizations and public figures responded favorably, and the march brought the largest number of protesters yet, a majority of them White and middle class. The two dozen families of victims who opened the march were followed by 10,000 protesters holding banners of a wide range of political organizations, including labor unions, antiracist organizations, undocumented migrants' groups, *quartiers populaires* organizations, anticapitalist parties, anarchist and libertarian groups, and environmentalist activists. To the organizers, the symbolism of having all these groups walk *behind* families of victims was key in ensuring that the families' claims and grievances would remain front and center.[47]

In parallel, some Truth and Justice actors worked to lobby political parties, in particular the new left-wing party, La France insoumise (LFI), founded in 2016 by former socialist Jean-Luc Mélenchon. Wary of cooptation, the activists did not ask simply the party to endorse the movement's grievances. Instead, they insisted on taking up space and raising their voice in the party's events, even when uninvited. In May 2018, the committee Truth for Adama "hijacked" a leftist protest, organized by the LFI along with fifty other left-wing groups, to condemn Macron's policies. While the demonstration did not center questions of racialized policing, Truth for Adama published a call for residents of marginalized neighborhoods to show up and take over the front rows (*cortège de tête*) of the Parisian protest. Their hijacking of the highly symbolic *cortège de tête*, in a demonstration that gathered over 30,000 people, was a powerful move vis-à-vis the left, a message that the left cannot ignore the grievances of racialized and marginalized communities and must follow their lead. In my interview with a member of the Adama committee, the activist explained that the goal was "to ensure that the question of police violence in marginalized neighborhoods is central to the left . . . to tell politicians, you cannot look away, it must be at the heart of your discourse."[48]

These sustained efforts pressured left-wing parties to articulate a position on these issues. By 2018, representatives of all the major left-wing parties attended the annual commemoration of Adama Traoré's death, including the Socialist Party, EELV (environmentalists), LFI, and the communist party. Around the same time, LFI elected representatives started introducing law bills and amendments that endorsed long-standing demands of the movement. They planned their law bills in coordination with Truth and Justice activists, a testimony to the movement's growing leverage within the political left.

Hatred and Violence against the Republican Police

Throughout the second half of the 2010s, as condemnations of police violence were gaining visibility in the media, police unions promoted a counternarrative, which portrayed the police as victims of what they called "anti-cop hatred" and "anti-cop violence." While unions had responded to the racial profiling campaign by discrediting their reform proposals, they countered the rise of public figures speaking up about police brutality by discrediting them, as persons, arguing that they were complicit in a dangerous new trend of hatred and violence targeting law enforcement.

In May 2016, the right-wing union Alliance Police Nationale called for a demonstration against what it called an "irresponsible and relentless attempt to portray police officers as savage brutes who hit blindly on the youth," denouncing a "demagogic ideology that promotes hatred and violence against the republican police."[49] In the context of the securitarian frenzy that followed the 2015 terrorist attacks, they demanded expanded powers to use force.

This discourse was soon picked up by nonunionized officers who launched a protest movement dubbed Angry Police (*policiers en colère*) after two police officers were attacked with Molotov cocktails and severely injured in 2016. The angry officers criticized both police unions and the institution for doing too little to protect them and demanded stronger protections against violence targeting law enforcement. This movement continued to grow over the following years and was joined in 2017 by a coalition of Angry Police Wives (*femmes de policiers en colère*), thus further promoting the narrative portraying police officers, and their whole families, as victims of alarming rates of hatred and violence.

The police's response to the Truth and Justice movement went beyond criticizing their claims. The police also sought to discredit the movement leaders by criminalizing the most visible figures. The repression that the Traoré family faced is, in this regard, emblematic. As Assa Traoré and the committee Truth for Adama gained unprecedented public attention, the police intensified their attempts to discredit the whole family. Unnamed police sources told journalists that the Traoré family was "a mafia" in their hometown Beaumont. Adama Traoré was posthumously criminalized, with rumors accusing him of having raped a former cellmate. His brother, Bagui, was charged with attempted murder, with police accusing him of leading and instigating the "riots" that erupted following Adama's death (after five years in pretrial detention, he was acquitted). Assa Traoré was sued by the three officers who arrested Adama, after she published a text in which she named them and said they had killed her brother "by crushing him under the weight of their bodies." She was convicted of violating the officers' presumption of innocence and required to remove two social media posts. The ruling also required her to post the judicial decision on the Truth for Adama page and to pay the officers their legal expenses.[50] Thus, while the pathway to credibility that the movement took helped impose previously discredited actors as vocal political figures, it also made them more vulnerable to targeted retaliation.

The Problem Is Not That Some Officers Don't Follow the Rules, It's That the System Is Bad

In December 2016, in response to the pressure by police unions and by the Angry Police movement, the socialist government proposed a bill—dubbed the Public Security Law—that would significantly expand police powers to use lethal force. Until then, officers could use force only in self-defense, that is, when strictly necessary and proportionate to defend themselves or others from an imminent threat.[51] The bill expanded police authorization to use lethal force to situations in which a person or a vehicle refuses to stop, if "they are susceptible, in their escape, to jeopardize the physical integrity of others."[52]

The Public Security Bill was strongly criticized by human rights groups,[53] judges' and lawyers' unions,[54] and the Rights Defender,[55] who warned that the bill risks increasing police-involved deaths and makes police accountability more difficult. Nevertheless, in the context of a new securitarian consensus following the 2015 terrorist attacks, these warnings were ignored. All major political parties, except for LFI, supported the bill, including socialists, centrists, republicans, and the far right.

By that time, Truth and Justice leaders had gained enough public visibility to be able to promote their analyses during the debates around the bill. Amal Bentounsi's collective Urgence Notre Police Assassine launched a petition calling on parliamentarians to vote against the bill, warning that it represents a "license to kill" (*permis de tuer*). The petition collected over seventy thousand signatures. To raise public attention around it, Amal Bentounsi contacted Member of Parliament Pouria Amirshahi, to ask if he would be willing to present the petition in parliament. Amirshahi was part of a group of socialist *frondeurs* who criticized their party's policies under Hollande. He had recently spoken about the Adama Traoré case in Parliament and seemed like he could be an ally.[56] "I had never done this before, to contact an MP like this,"[57] Amal told me. The elected representative agreed, and they coordinated their actions. On the day that the National Assembly was due to vote on the bill, the collective Urgence Notre Police Assassine organized a rally in front of the National Assembly to symbolically present the petition to Parliament. Pouria Amirshahi joined the rally, along with two other representatives, to express his support for the petition. Right afterward, in Parliament, he filed a motion to reject the bill and gave a thirty-minute speech condemning the laws and policies that foster police violence and impunity.

His speech endorsed a structural analysis of police violence, which blamed institutional policies and laws rather than bad actors. He started by naming recent victims of police violence, Rémi Fraisse, Adama Traoré, Théo Luhaka, and arguing that police violence happened not only during demonstrations but also "in certain low-income neighborhoods where social segregation is manifested through racism." Then, he said that the bill would increase the number of those killed by the police and consolidate police officers' "feeling of impunity" that lead some "to believe they are authorized to shoot on sight, to kill, to choke, to beat, to bully, to rape, to humiliate." Responding to the government's claims that misconduct cases were isolated incidents, the representative said, "The problem is not just that some officers don't follow the rules; it's that the system itself is bad and allows officers to break free from the laws."[58] Although the motion to reject was voted down, and the bill passed into law by a large margin,[59] this joint action was significant in that it introduced the movement's structural analysis in the legislative arena.

Echoing the police unions' rhetoric, the government retorted by arguing that the police are victims of violence, not perpetrators. In his statement responding to Pouria Amirshahi, Interior Minister Bruno Le Roux started by reiterating his full support for the police. Then, he said, "I want to start by giving some numbers that reflect the heavy price that our security forces pay each year." He claimed that in 2016, twenty-six police officers died and sixteen thousand were injured in the course of their duties. He admitted that misconduct can happen, but affirmed that "every time, investigations are conducted and sanctions are delivered," noting that 5,500 disciplinary sanctions were given to police officers in 2016. This remained the staple response of the government, including after Macron's movement took power. All reform proposals to address police violence were systematically rejected with the argument that the police are, in fact, facing increasing violence and need stronger protection.

This argument was made possible by the police's continued control over the production and dissemination of official data. When Bruno Le Roux cited the numbers of police officers who died in the course of their duties and the number of disciplinary sanctions, these data had not yet been published. When they did get published several months later, it appeared that only three out of the twenty-six police deaths he mentioned were due to assaults by individuals, the majority was caused by traffic accidents or sports injuries.[60] Only a fraction of all disciplinary sanctions were for misconduct targeting individuals, even though these were the majority of complaints—most disciplinary measures were for misconduct in the private sphere or disobeying orders.[61] Having thus dismissed the few parliamentarians opposing the bill, the government put it to a vote in February 2017; it passed with a large majority. As many had feared, this law led to an unprecedented increase in police killings. While in previous decades there were on average fifteen police-caused death per year, the numbers started increasing in the 2010s. Then, in each of the years 2021, 2022, 2023, and 2024, over fifty people died during police interventions.[62] Lethal shootings against moving vehicles increased fivefold.[63]

In sum, the Truth and Justice movement built their credibility in the political field by using the legitimacy of families of victims as *les premiers concernés* (the most affected) to take space in leftist settings. Their goal was not only to get politicians to endorse their reform proposals, but also to gain a seat at the table and become unavoidable political interlocutors. This helped them introduce their structural analysis of police violence and impunity in the political arena. It also made the most visible leaders vulnerable to retaliation, with police unions accusing them of promoting anticop violence and hatred.

Maintaining Political Leverage

By the end of the 2010s, the issues of discriminatory stops, police violence, and impunity had become salient political issues, with left-wing politicians promising reforms in their electoral platforms and legislators repeatedly introducing law bills to address the issues.

At the same time, it became increasingly unlikely that change would happen through electoral politics. The 2017 election of Emmanuel Macron's "neither right nor left" party, LREM, reshaped the political field, marking the precipitous decline of the two political parties that had dominated French politics for decades, the Republicans and the Socialists. At the same time, the far right continued to rise. Macron admitted, during his electoral campaign, that "there are way too many identity checks, with real discrimination," and stated, "there is no good argument to justify police violence."[64] Nevertheless, his party rejected all reform proposals and continued enacting securitarian laws that granted more powers and resources to the police.

In this context, movement actors sought to sustain political pressure via routes other than electoral politics. The pathway that each mobilization took to place their issues on the political agenda set them on distinct trajectories for maintaining political leverage.

The campaign against racial profiling had placed their issue on the political agenda by establishing *contrôles au faciès* as a reality and then gaining endorsements for their reform proposals. They were reliant on their political allies to move the issue forward in the political arena. As a result, when the socialists reneged on their promises for reform, and then Macron came to power, the window of opportunity for the reforms to pass closed. The campaign's key reform proposal, stop forms, became an issue that opposition leaders sporadically raised, and the majority systematically rejected. The campaign had little control over when these proposals would be discussed, or how the issue would be framed in the political debate. Given their limited leverage in the policy field, campaign leaders focused their resources on litigation. This allowed them to maintain the issue in the public debate. In 2021, several organizations launched a class action lawsuit against the state for discriminatory stops. Two years later, the administrative court ruled that *contrôles au faciès* exist but that the court cannot order the state to change its practices.

For its part, the pathway that the Truth and Justice movement took to access the political field allowed it to maintain some (limited) leverage over the political arena. Even as the opportunities to pass legislative reforms closed, movement leaders used their public profile to impose their presence in leftist spaces, where they continued promoting their analyses of racialized police violence. They focused their efforts on lobbying the new left-wing party La France insoumise and expanding their influence over grassroots protest movements. Some Truth and Justice leaders worked to build alliances with the Yellow Vests, an eclectic protest movement that emerged in 2018, initially to protest fuel price hikes, later shifting to demand profound political and institutional changes. When the Yellow Vest protesters, for the most part White people living outside of urban centers, were subjected to harsh police repression, the Truth and Justice movement saw an opportunity to build alliances and expand political support against police violence and impunity. As they had done with labor and environmental movements, activists insisted that the struggle against police violence had to go beyond a critique of protest policing and include an attention to routine policing practices targeting racialized people living in marginalized neighborhoods.

The movement's efforts to strengthen their influence in grassroots movements allowed activists to increase their mobilizing capacity in the street and thereby to maintain some leverage over the political agenda.

When, in May 2020, the video of George Floyd's killing in Minneapolis sparked outrage throughout the world, Truth and Justice leaders were able to capitalize on the media attention around this case to mobilize massively. Despite COVID restrictions, in June 2020, several demonstrations took place all over France to denounce police violence and racism, the most important of which was in Paris, where 20,000 people gathered. These protests came on the heels of a period of increased media attention on policing and racism. In May, the Rights Defender published his opinion describing the "eviction of undesirables" as systemic discrimination. And in June, a journalistic investigation revealed that thousands of police officers exchanged racist and sexist messages on a Facebook group.[65]

Faced with mounting pressure, Interior Minister Christophe Castaner organized a press conference titled "the question of racism and accusations toward the police." Responding to those who drew parallels between the United States and France, the minister started by saying, "I would like us all to remember that France is not the United States,"[66] adding "there is no racist institution or targeted violence." Still, he admitted, "too many have failed to uphold their Republican duty." He promised "zero tolerance against racism" in the police, a ban on chokeholds, and a "profound reform" of the police investigative bodies.[67] These statements were significant; for the first time, an Interior minister acknowledged accusations of racialized policing and suggested that reforms were needed to combat racism within the institution and to reduce police-caused deaths. While he rejected the concept of institutional racism, the fact that he explicitly addressed it illustrates the ability of the movement to impose their analysis in the political debate, and to demand a political response. Unsurprisingly, under pressure from police unions, Castaner was replaced, less than a month later, by hard-liner Gérald Darmanin.

Conclusion

Despite an unfavorable political context, marked by the securitarian consensus that followed the 2015 terrorist attacks, movement actors managed to introduce and sustain their grievances on the political agenda. This success relied, in large part, on their ability to introduce and disseminate their knowledge claims in the political arena. To do this, each coalition took a different pathway. The racial profiling campaign aligned with the political field's epistemic rules (relying on credentialed experts and quantitative methods) to establish the truth of a previously contested claim, whereas the Truth and Justice movement challenged the dominant hierarchy of credibility (raising the profile of discredited actors) to turn its leaders into unavoidable interlocutors in the political arena.

Each pathway created distinct opportunities and constraints in the political arena. The campaign against racial profiling drew on the widespread recognition of the "reality" of racial disparities in police stops to seek a broad range of political endorsements for reform. Activists' advocacy work turned *contrôles au faciès* from a nonissue to a recurring political issue. Because the campaign's study proved widespread racial disparities, but remained uncertain about their causes, when politicians introduced the issue in the political arena, it was framed in terms that aligned with the dominant understanding of racialized policing as a problem of biased officers. Political opponents responded by arguing that accusing police officers of being racists is unfair and dangerous. The conversation around *contrôles au faciès* remained confined to the question of what to do about biased officers, with little engagement with the legal, institutional, and structural factors underlying racial profiling practices.

In the Truth and Justice movement, leading figures worked to increase their public profile in order to impose themselves in the political left as a voice that can no longer be ignored. By insisting that they be included and heard in political settings, they introduced their claims on their own terms, emphasizing the systemic and structural nature of racialized policing. They gained fewer allies in the field of electoral politics, but they promoted their analyses in leftist protest movements, which helped them increase their capacity to mobilize in the streets. This helped them maintain some leverage to shape the public debate. However, because their approach relied on leading figures being vocal and taking up space, when opponents developed counterarguments, they centered on delegitimizing them, as persons, for being anticop haters, thus exacerbating the violence vulnerable groups already suffered. This demonstrates that the pathway to credibility shapes not only the claims activists are able to introduce in the political field but also the strategies that opponents develop and the risks that activists and victims face.

Conclusion

On June 27, 2023, the video of a policeman shooting and killing Nahel Merzouk, a seventeen-year-old French boy of Algerian origin, went viral online. Captured that morning by passers-by, the footage showed a yellow car stopped on the side of a road with the driver's window open. Two policemen are seen standing on the sidewalk with their guns pointed inside the vehicle directly at the driver. One officer can be heard shouting, "You're gonna get a bullet in your head" (*tu vas te prendre une balle dans la tête*). Then, almost simultaneously, the car speeds up, one officer screams "shoot" (*shoote*), and the other fires his gun directly at the driver. While the officers initially claimed that Nahel was speeding directly at a policeman and endangering his life, the footage clearly showed that there was no one in front of the car when Nahel was shot.

The images of Nahel Merzouk's killing triggered widespread outrage and anger. An uprising erupted in Nanterre, the banlieue on the outskirts of Paris where Nahel grew up and was killed. Soon, the revolt spread to other neighborhoods across the country. For over a week, every night, young people burned cars and trash cans, vandalized public buildings, and looted stores.

France had not witnessed an urban uprising of this scale since 2005, when revolts erupted in marginalized neighborhoods (*quartiers populaires*) following the deaths of teenagers Zyed Benna and Bouna Traoré. Many journalists and commentators drew parallels between the two events. Both were triggered by the death of Black and Arab teenagers in *quartiers populaires* during police interventions. Both were led by marginalized young men who protested the routine brutality and racism they experienced at the hands of the police. And both spread beyond the victims' neighborhood to affect the whole country.[1]

While the parallel between 2005 and 2023 highlights the continued crisis of racialized policing in France, it also sheds light on the significant transformation of the public and political debate around policing and inequality. In 2005, government officials unanimously framed the rebellion as a problem of "urban violence" and ignored the racialized policing practices that triggered it. Nicolas Sarkozy, who was the Interior minister at the time, declared that there was no need for an investigation into the teens' deaths and communicated exclusively on the damages caused by the "riots" and on the police response to quell them. While the left-wing opposition criticized Sarkozy's repressive response to the riots, they did not mention police brutality or racism in their public statements on the events. The mainstream media debate focused on whether the uprising was caused by inherent violent immigrant cultures, or by social exclusion and segregation. Despite decades of collective action against police brutality and racism, within racialized communities in *quartiers populaires* their grievances and analyses remained absent from the conversation.

In contrast, in 2023, government officials denounced the police killing, and much of the public debate was centered on issues of police brutality, racism, and impunity. President Emmanuel Macron condemned the policeman's actions, calling it "inexplicable and unforgiveable."[2] Interior Minister Gérald Darmanin, who was Sarkozy's spokesperson before joining Macron's government, called the footage "extremely shocking."[3] The government promised that justice would be done, and within a couple of days, the policeman who shot Nahel Merzouk was placed under investigation for homicide and maintained in pretrial detention, an extremely rare occurrence in cases of deaths at the hands of the police.

The reactions of the leftist opposition were also starkly different from 2005. A few days after Nahel's killing, ninety left-wing parties, labor unions, and NGOs released a joint text, titled "Our Country Is Grieving and Angry," in which they expressed solidarity with the "revolts" and argued that the tensions between the police and the population stem from a history "marked by injustice, prejudice, violence, discrimination, sexism and a systemic racism that cuts through society as a whole and is not yet eradicated."[4] The organizations called for immediate action to respond to "the demands of the affected population," citing four key measures: repealing the 2017 Public Security Law that expanded police powers to use lethal force; engaging in a "profound reform of the police, their intervention methods, and their weaponry"; replacing the IGPN with an independent investigative body; and investing more resources in the struggle against racism, including in the police.

There were also noticeable differences in the media coverage of the two uprisings. Like in 2005, the 2023 revolts were primarily framed as "urban violence," but the press also extensively discussed police violence and racism.[5] Left-leaning and centrist newspapers published their own analyses about "why the police kill"[6] or why France failed to pass reforms to address "racism and violence in the police."[7] Terms such as "systemic racism," which were completely absent from the coverage of the 2005 revolts, were now used and debated in mainstream media.[8] Large press outlets published several pieces by well-known scholars, who pointed to "systemic racism" in the police (Patrick Simon in *Libération*);[9] discussed France's "long history of racialization of police dominance" (Emmanuel Blanchard in *Le Monde*);[10] pointed to the legalized "ascendency of the police over postcolonial youth" (Fabien Jobard in *Le Monde*);[11] and explained the "legitimate anger" of the uprising (Didier Fassin in *Libération*).[12]

These shifts in the public debate about policing and inequalities would not have been possible without the work of activists, researchers, victims, and journalists who produced independent data and analyses on racialized policing practices. The police hold significant epistemic power, which gives them disproportionate control to determine what is known, and what remains unknown (and sometimes unknowable) about policing and inequalities. In 2005, the government relied on its monopoly over the production of crime statistics to impose its reading of the events, highlighting the numbers of cars burned, buildings vandalized or officers injured, while not releasing any data on police use of force. The police drew on the assumed credibility of officers and on the institution's privileged access to the media to control the narrative and to silence and discredit those contesting their action.

But while the police's epistemic power is a formidable tool to silence and discredit the grievances of targeted communities, I have shown that it can be challenged and disrupted. Since the late 2000s, activist coalitions have released research demonstrating widespread racial disparities in identity checks, documented institutional practices of police harassment targeting Black and Arab men, and uncovered the mechanisms sustaining police impunity. These efforts were key in overcoming political denial and placing the issues of police violence and racism on the agenda.

In this conclusion, I use the 2023 uprising to illustrate the relevance of the theoretical framework developed throughout the book, for understanding how the police's epistemic power operates, how activists challenge it, and with what consequences for the public and political debate. Through a comparison of the way the 2005 and 2023 revolts were framed and debated, I draw out the key insights of the book, highlighting the ways in which the movement's knowledge production contributed to shifting the terms of the debate. The analysis brings out the central argument of the book: that different modes of knowledge production have distinct implications for how activists define the problem and for their influence on media, political, and judicial debates. While the chapters have focused on comparing the strengths and trade-offs of different modes of knowledge production, here, I show that the combination of different epistemologies was essential for the movement as a whole.

Which Numbers Count? Official and Unofficial Statistics

The police's control over the production and dissemination of statistics on crime and policing is one of the main sources of their epistemic power. In France, as in many other countries, law enforcement agencies release only a carefully selected set of data, which help portray their work as necessary to combat crime while obscuring the ways in which they reproduce social and racial inequalities. For a long time, this allowed the police to channel public attention toward crime and disorder and to portray revolts against police brutality as senseless "urban violence." It helped them dismiss any allegations of discrimination and prevent issues of racialized policing from reaching the political agenda.

Throughout the late 2000s and 2010s, the movement against racialized policing increased its ability to produce independent statistical measures of policing practices, to make up for missing or incomplete police data. Given that statistics are widely considered to be the most credible and reliable form of data, activists' ability to generate quantitative data represented an important challenge to the police's epistemic power. When the campaign against racial profiling released the result of their study quantifying disparities in police stops, it became untenable for politicians, government officials, and police leaders to continue denying the reality of racial profiling. This opened a window for campaign leaders to introduce new legal claims and to place their policy proposals on the legislative agenda.

However, like any mode of knowledge production, quantitative epistemologies have important limitations. While statistics are essential to establish the existence of disparities or the prevalence of specific practices, they are often insufficient to determine the social mechanisms that underlie these trends. Quantitative epistemologies also tend to capture the aspects of racialized policing that are amenable to quantitative measurement, which can focus the debate on some aspects of the problem to the detriment of others.

The public debates surrounding the 2023 uprising illustrate the potential and limitations of quantitative epistemologies. Activists and left-wing politicians claimed that Nahel Merzouk's killing was not an isolated incident but was part of a worrying rise in police killings. This increase, they argued, was caused by the 2017 Public Security Law that significantly expanded the police's right to use lethal force, including by authorizing officers to shoot at a vehicle that doesn't comply with an order to stop, if it is susceptible to cause bodily harm in its escape. Interior Minister Gérald Darmanin denied the claim, stating, "police use of firearms, and the number of people who died as a result, has decreased since 2017." Like scores of government officials before him, he relied on the authoritativeness of his ministry, as the state agency producing statistics about policing practices, to assert the credibility of his claim.

However, unlike his predecessors, the minister's statement was quickly discredited on the basis of a database of police-involved deaths in France created by the independent media *Basta*. Contradicting the minister's claim, *Basta*'s database showed that, since 2017, fatal police shootings targeting moving vehicles had increased fivefold. Left-wing politicians drew on these statistics to debunk Darmanin's claim and call for repealing the 2017 law. Media outlets, too, published articles debunking the minister's statement, with titles such as, " 'The Number of Police Shootings Has Decreased since 2017': Why This Statement by Gérald Darmanin Is False."[13]

Like the racial profiling study, the police killings database made it difficult for the government to blatantly misrepresent trends or maintain blanket denials. It also pressured the police to publish their own data. On the heels of the publication of *Basta*'s database in 2018, the police inspection service IGPN started publishing annual reports with data on police use of force and police-involved deaths. The 2021 report showed an increase in the number of police shootings targeting moving vehicles since 2017, thus corroborating *Basta*'s independent finding. Most of the media coverage drew on both the scholarly study and the IGPN report to debunk Darmanin's claim.

Faced with this challenge to their epistemic power, police leaders sought to discredit *Basta*'s database. In an article on *FranceInfo* titled "True or False? Are There Really Five Times More Lethal Police Shots Following Refusals to Stop since the 2017 Law?," unnamed police sources warned that "*Basta* is not an official source. It's a media that is clearly marked on the left, and which is therefore not neutral." The article further suggested that official data, while more authoritative, was not conclusive because it was still incomplete:

> In reality, there are no official numbers. True, there is an IGPN report published in 2021, which documents police use of firearms directed at moving vehicles, that is, in response to a refusal to stop. But this report does not break down fatal and non-fatal shots. FranceInfo has therefore contacted the Interior Ministry to obtain these numbers, and they answered that these numbers are "being compiled."[14]

By insisting that official numbers were not yet complete, while delaying the publication of these numbers to an unspecified date, the police sought to rely on their control over the production and dissemination of official data to dismiss critiques. But in a context where nonstate actors competed with the police to produce statistics on policing practices, such dismissals became increasingly untenable, and Darmanin soon stopped claiming that police shootings had decreased since 2017.

Right-wing and far-right political parties and police unions adopted a different strategy to regain control over the narrative. They admitted that police-involved deaths had increased but suggested that this was caused by rising cases of drivers refusing to comply with orders to stop, which endangered others.[15] As they had done following the publication of the racial profiling study, when faced with evidence they could not discredit, they shifted from denying to acknowledging the reality of the policing patterns uncovered, while placing the blame on victims. Although a scholarly study had demonstrated that the fivefold increase in police shootings could not be attributed to a rise in refusals to stop,[16] the unions' claim still gained traction in the public debate, with mainstream media discussing at length the increasing dangers officers face during traffic stops.

These struggles over quantitative data are not unique to France, but they may take different forms depending on the context. In France, the epistemic power of the police relies in large part on obscuring police actions by limiting the collection and publication of data. As a result, activists have focused on generating independent statistics to make up for missing data and shed light on policing practices. In contrast, many police forces in the United States are producing and circulating massive amounts of data, on the basis of which they construct truth narratives about criminal threats and the necessity of a tough police response. These data document law enforcement actions, but also the people targeted, with the construction of databases on alleged "gang members," "terrorists," or "criminal aliens."[17] In this context, activists' knowledge work has focused on escaping state surveillance and making racialized communities invisible to the police gaze.[18] Much activism consists in resisting the implementation of new police databases or calling for their abolition.[19]

This suggests that movement actors should carefully weigh the pros and cons of calling on the police to collect more data. While such reforms may seem like necessary and reasonable measures to increase police transparency and allow for evidence-based practices, they also bolster the epistemic power of the police by further increasing their legitimacy as the primary, and often sole, producer of data on crime, disorder, and policing. Activists should also be vigilant about the potential of police statistics to reinforce and normalize racialized criminalization, as these data rely on law enforcement practices that are racially biased.[20] Rather than calling on state institutions to collect more data, the way forward might be to carve avenues for a variety of actors to produce quantitative knowledge and to work on bolstering the credibility and visibility of independent data. Paradoxically, countries with strong institutional opacity like France might offer more incentives for researchers and activists to participate in the production, curation, and dissemination of statistics, than countries that release massive amounts of administrative data.[21]

What Really Happened? Making Police Violence Visible

In addition to producing statistical knowledge, movement actors have sought to document police interventions. This is essential, because when Black and Brown men denounce police actions, their testimonies are given less credit than those of officers. As I have shown, one of the dimensions of the police's epistemic power is that, in courts, as in the political sphere and media debate, officers benefit from a presumption of credibility, while the communities they target suffer from a credibility deficit.[22] This makes it difficult for victims to make their claims heard and believed.

Movement actors have sought to disrupt the police's credibility by collecting evidence of police interventions to make abusive patterns of practice visible. Such grounded epistemologies—efforts to document police actions in a local space—are a central activist strategy around the world. One of the most common forms is copwatching, which involves observing (and often filming) police actions and using the evidence in legal proceedings and political advocacy.[23]

In the neighborhood mobilization discussed in chapter 3, local actors established a fact-finding process to document the routine interactions between Black and Arab teenagers and a local police unit. By systematically collecting testimonies of victims and witnesses, photos and videos of the interactions, and medical certificates of the injuries sustained, they produced evidence of the routine, repeated abuses targeting racialized youth in the neighborhood. This made it untenable for the judiciary to keep dismissing allegations of misconduct without investigation. It helped the coalition cast doubts on the police narrative and allowed them to garner media attention on the issue of discriminatory police harassment.

While grounded epistemologies are essential to substantiate the testimonies of policing victims and cast doubts on fabricated police accounts, they also have important limitations. As the neighborhood mobilization showed, fact-finding projects require significant investment on the part of vulnerable populations, who may not have the resources to commit to such projects. They also expose them to police retaliation, which can take the form of increased police harassment or criminal indictments.

Moreover, while grounding knowledge production in the experiences of those affected by policing generates evidence that closely matches their experiences and concerns, it does not necessarily result in their empowerment. In his investigation of Marxist movements, Hoffman argues that "the simple act of posing a carefully crafted and ordered question or set of questions in certain institutional or geographical contexts . . . *can* invite others to appraise their political situations differently."[24] My study suggests that, while asking questions and collecting narratives can help people think about their situation differently, it is not enough to lead to politicization. Modes of knowledge production that center the gaze of external actors—lawyers collecting testimonies, activists watching police interactions—run the risk of reproducing dynamics of power whereby victims of oppression are seen as objects of research rather than as political subjects in their own right.

In recent years, activists have increasingly relied on citizen footage of police interventions to document police abuses. Nahel Merzouk's killing became a rallying cry, like George Floyd's in 2020, because his death was captured on camera and viewed by millions. Many commentators suggest that the proliferation of smartphones is fundamentally changing the visibility of police actions and the ability of police forces to dominate the narratives of events. Since almost anyone can use their smartphone to film a police intervention and post it on social media, some have argued that the public now has the ability to constantly document police actions, thus placing the police under a new "regime of visibility."[25] To put it in the terms I've been using in this book, this argument suggests that filming the police is a mode of knowledge production that allows ordinary citizens to powerfully challenge the epistemic power of the police.

It is undeniable that videos are powerful to discredit fabricated police narratives. When Nahel Merzouk was killed, the first media stories were all based on the police's official narrative, according to which Nahel was speeding directly at a police officer who was standing in front of the car, putting his life in danger. This self-defense narrative was quickly discredited when videos of the shooting started circulating online. The three videos, which were taken from two different angles, showed that, when the car sped up, both police officers were on the sidewalk, by the driver's window, and that there was no one standing in front of it. The footage had an immediate and powerful effect; it provided visual evidence that discredited the police narrative. Media outlets posted the footage, arguing that it contradicted the official account, and cited growing anger and demands for the truth.

However, as I have argued throughout the book, any mode of knowledge production entails trade-offs, highlighting some aspects of racialized policing and obscuring others. Who watches the police, where they look, and what they can see, shape which aspects of policing are made visible. Applying this insight to citizen footage suggests that we should be cautious not to place excessive expectations on this technology to fundamentally transform the epistemic power relationship between the police and their targets. While this requires a longer discussion, here, I want to draw attention to a few points of vigilance when considering the potential and limitations of relying on citizen footage.

One issue we should be attentive to is that citizen footage provides a small and biased sample of police interventions. There are systematic biases in *who* is able to film the police. During my fieldwork, I often spoke with young men who were frustrated by the advice they received from some lawyers and NGOs to film police interventions. In their experience, when young Black or Arab men from low-income neighborhoods tried to film the police, police officers got angry and used threats, intimidation, and sometimes violence. Most were not willing to take the risk of having their phones destroyed, being beaten, or even shot with rubber bullets. Groups that the police do not perceive as their primary targets, for example, White women or older people, can more safely film police actions, but because they are less exposed to police violence and racism, they are also less likely to feel the need to record police interventions they encounter in their daily lives.

There are also systemic biases in *where* police intervention can be filmed. At large protests, the crowds make it more likely that there will be people recording police use of force. There are journalists with professional equipment for capturing image and sound, and participants are usually alert to the issue and may more readily have the reflex to take their phones out when the police clash with protesters. In contrast, in marginalized neighborhoods, there may be fewer people around when the police intervene, especially at night. Passers-by are more likely to be vulnerable to police retaliation and thus be reluctant to film. Because the most marginalized social spaces are the least amenable to filming the police, there is a systematic bias in the types of police interventions that get captured on camera—they are more likely to happen in crowded spaces such as protests or busy urban roads. Capturing videos is also nearly impossible for police actions that take place inside police vehicles or in police custody.

Once a video is taken, the *ability to circulate it* is unequally distributed. As studies have shown, most footage of police violence that is posted online doesn't circulate widely; only social media users with a large follower base have the capacity to make videos go viral.[26] As a result, many videos never circulate widely enough to be picked up by mainstream media, activists, or politicians. The social networks of victims and witnesses, and their ability to reach out to influential movement leaders is essential to disseminate existing videos.

These constraints on who can film police actions, where they can safely do so, and their capacity to circulate it widely online, result in systematic biases in the footage that goes viral. It amplifies police brutality that happens in crowded places (protests, high-traffic roads) or that targets people with social networks connecting them to influential people, and it downplays routine police violence in working-class neighborhoods targeting the most marginalized communities.

Another limitation of videos is that they focus the attention on the minute details of one police intervention, thus allowing power holders to portray the case as an isolated incident, a one-off blunder. After the video of Nahel Merzouk's killing was published, journalists and commentators scrutinized the interaction second-by-second to discuss whether the officers acted lawfully in this one instance. While the footage showed clearly that, when Nahel was shot, the car was not speeding directly at anyone, it left many questions unanswered, namely, about the events that led to the traffic stop and about what happened inside the vehicle. The two officers told investigators that Nahel had been driving dangerously for twenty minutes before the footage was taken, speeding and running over a red light, endangering one pedestrian and one cyclist in the process. They also claimed that they did not say "you're gonna get a bullet in your head" (*tu vas te prendre une balle dans la tête*) and "shoot" (*shoote*), but rather, "put your hands behind your head" (*mains derrière la tête*) and "cut [the engine]" (*coupe*). The officer who fired said that he did so because he worried the car might pull along his colleague whose arms were inside the vehicle, or run over a passing pedestrian. This account, and its compatibility with the video evidence, were discussed at length.

Thus, on its own, video footage can channel the conversation toward a focus on the detailed facts of one individual incident, making it difficult to contextualize the case within broader patterns of racialized police violence.

Activists' ability to move the conversation beyond individual cases hinges on their capacity to draw on other forms of knowledge that allow them to generalize from the few cases that garner media attention to expose patterns of practice. In France, the movement's work to produce and mobilize various forms of knowledge—statistics about broader policing patterns, grounded analysis of neighborhood dynamics, experiential knowledge of policing victims—was key in this regard.

More broadly, surveillance scholars have pointed to the complexities involved in countering police surveillance through the same technology that the state and corporations use to establish and reinforce surveillance capitalism.[27] Bärbel Harju's study of a copwatching initiative in Germany shows that, when these concerns are taken into account from the start, the risk of reinforcing surveillance can be tempered, for example by designing platforms that do not keep track of any personal or identifiable data. In this way, she suggests, these practices "can be understood as more than actual practices of technology-enhanced counter-surveillance, and become a subversive practice of re-imagining dominant narratives and hierarchies."[28]

Who Can Speak? Policing Victims as Unavoidable Interlocutors

A central mechanism of the police's epistemic power is their ability to discredit the groups they target. State and police representatives regularly use their excess credibility and their privileged access to the media to frame victims and their allies as criminal and untrustworthy. For decades, this allowed the police to keep the voices of victims out of the media and political debate. During the 2005 uprising and in previous protests, the testimonies and analyses of protesters, and more broadly of the populations most targeted by racialized policing, were absent from mainstream debates.

To challenge the police's ability to silence the communities they target, the Truth and Justice movement worked not only to collect and disseminate victims' testimonies, it also raised their profile as knowers in their own right. Families of victims of police killings took over the movement's leadership and promoted their own analyses of their loved ones' deaths, and of the structures of oppression they are embedded in. This liberation epistemology, which challenges dominant notions about who is recognized as a knower and how knowledge should be produced, is significant for several reasons.

As standpoint theorists have shown, when we take the lives of marginalized groups as the starting point of inquiry, we see particularly significant problems to be explained, which are not visible to those in dominant positions.[29] The experiences of families in their quest for justice shed light on a host of actors and institutions that sustain racialized police brutality, including police chiefs, investigative judges, prosecutors, medico-legal experts, journalists, and others. This helped the movement raise new questions and move the conversation from an attention to officers' behaviors to an analysis of the system-wide structures through which racist state violence is maintained.

When movements center not only the testimonies but also the analyses of victims, the oppressed move from being sources of data to be interpreted and analyzed by others, to being "lay experts"[30] whose voice and analysis cannot be ignored. Some of the leading figures of the Truth and Justice movement have become unavoidable political interlocutors, regularly invited on TV and radio shows for their expertise on the issue of police violence. During the 2023 uprising, Amal Bentounsi, who lost her brother in 2012 and had become by then one of the most prominent figures of the movement, was invited onto the news TV channel BFMTV. She spoke of the movement's calls to abolish the Public Security Law, reminding viewers that, before the bill was voted into law, she launched a petition against it, which collected 77,000 signatures. She also spoke of the stark increase in police killings since 2017, saying that deaths during traffic stops targeted "in majority racialized young men."[31]

The work of Amal Bentounsi and others helped pave the way for newly affected families to be heard and seen. Immediately following the killing of Nahel Merzouk, established Truth and Justice actors helped his mother, Mounia, become a key voice in the media coverage of her son's killing. On the day of Nahel Merzouk's death, Assa Traoré, by then the most prominent figure of the movement, reached out to Mounia Merzouk and invited her to appear in an Instagram live on her account. In the live, the grieving mother spoke of her pain at losing her only child. That very morning, she said, he gave her "a big kiss" and told her he loved her, before they both went out of their home. She recalled how, an hour later, she was told that police had shot him. "What am I going to do? I lived for him, I bought him everything, I gave him everything, everything, everything, [and then] a son of a bitch away takes my son!"[32] The next day, Mounia Merzouk appeared in an interview on public TV channel France 5, where she expressed her anger at the officer who took her son's life. "He saw an Arab face, a kid, he decided to take his life," she said, adding "How long will this last? How many more children will be lost? Tell me, how many children will be lost? How many mothers will be like me? How many mothers? What do they expect?"[33] With the help of other families of victims, she organized a vigil (*marche blanche*) to be held two days after Nahel's death, in Nanterre. At the protest, which was attended by over 6,000 people, she led the march, wearing a white T-shirt with the words "Justice for Nahel" printed on it. The march was covered in all mainstream media, and her picture with a fist raised become a symbol of the rallying cry "Justice for Nahel."

This public visibility of the sisters and mothers of the men killed by the police helps humanize marginalized communities and makes it more difficult for government officials to dismiss their grief and grievances. While in 2005, no government representatives expressed solidarity with the victims and their families, in 2023, President Emmanuel Macron's first public address focused on condemning Nahel Merzouk's killing and expressing the nation's sympathy to his loved ones:

> First of all, I want to say the emotion of the whole nation, after what happened and the death of the young Nahel, and to say to his family our complete solidarity and the affection of the nation. We have a teenager who was killed, it is inexplicable and unforgiveable, and first of all, [my] words are words of affection, of shared pain, of support for his family and loved ones.[34]

Raising the public profile of victims also introduces their perspectives in the public debate, which helps challenge the police's control over the narrative of contested incidents. While in 2005, the testimony of the surviving victim was covered only in one outlet, eleven days after the tragedy, the testimonies of the two passengers who were in the car with Nahel Merzouk were published in all mainstream media within a couple of days. Their accounts provided important context about the fatal police shot, which was neither visible in the videos nor mentioned in the officers' accounts. Both witnesses explained that the police officers were immediately aggressive when Nahel stopped the car and opened the window. According to them, the officers drew their guns and pointed them at the driver, shouting at him to cut the engine and threatening, "you're gonna get a bullet in your head." The policemen then used their rifle butts to hit Nahel several times. One of those blows rattled Nahel, who took his foot off the brake pedal, moving the car forward. This account seemed to be corroborated by one of the videos that was posted online, which showed the officers moving their arms back and forth through the driver's window right before the car speeds forward. Thus, in addition to legitimizing policing targets as victims, the movement's capacity to introduce their perspectives in the public debate provides important contextual information about how police interactions unfold.

Liberation epistemologies do more than cast doubts on police narratives; they also lay bare the systems of oppression within which police brutality is embedded. This is true beyond France. In Brazil, mothers have been organizing to demand justice for their sons killed and disappeared by the police. As Jaime Amparo Alves shows, their work made visible the scale of police brutality in the favelas, and it also disrupted the dominant ideology about race in Brazil, where the state denies the persistence of racism. The mothers' strategy of occupying central squares in the city and renaming them Black square, helped expose the city for its anti-Blackness, and challenge the racial order in which Blackness equals placelessness.[35] It shed light on the way mundane police interventions and spatial segregation produce race.

We should be careful not to romanticize bottom-up epistemologies, however. Like any mode of knowledge production, victim-led models have important limitations. While they raise important questions, they cannot provide all the answers on their own. In France, families of victims drew on their experiences to connect their personal tragedies to broader systems of oppression, but they also relied on the work of scholars and journalists who produced statistics about police killings, lawyers who uncovered institutional policies about police use of force, and physicians who debunked fabricated autopsy reports. Combining their bottom-up epistemology with other modes of knowledge production was essential for the Truth and Justice movement to explain the mechanisms through which large-scale systems of oppression result in police killings.

We should also keep in mind that centering policing victims means placing significant burdens on them. Carrying the responsibility of leading the movement while also bearing the weight of their grief leads many to suffer from burnout, depression, and anxiety. This is particularly acute in France, where the relatively small number of active families means that a handful of people carry a disproportionate responsibility to sustain the whole Truth and Justice movement. The state's social safety net provides insufficient support. The families I worked with talked about the difficulties they faced when seeking adequate mental health services, their struggles keeping up paid employment alongside their activism, and the disdain they experienced from state authorities when they demanded justice.

Those who gained public visibility were also vulnerable to threats, retaliation, and attacks on their reputation. The most prominent figures of the movement have all been exposed to smear campaigns, lawsuits, and death threats. Like other families of victims before her, when Mounia Merzouk started getting media attention, a campaign to discredit and delegitimize her emerged. Right-wing and far-right commentators suggested that her grief wasn't genuine, noting that she was photographed smiling or chanting during the vigil for Nahel. They presented her son as a criminal, claiming that he was "well-known to the police," that "he had a lengthy criminal record" (which is untrue), with some even saying he was a multirecidivist, drug dealer, and armed robber. Many newspapers fact-checked these allegations, revealing that the victim had no prior convictions and had been charged only once for a refusal to comply during a stop. Still, these smear campaigns take an immense toll on families of victims.

This suggests that movement actors should be attentive to building alternative infrastructures capable of providing the kind of holistic support policing victims need, including help in their quest for justice in courts, but also physical and mental health services, financial support for housing and food, and help finding stable employment. This is what the Mutual Aid Network for Truth and Justice is attempting to do in France. Created in 2020, it brings together various collectives of victims of state violence to share information, pool support, and strategize collective action.[36]

Antiracism without Races

In France, the antiracialist ideology, which promotes an ethos of "indifference to difference" and forbids the collection of racial data, complicates activists' efforts to make visible the role of race in policing. Although postcolonial immigrants and their children have been organizing against the police's racist practices since the 1970s, for decades, they struggled to make their grievances heard. On the rare occasions when the issue was brought up in the political arena, governments systematically denied any discrimination in policing, arguing that claims of unequal treatment were not backed up by evidence. Given the restrictions on producing racial statistics, there was little activists could do to produce such evidence.

In contrast, by 2023, the question of racism in policing had become a salient—and polarizing—political issue. During the uprising, a significant section of the left, including political parties, unions, and intellectuals, framed Nahel Merzouk's death as illustrative of "a problem of racism in the police."[37] While the government initially ignored these statements, it responded publicly when the United Nations High Commissioner for Human Rights expressed concern over Nahel's killing and encouraged France "to seriously address the deep issues of racism and discrimination in law enforcement."[38] The Ministry of Foreign Affairs released a statement saying, "any accusation of racism or systemic discrimination by the police is totally unfounded. . . . France and its police forces combat racism and all forms of discrimination with determination."[39] Still, the question of police racism remained salient in the media and political debates, with the political left leading the charge.

The emergence of this question in the public debate illustrates one of the key achievements of the movement. While antiracialism makes it difficult to name and measure racial inequalities, it does not make it impossible. Although there is almost no administrative data to draw on to measure racial inequalities in policing, movement actors have developed various approaches to produce knowledge about the racialized dimension of French policing. This has given them leverage to push the left to overcome its historical reluctance to address racial oppression.

In the late 2000s, the campaign against racial profiling launched France's first study quantifying racial disparities in police stops. In the absence of administrative data about identity checks, campaign leaders used a methodology that relied on observing hundreds of police stops in crowded spaces to measure the disproportionate targeting of people perceived as Black or Arab. The study demonstrated widespread racial disparities, which allowed activists to overcome decades of political denial. Almost overnight, politicians on the right and on the left admitted the "reality" of *contrôles au faciès* (discriminatory stops), mainstream media announced that racial profiling was now scientifically proven, and courts started looking into the state's responsibility for discriminatory stops. As we saw, while the quantitative methodology helped activists establish the credibility of their data, the study's findings were interpreted narrowly, as evidence of biased officers making decisions about whom to stop based on racial prejudice.

In the second half of the 2010s, other modes of knowledge production helped the movement push for a more structural understanding of racialized policing, which went beyond condemning racist cops. The neighborhood mobilization drew on the records uncovered in a criminal investigation to demonstrate that the disproportionate targeting of Black and Arab men did not simply reflect the behavior of a few officers. In the twelfth arrondissement, it resulted from an institutional policy of "evicting undesirables" from public spaces, which required officers to harass racialized young men in their own neighborhoods. Based on this evidence, they launched France's first lawsuit against the state for "systemic discrimination" in policing, which helped move the judicial and political debates beyond discussions of individual bias. In 2020, the state-appointed Rights Defender condemned what they called institutional and systemic discrimination in policing, and in 2023, they launched research projects on the police practice of "evicting undesirables."[40]

In parallel, leading figures of the Truth and Justice movement imposed their presence in leftist spaces, claiming that it was necessary for the communities most targeted by police violence to have a seat at the table. There, they pushed for a historically grounded, structural analysis of racialized policing, attentive to the role of the state in maintaining racial hierarchies. They emphasized the continued legacy of France's colonial history, linking the personal trajectories of victims of police killings to the broader history of colonialism.

In promoting their structural analysis of police racism, movement actors have been careful to conceptualize *racism* without endorsing essentializing notions of *races* as natural, biological differences. They promoted a language that emphasizes the process whereby dominant groups assign a racialized identity to oppressed groups, describing victims of racism as "people perceived as Black or Arab," or as "racialized people" (*les personnes racisées*). This language is now becoming the dominant way for leftists to talk about racism. This allows them to highlight the social processes of racialization and exclusion while aligning with the antiracialist rejection of racial categories.

Combined, these different modes of knowledge production strengthened the movement's capacity to promote an analysis of racism as a system of oppression. Paradoxically, although the police are one of the most opaque state institutions, holding significant epistemic power, antipolice activism became a central issue around which the antiracist movement has coalesced. In the early 2020s, an increasing number of left-wing parties endorsed an institutional and systemic analysis of racialized policing (with the notable exception of the socialist party). In their media interviews following Nahel Merzouk's killing, leaders of La France insoumise, which became the strongest left-wing party in French Parliament in 2022, explained:

> When we say "the police kill" or "there is a problem of structural racism in the police," this does not mean that all the people that belong to the police force kill or are racists. . . . It means that there's an organization, a structure, a doctrine, and resources, which result, in the end, in an institution that cannot properly accomplish the role it was given. It's a systemic issue. It's not just the actions of a few isolated individuals, but the result of a system that produces these situations and protects [wrongdoers] when they happen.[41]

Some politicians started making parallels between contemporary police violence targeting immigrants and their descendants and colonial policing practices. This frame was also increasingly adopted by public intellectuals who had previously refrained from endorsing postcolonial analyses—a testament to the fact that these analyses became speakable in mainstream settings. For example, Fabien Jobard, one of the most respected experts on policing in France, was reluctant to link contemporary policing practices to France's colonial history when he coauthored the racial profiling study in 2009. At the time, he believed that such claims were so controversial that they would discredit the whole report. In contrast, the opinion piece he published following the killing of Nahel Merzouk in *Le Monde* was centered on the colonial legacies of contemporary policing. The article, titled "Lawmakers Have Entrenched the Ascendency of the Police over Postcolonial Youth," argued that "asking whether police officers are racist or not doesn't really help understand what's happening." Instead, the author explains, "the police is a site for the perpetuation of the colonial relation on our land." He traced this perpetuation to the way postcolonial migration was handled in the metropole, through housing in underresourced suburbs combined with policing logics of containment, control, and a permanent obligation of deference inherited from the Algerian war.[42] This opinion piece was part of a broader trend whereby public intellectuals who had previously refrained from endorsing postcolonial analyses were now increasingly highlighting the continuities of colonial policing in contemporary practices, thus demonstrating a shift in what is sayable and hearable in scholarly and political circles.

Racist Backlash

The movement's success in placing the issue of police racism on the agenda has been met with fierce backlash. As the proliferation of evidence made it untenable to keep denying that the police disproportionately target racial minorities, the right has shifted from denial to justifying these practices. Politicians and media hosts portray the police as the last bastion against an existential threat posed by immigration, which is framed as a source of crime and terrorism, and a danger to the survival of the Republic.

While in 2005 the right blamed the uprising on immigrant cultures and failures of parental authority, in 2023 they went further and framed those with origins outside of Europe, no matter how many generations removed, for being inherently violent and un-Republican. When Interior Minister Gérald Darmanin noted that 90% of those arrested during the revolts were French citizens, right and far-right politicians unanimously criticized his "blindness" to the "immigration problem," explaining that, while the rioters were French on paper, they were foreign in their values and beliefs. The president of the Republican group in the Senate, Bruno Retailleau, said "there is obviously a link between these events and immigration," explaining that the rioters might be French citizens, "but unfortunately, for the second, third, generation, there is a sort of return to their ethnic origins."[43] The Republican party leader, Eric Ciotti, concurred and called for stripping rioters of their French citizenship when they have dual nationality, and taking away state benefits from their families. Marine Le Pen, the head of the far-right party Rassemblement National, commented, "[the Interior minister] knows very well that a supermajority of the people involved don't feel French (*se sentent étrangers*) or are of foreign origin," arguing that they are motivated by "a hatred of France" and not by any political will.[44]

Even more worrying, the far right endorsed a belligerent rhetoric, warning of an upcoming racial civil war. On the same day as the United Nations called on France to look into its deep-seated issues of racism, the former presidential candidate and far-right figure Eric Zemmour said, "we are in the premises of a civil war," which he described as "an ethnic, racial war." Echoing the war-mongering discourse, two of the largest police unions, Alliance and UNSA Police, published a press release describing the police as "at war" with "hordes of savages." The text, titled "Enough Is Enough," called for a "struggle against those 'pests'" (*nuisibles*) and demanded the full incapacitation of all those arrested.[45] While in 2005 the right blamed immigrant "cultures" and a failure of parental authority, in 2023 they used explicitly racist language (savages, pests) to condemn racialized groups as inherently violent and un-French.

The police unions' press release further threatened that, in the absence of "concrete measures of juridical protection for the Policeman, of adequate penal response [against rioters], of substantial means [for the police]," they would "enter in resistance" against the state. This threat is part of a broader trend, whereby right-leaning and far-right police unions are increasingly framing the police not as a public service institution, but as a political faction, willing to use any means necessary to defend its interests, even against the state. In the context of an increasingly popular far right, this rhetoric is finding a strong echo among the French public. When far-right politician Jean Messiha started an online crowdfunding campaign to support the officer who shot Nahel Merzouk, it collected 1.6 million euros within a few days.

This shift, from denying and dismissing claims of racism to owning and justifying racist state practices, echoes broader trends in Western Europe and North America. In many countries, the right and far right are responding to the growth of movements contesting racialized state violence with overtly racist rhetoric and policies. This backlash foreshadows the implementation of increasingly brutal state policies targeting groups defined by their ascribed race, ethnic origin, or religion, through police repression, incarceration, and deportation.

Where Do We Go from Here?

As I write these final lines in March 2025, the political horizon seems bleak for those of us invested in the struggle for justice, equality, and safety from harm. The French movement against racialized policing, like similar movements across the world, made significant advances in the 2010s, but it is now facing a severe backlash. Police brutality is increasing, the rise of the far right is accelerating rapidly, and like other Western countries, the government is intensifying its repression of progressive movements.

This does not mean that all hope for transformative change is gone forever. Social change happens in cycles, and sooner or later, another wave of activism will emerge, which will build on the advances the 2010s generation achieved. My hope is that the key lessons of this book will be of use to activists, lawyers, victims, and scholars invested in reducing the harms of policing on marginalized communities.

One lesson is that, to understand what it takes to challenge an institution as mighty as the police, when its victims are some of the most marginalized and discredited groups in society, we must go beyond examining what the police do, and also analyze the *power relation* between law enforcement and the communities they target. This means overcoming the artificial division, common in the research field, between those who study the police and those who study marginalized communities, a move many scholars are now making.

Paying attention to power relations requires that we break down the mechanisms through which the police consolidate their dominance, and the avenues people can take to disrupt it, so we can better understand the dynamics of stability and change in the politics of policing. In this book, I focused on one dimension of this power relation—epistemic power— and proposed conceptual tools to analyze how it operates to protect the police from political challenge, how movements confront and challenge it by producing their own evidence, and the consequences of this struggle over knowledge on the public debate about police violence, racism, and accountability.

This analysis suggests that we should think deeply about the implications and trade-offs of our methods of knowledge production and anticipate their limitations. While statistics are often essential to introduce the question of racial inequality in the public debate, quantitative epistemologies are insufficient, on their own, to capture the institutionalized practices and social structures that sustain these inequalities. Evidence of institutional policies and historical legacies are also needed to uncover the mechanisms that lead to unequal outcomes.

Epistemologies that center the experiences of victims can help shed light on how multiple institutional and social forces participate in sustaining racialized policing and the structures of oppression it reproduces. But we should not assume that research projects involving marginalized communities are always empowering. The public exposure they entail for victims increases their vulnerability to repression and retaliation. We must also remain attentive to the difference between using people's testimonies as data and elevating their voices and analyses as knowers. Both can be helpful, but only the latter contributes to building power from the ground up. Fostering approaches that amplify the voices of impoverished and racialized communities is essential; only then can those most affected control how their grievances are framed when they are introduced in the public and political arena. Regardless of our preferred methods, we should be careful not to embrace new technologies without assessing how they contribute to sustaining capitalist and racist structures.

We should also remain attentive to the fact that many research projects—this book included—tend to obscure the harms suffered by groups that are too small, or too isolated spatially, to be easily included in research. For example, Roma or Traveler communities are present in the movement, but their experiences and analyses remain marginal in knowledge production. The same goes for residents of France's overseas territories, who are subjected to high levels of police brutality but often struggle to be included in the Paris-centered movement. Addressing this requires incorporating an attention to the most marginalized groups at the stage of designing knowledge projects.

Another key lesson is that, while anyone invested in producing knowledge will understandably defend their approach, we should be aware that it is often the combination of various modes of knowledge production, including from groups we might disagree with epistemologically or politically, that transforms the public debate. Mainstream approaches are essential to overcome political denial and place issues on the agenda, and counterhegemonic approaches are necessary to move beyond the dominant understanding of policing and to uncover the systems of oppression they perpetuate. The goal should be to multiply the sites of knowledge production so a diversity of epistemic approaches can flourish. This requires investing in research infrastructures that foster independence from the state and corporate interests, and hence to come up with alternative funding structures. This is especially critical at a time when the future of academic research is uncertain.

Ultimately, resisting the epistemic power of the police and making racialized police violence visible will not be sufficient to transform policing. But it is an essential step in the struggle toward imagining and building societies that are more equal, just, and safe for everybody.

Acknowledgments

In the process of researching and writing this book, I have received support from many people who contributed with their insights, feedback, guidance, and care.

First and foremost, I would like to extend my deepest gratitude to the movement actors who kindly included me in their work and were generous enough to share their experiences and analyses with me. Everything I learned during this research, I owe to them. While I can't name all the brave and brilliant activists, lawyers, and victims who influenced my thinking, I am particularly indebted to Ramata and Fatou Dieng, Farid El Yamni, Amal Bentounsi, Aurélie Garand, Assa Traoré, and Awa Gueye, who lost their brothers to police violence and have been fighting for truth and justice ever since. Their work, alongside other actors of the Truth and Justice movement, never ceases to inspire me. I am also indebted to all the members of the campaign against racial profiling for involving me in their advocacy, litigation, and organizing work and for generously sharing their insights about antidiscrimination work in France. I would like to thank in particular Sarah, Adam, and Slim Ben Achour, whom I spent countless hours with. My deepest gratitude goes to the twelfth arrondissement youth counselors Malik and Paul, and to the plaintiffs, parents, and local activists who welcomed me in their coalition and shared their stories and analyses with me. Each and every one of them taught me so much. I am grateful for their participation in my research, but more importantly, for the incredible work they do promoting a more just, more equal, and more inclusive world.

In academia, I was fortunate to have a large and supportive group of mentors, colleagues, and friends who helped at various stages of the project. At the early stages, my graduate school mentors played a key role in guiding me through what was my first large research project. John Hagan provided unfaltering support and constant encouragement. Aldon Morris gave me sharp feedback and listened patiently when I was feeling less than confident about academia as a career. Laura Beth Nielsen was always up for discussing ideas in what were consistently stimulating meetings. And Liora Israël provided me not only with constructive feedback but also with her expertise and networks in France's academic and activist field. Other scholars were generous enough to read and comment on parts of the project, including Mary Pattillo, Charles Camic, Robin Stryker, Andrew Papachristos, and Monica Prasad.

Once I started writing the book, many colleagues and friends helped by reading drafts, listening as I tried to make sense of my arguments, and brainstorming with me. No one has read more drafts of this book than my friend and colleague Jane Pryma, who has probably seen every iteration of every chapter I ever wrote (and there were more than I care to admit). Marie Laperrière comes as a close second; she, too, has read and commented on countless versions of the book. I often joke that both Jane and Marie should be listed as coauthors.

One of the most important moments in crafting the manuscript was the book workshop I organized in 2023 with the support of the University of Washington. I am incredibly grateful for the brilliant scholars who read an early version of the manuscript and gave me incisive and constructive feedback: Michael Rodríguez-Muñiz, Oliver Rollins, Vincent-Arnaud Chappe, Michael McCann, Monica Bell, Michèle Lamont, and Neil Gross. Each one of them gave me invaluable feedback that helped me improve the writing and clarify my main arguments. Their deep engagement with the manuscript helped me figure out what exactly I wanted the story to be about, who I wanted the audience to be, and how to let the narrative drive the writing.

One of my favorite things about academia is the diversity of writing groups and workshops one can join. I have benefited immensely from them at each institution of higher education I've been a part of. At Northwestern, I received productive feedback from members of the Crime, Law, and Society workshop; the Race and Society workshop; the Comparative Historical Social Science workshop; and the interdisciplinary writing groups organized by the Graduate School. At the Centre Maurice Halbwachs, the friendship and support of my fellow graduate students Hamza Esmili and Bérangère Savinel kept me sane when fieldwork was difficult. At Brown University, I benefited from the feedback of my postdoc peers at the Watson Institute, in particular Gabriel Koehler-Derrick, Madeline Woker, and Aalyia Sadruddin. At the University of Washington, the informal writing group I organized with fellow junior faculty Jelani Ince, Theresa Rocha Beardall, and Rawan Arar, the Law, Societies, and Justice workshare, and my colleagues Katherine Beckett and Smadar Ben Natan, helped me move this project forward while navigating the first years on the tenure track. And at Sciences Po, support and advice from my colleagues, including Mirna Safi, Lidia Panico, Zachary Van Winkle, Bastian Betthäuser, and Jen Shradie, helped me bring the book to an end.

Many other friends have read chapters, provided feedback, and helped me think through my arguments when I felt stuck, including Amy Swanson, Dalia Abdelhameed, Yannick Coenders, Mary Ellen Stitt, Ari Tolman, Erica Banks, Melike Arslan, Noga Rotem, Dina Waked, Arif Camoglu, Laurent Gayer, Anthony Pregnolato, Paul Le Derff, Jérémie Gauthier, Aline Daillère, Noha Roushdy, Ramy Sabry, and Allanah Karas. Special thanks to Ole Hexel, who spent countless hours listening to me try to figure out the story I wanted to tell, and to Yara Sallam, who found the title for the book.

As I was finalizing the manuscript, it was a pleasure to work with the team at Stanford University Press, in particular my editor Marcela Maxfield, who was particularly helpful and efficient.

To all of them, and to my family and friends who provided care and love throughout the (many) years it took to finalize this book, I am profoundly grateful.

Notes

Introduction

1. Fabien Jobard et al., "Measuring Appearance-Based Discrimination: An Analysis of Identity Checks in Paris," *Population* (English edition) 67, no. 3 (2012): 349; Défenseur des droits, "Enquête sur l'accès au Droit Volume 1: Relations Police / Population, Le Cas Des Contrôles d'identité," 2017; Nicolas Jounin et al., "Le faciès du contrôle: Contrôles d'identité, apparence et modes de vie des étudiant(e)s en Île-de-France," *Déviance et Société* 39, no. 1 (2015): 3.

2. Pseudonym.

3. Pseudonym.

4. The national origin has been changed.

5. Interview with Joseph, May 24, 2018.

6. Jacques de Maillard and Mathieu Zagrodzki, "Styles of Policing and Police-Public Interactions: The Question of Stop-and-Search by Police Units in France," *International Journal of Police Science and Management* 23, no. 2 (2021): 157–67; Didier Fassin, *Enforcing Order: An Ethnography of Urban Policing* (Polity Press, 2013); Jérémie Gauthier, "Origines contrôlées: Police et minorités en France et en Allemagne," *Sociétés contemporaines* 97, no. 1 (2015): 101; Aline Daillère, "La justice dans la rue: Du pouvoir contraventionnel des policiers" (Mémoire de Master 2 de Science politique, "Politiques de prévention et sécurité"), Université de Versailles-Saint-Quentin-en-Yvelines, 2019; Jacques de Maillard, "Experiencing Police Stops in France: Low-Level Tensions, Trust and Citizenship," *European Journal of Policing Studies* 6, no. 1 (2023): 5–26.

7. Aline Daillère, "L'amende forfaitaire, arme du (non-)droit," *Champ pénal*, no. 26 (2022); Collectif Contre le Contrôle au Faciès, "Les maux du déni cinq ans de contrôles abusifs rapportés par les victimes et leurs familles, 2011–2015" (2016);

Human Rights Watch, "'La base de l'humiliation,' les contrôles d'identité en France" (2012).

8. Ivan du Roy and Ludo Simbille, "Entre 1977 et 2022, 861 morts suite à l'action des forces de l'ordre d'interventions policières ou du fait d'un agent des forces de l'ordre," *Basta!*, https://bastamag.net/webdocs/police/.

9. Ivan du Roy and Ludo Simbille, "'Refus d'obtempérer,' 'malaises' en detention . . . 52 décès liés à une intervention policière en 2024," *Basta!*, June 26, 2025.

10. While the total number of police-involved deaths may seem small compared with US rates, they represent a significant and rising proportion of all homicides (1.5% in 2016, 2.7% in 2022).

11. Fabien Jobard, *Bavures policières: La force publique et ses usages*, Textes à l'appui (La Découverte, 2002); Howard Becker, "Whose Side Are We On," *Social Problems* 14, no. 3 (1967): 239–47.

12. Dominique Monjardet, "Gibier de recherche, la police et le projet de connaître," *Criminologie* 38, no. 2 (2005): 13–37; Fassin, *Enforcing Order*; Jobard, *Bavures policières*.

13. The law bans the collection and use of personal data that directly or indirectly capture racial or ethnic origin. Limited exceptions apply when the data are collected for research purposes, and only after obtaining approval from a national authority, which examines requests on a case-by-case basis.

14. Jan Terpstra, "Two Theories on the Police—The Relevance of Max Weber and Émile Durkheim to the Study of the Police," *International Journal of Law, Crime, and Justice* 39, no. 1 (May 2011): 1–11.

15. Magda Boutros, "The Epistemic Power of the Police," *Theoretical Criminology* 28, no. 4 (2024): 495–515.

16. David Theo Goldberg, *The Threat of Race: Reflections on Racial Neoliberalism* (Wiley-Blackwell, 2009).

17. Magda Boutros, "Antiracism without Races: How Activists Produce Knowledge about Race and Policing in France," *Social Problems* 71, no. 1 (2024): 1–17.

18. Some recent studies include Michelle Phelps, *The Minneapolis Reckoning: Race, Violence, and the Politics of Policing in America* (Princeton University Press, 2024); Salwa Ismail, "The Egyptian Revolution against the Police," in *The Affective Dynamics of Mass Protests: Midān Moments and Political Transformation in Egypt and Turkey*, ed. Bilgin Ayata and Cilja Harders, Routledge Studies in Affective Societies (Routledge, 2024); Jaime Amparo Alves, *The Anti-Black City: Police Terror and Black Urban Life in Brazil* (University of Minnesota Press, 2018).

19. Abdellali Hajjat, "Le MTA et la 'grève générale' contre le racisme de 1973," *Plein droit* 67, no. 4 (2005): 35; Rachida Brahim, *La race tue deux fois: Une histoire des crimes racistes en France (1970–2000)* (Éditions Syllepse, 2020).

20. Sophie Béroud et al., eds., *Engagements, rébellions et genre: Dans les quartiers populaires en Europe, 1968–2005* (Editions des Archives contemporaines, 2011); Abdellali Hajjat, "Rébellions urbaines et déviances policières," *Cultures et Conflits*, no. 1 (2014): 11–34.

21. Erik Bleich, "Antiracism without Races," *French Politics, Culture, and Society* 18, no. 3 (2000): 48–74.

22. Goldberg, *Threat of Race*.

23. Martin Thomas, *Violence and Colonial Order: Police, Workers, and Protest in the European Colonial Empires, 1918–1940*, first paperback ed. (Cambridge University Press, 2015); Laleh Khalili and Jillian Schwedler, *Policing and Prisons in the Middle East: Formations of Coercion* (C. Hurst, 2010).

24. Mathieu Rigouste, *L'ennemi intérieur: La généalogie coloniale et militaire de l'ordre sécuritaire dans la France contemporaine*, La Découverte-poche (La Découverte, 2011).

25. Alana Lentin, *Racism and Anti-Racism in Europe* (Pluto Press, 2004).

26. Anthony Pregnolato, "La ligue des droits de l'homme face aux violences policières," *Matériaux pour l'histoire de notre temps* 137–38, no. 3–4 (2020): 87–96; Philippe Juhem, "SOS-Racisme, histoire d'une mobilisation 'apolitique': Contribution à une analyse des transformations des représentations politiques après 1981" (Université de Nanterre Paris X, 2007).

27. Ahmed Boubeker and Abdellali Hajjat, eds., *Histoire politique des immigrations (post)coloniales: France, 1920–2008* (Éditions Amsterdam, 2008); Foued Nasri, "La dénonciation des pratiques policières à Lyon à la fin des années 1970: Socio-Histoire locale de la formation d'une cause," *Champ pénal*, no. 26 (2022); Mogniss Hamed Abdallah, *Rengainez, on Arrive! Chroniques des luttes contre les crimes racistes ou sécuritaires, contre la hagra policière et judiciaire (des années 1970 à nos jours)* (Libertalia, 2012).

28. Abdellali Hajjat, *La marche pour l'égalité et contre le racisme* (Éditions Amsterdam, 2013).

29. Hajjat, *La marche pour l'égalité*; Saïd Bouamama, "Extrême gauche et luttes de l'immigration postcoloniale," in *Histoire politique des immigrations (post)coloniales: France, 1920–2008*, ed. Ahmed Boubeker and Abdellali Hajjat (Éditions Amsterdam, 2008).

30. Soline Laplanche-Servigne, "Quand les victimes de racisme se mobilisent: Usage d'identifications ethnoraciales dans l'espace de la cause antiraciste en France et en Allemagne," *Politix* 108, no. 4 (2014): 143–66; Pauline Picot, "Quelques usages militants du concept de 'racisme institutionnel': Le discours antiraciste postcolonial (France, 2005–2015)," *Migrations Société* 163, no. 1 (2016): 47–60.

31. For a more comprehensive overview of the movement, see Anthony Pregnolato, "L'espace des mobilisations contre les violences des forces de l'ordre en France depuis les années 1990," *Mouvements* 92, no. 4 (2017): 38–47; Anthony Pregnolato, "Rébellions urbaines et mobilisations contre les violences policières dans la région parisienne (2005–2018)" (PhD diss., Université Paris Nanterre, 2021).

32. The term *islamo-gauchiste* is reminiscent of the slur *judéo-bolchévique*, which was used in the 1930s to promote both anti-Semitism and anticommunist sentiment.

33. Mediapart, *Allô Place Beauveau?*, www.mediapart.fr/studio/panoramique/allo-place-beauvau-cest-pour-un-bilan; *Basta!*, "Le nombre de personnes tuées par un tir des forces de l'ordre a doublé depuis 2020," June 28, 2023.

34. Fabien Jobard, "Colères policières," *Revue Esprit*, no. 423 (2016): 55–63.

35. Hajjat, *La marche pour l'égalité et contre le racisme*; Foued Nasri, "Permanences et discontinuités dans les mobilisations associatives des héritiers de l'immigration maghrébine au sein de l'agglomération lyonnaise: Le cas de Zaâma d'Banlieue et Des Jeunes Arabes de Lyon et Banlieue (1979–1998)" (Institut d'études politiques de Paris, Sciences Po, 2013); Pregnolato, "Rébellions urbaines et mobilisations contre les violences policières dans la région parisienne (2005–2018)"; Phelps, *Minneapolis Reckoning*; Megan Mink Francis, "The Price of Civil Rights: Black Lives, White Funding, and Movement Capture," *Law and Society Review* 53, no. 1 (2019): 275–309.

36. Boubeker and Hajjat, *Histoire politique des immigrations (post)coloniales*; Pregnolato, "L'espace des mobilisations contre les violences des forces de l'ordre en France depuis les années 1990"; Nasri, "La dénonciation des pratiques policières à Lyon à la fin des années 1970."

37. Pregnolato, "La ligue des droits de l'homme face aux violences policières"; Éric Agrikoliansky, "Usages choisis du droit; Le service juridique de la ligue des droits de l'homme (1970–1990): Entre politique et raison humanitaire," *Sociétés contemporaines* 52, no. 4 (2003): 61.

38. Abdallah, *Rengainez, on Arrive! Chroniques des luttes contre les crimes racistes ou sécuritaires, contre la hagra policière et judiciaire des années 1970 à nos jours.*

39. Bouamama, "Extrême gauche et luttes de l'immigration postcoloniale."

40. Pregnolato, "Rébellions urbaines et mobilisations contre les violences policières dans la région parisienne (2005–2018)."

41. Tony Cheng, *The Policing Machine: Enforcement, Endorsements, and the Illusion of Public Input* (University of Chicago Press, 2024); Jobard, *Bavures policières*; Joanna C. Schwartz, "Police Indemnification," *SSRN Electronic Journal*, 2013.

42. Cédric Moreau de Bellaing, *Force publique: Une sociologie de l'institution policière*, Collection Études Sociologiques (Economica, 2015).

43. Jobard, *Bavures policières*; Ivan du Roy and Ludovic Simbille, "Décès suite à une intervention policière: Les deux-tiers des affaires ne débouchent sur aucun procès," *Basta!*, July 16, 2020.

44. See, for example, Anthony Pregnolato, "Les violences policières en procès: Mort d'Amine Bentounsi; La condamnation exceptionnelle du policier Saboundjian," *Lien social et Politiques*, no. 84 (2020): 163.

45. Roy and Simbille, "Décès suite à une intervention policière: Les deux-tiers des affaires ne débouchent sur aucun procès."

46. Jobard, "Colères policières"; René Lévy, "La police française à la lumière de la théorie de la justice procédurale," *Déviance et Société* 40, no. 2 (2016): 139.

47. Jérôme Berthaut, *La banlieue du "20 Heures": Ethnographie de la production d'un lieu commun journalistique*, L'ordre Des Choses (Agone, 2013); Paul Le Derff, "Faire voir, faire parler, faire taire: La publicisation des faits policiers mortels en

France (1990–2016)" (PhD diss., Université de Lille, 2023); see also, in the United States, Regina G. Lawrence, *The Politics of Force: Media and the Construction of Police Brutality* (University of California Press, 2000).

48. Brahim, *La race tue deux fois*; Trica Danielle Keaton, *You Know You're Black in France When: The Fact of Everyday Antiblackness* (MIT Press, 2023); Lentin, *Racism and Anti-Racism in Europe*; Patrick Simon and Amy Jacobs, "Statistics, French Social Sciences, and Ethnic and Racial Social Relations," *Revue Française de Sociologie* 51, Supplement: An Annual English Selection (2010): 159–74; Cathy Lisa Schneider, *Police Power and Race Riots: Urban Unrest in Paris and New York* (University of Pennsylvania Press, 2014); Audrey Célestine, "French Caribbean Organizations and the 'Black Question' in France," *African and Black Diaspora: An International Journal* 4, no. 2 (July 2011): 131–44.

49. Goldberg, *Threat of Race*, 31.

50. Brahim, *La race tue deux fois*.

51. Pregnolato, "Rébellions urbaines et mobilisations contre les violences policières dans la région parisienne (2005–2018)."

52. Mustafa Emirbayer, "Manifesto for a Relational Sociology," *American Journal of Sociology* 103, no. 2 (September 1997): 281–317.

53. Terpstra, "Two Theories on the Police—The Relevance of Max Weber and Émile Durkheim to the Study of the Police."

54. Egon Bittner, "Florence Nightingale in Pursuit of Willie Sutton: A Theory of the Police," in *The Potential for Reform of Criminal Justice*, ed. Herbert Jacob, Sage Criminal Justice System Annuals (Sage, 1974), 11–44; see also, Steven Lukes, *Power: A Radical View*, 2nd ed. (Palgrave Macmillan, 2004).

55. Bittner, "Florence Nightingale in Pursuit of Willie Sutton."

56. Jobard, *Bavures policières*.

57. Ian Loader and Aogán Mulcahy, *Policing and the Condition of England: Memory, Politics, and Culture*, Clarendon Studies in Criminology (Oxford University Press, 2003); Neil Walker, "Defining Core Police Tasks: The Neglect of the Symbolic Dimension?," *Policing and Society* 6, no. 1 (1996): 53–71.

58. Loader and Mulcahy, *Policing and the Condition of England*, 46.

59. Patrick J. Carr, Laura Napolitano, and Jessica Keating, "We Never Call the Cops and Here Is Why: A Qualitative Examination of Legal Cynicism in Three Philadelphia Neighborhoods," *Criminology* 45, no. 2 (2007): 445–80; David S. Kirk and Mauri Matsuda, "Legal Cynicism, Collective Efficacy, and the Ecology of Arrest," *Criminology* 49, no. 2 (May 2011): 443–72; Julien Talpin et al., *L'épreuve de la discrimination: Enquête dans les quartiers populaires*, 1st ed., 2021, Collection "Le Lien Social" (Presses Universitaires de France, 2021).

60. Cevipof, "En quoi les français ont-ils confiance aujourd'hui?" vague 12b, May 2021.

61. Boutros, "Epistemic Power of the Police."

62. For a review of the relevant scholarship, see Charles Camic, Neil Gross, and Michèle Lamont, eds., *Social Knowledge in the Making* (University of Chicago Press, 2011).

63. Alfred Archer et al., "Celebrity, Democracy, and Epistemic Power," *Perspectives on Politics* 18, no. 1 (March 2020): 27–42.

64. Linsey McGoey, *The Unknowers: How Strategic Ignorance Rules the World* (ZED, 2019), 3.

65. The concept of epistemic power is closely related to epistemic injustice, which Fricker defines as "a wrong done to someone specifically in their capacity as a knower"; Miranda Fricker, *Epistemic Injustice: Power and the Ethics of Knowing* (Oxford University Press, 2007).

66. Simone Browne, *Dark Matters: On the Surveillance of Blackness* (Duke University Press, 2015), 16.

67. Andy Clarno, Janaé Bonsu-Love, Enrique Alvear Moreno, Lydia Dana, Michael De Anda Muñiz, Ilā Ravichandran, and Haley Volpintesta, *Imperial Policing: Weaponized Data in Carceral Chicago* (University of Minnesota Press, 2024), 42.

68. Clarno et al., *Imperial Policing*.

69. Fabien Jobard, "Propositions sur la théorie de la police," *Champ pénal*, no. 9 (January 30, 2012).

70. Berthaut, *La banlieue du "20 Heures."*

71. Sandra Harding, "Rethinking Standpoint Epistemology: What Is 'Strong Objectivity'?," *Centennial Review*, (1992): 437–70; Patricia Hill Collins, *Black Feminist Thought: Knowledge, Consciousness, and the Politics of Empowerment*, 2nd ed., Routledge Classics (Routledge, 2009); Charles W. Mills, *The Racial Contract* (Cornell University Press, 1997).

72. Michael Rodríguez-Muñiz, "Intellectual Inheritances: Cultural Diagnostics and the State of Poverty Knowledge," *American Journal of Cultural Sociology* 3, no. 1 (2015): 89–122; Matthew Desmond, *Evicted: Poverty and Profit in the American City* (Crown, 2016).

73. Margaret Somers, "Where Is Sociology after the Historic Turn? Knowledge Cultures, Narrativity, and Historical Epistemologies," in *The Historic Turn in the Human Sciences*, ed. Terence McDonald (University of Michigan Press, 1996).

74. Browne, *Dark Matters*; Steven Epstein, *Impure Science: AIDS, Activism, and the Politics of Knowledge*, Medicine and Society (University of California Press, 1998); Aziz Choudry, *Learning Activism: The Intellectual Life of Contemporary Social Movements* (University of Toronto Press, 2015); David J. Hess, *Undone Science: Social Movements, Mobilized Publics, and Industrial Transitions* (MIT Press, 2016); María Isabel Casas-Cortés, Michal Osterweil, and Dana E. Powell, "Blurring Boundaries: Recognizing Knowledge-Practices in the Study of Social Movements," *Anthropological Quarterly* 81, no. 1 (2008): 17–58; Donatella della Porta and Elena Pavan, "Repertoires of Knowledge Practices: Social Movements in Times of Crisis," *Qualitative Research in Organizations and Management: An International Journal* 12, no. 4 (2017): 297–314.

75. Marcelo Hoffman, *Militant Acts: The Role of Investigations in Radical Political Struggles*, SUNY Series in New Political Science (State University of New York Press, 2019).

76. This definition is adapted from the definition of social knowledge developed by Charles Camic, Neil Gross, and Michèle Lamont, eds., *Social Knowledge in the Making* (University of Chicago Press, 2011).

77. Della Porta and Pavan, "Repertoires of Knowledge Practices."

78. These features build on the work of Camic, Gross, and Lamont, *Social Knowledge in the Making*.

79. For analyses of these conflicts, see Robert Benford, "Frame Disputes within the Nuclear Disarmament Movement," *Social Forces* 71, no. 3 (1993): 677–701; Zakiya Luna, "Who Speaks for Whom? (Mis)Representation and Authenticity in Social Movements," *Mobilization: An International Quarterly* 22, no. 4 (2017): 435–50; Amin Ghaziani and Kelsy Kretschmer, "Infighting and Insurrection," in *The Wiley Blackwell Companion to Social Movements*, ed. David A. Snow et al. (Wiley, 2018), 220–35.

80. Helen Reese and Garnett Newcombe, "Income Rights, Mothers' Rights, or Workers' Rights—Collective Action Frames, Organizational Ideologies, and the American Welfare Rights Movement," *Social Problems* 50, no. 2 (2003): 294–318; Myra Marx Ferree, "Resonance and Radicalism: Feminist Framing in the Abortion Debates of the United States and Germany," *American Journal of Sociology* 109, no. 2 (2003): 304–44; Zakiya T. Luna, "Marching toward Reproductive Justice: Coalitional (Re)Framing of the March for Women's Lives," *Sociological Inquiry* 80, no. 4 (2010): 554–78.

81. Michael Rodríguez-Muñiz, *Figures of the Future: Latino Civil Rights and the Politics of Demographic Change* (Princeton University Press, 2021).

82. Epstein, *Impure Science*.

83. Patrick Simon and Joan Stavo-Debauge, "Les politiques anti-discrimination et les statistiques: Paramètres d'une incoherence," *Sociétés contemporaines* 53, no. 1 (2004): 57–84.

84. For example, Stéphane Beaud and Gérard Noiriel, *Race et sciences sociales: Essai sur les usages publics d'une catégorie*, "Épreuves Sociales," Mettre les idées reçues à l'épreuve des réalités sociales (Agone, 2021).

85. For example, Simon and Stavo-Debauge, "Les politiques anti-discrimination et les statistiques."

86. Mirna Safi and Patrick Simon, "Les discriminations ethniques et raciales dans l'enquête Trajectoires et Origines: Représentations, expériences subjectives et situations vécues," *Economie et statistique* 464, no. 1 (2013): 245–75; Laure Bereni and Vincent Arnaud Chappe, "La discrimination, de la qualification juridique à l'outil sociologique," *Politix* 94, no. 2 (2011): 7–34.

87. Fabrice Dhume, "Du racisme institutionnel à la discrimination systémique? Reformuler l'approche critique," *Migrations Société* 163, no. 1 (2016): 33–46.

88. Olivier Le Cour Grandmaison, *Racismes d'État, États racistes: Une brève histoire* (Éditions Amsterdam, 2024).

89. Ann Juanita Morning, *The Nature of Race: How Scientists Think and Teach about Human Difference* (University of California Press, 2011).

90. Lentin, *Racism and Anti-Racism in Europe*; Goldberg, *Threat of Race*; Paul

Khalil Saucier and Tryon P. Woods, eds., *Conceptual Aphasia in Black: Displacing Racial Formation*, Critical Africana Studies (Lexington Books, 2016); Eduardo Bonilla-Silva, *Racism without Racists: Color-Blind Racism and the Persistence of Racial Inequality in the United States*, 3rd ed. (Rowman and Littlefield, 2010); Omar Slaouti and Olivier Le Cour Grandmaison, eds., *Racismes de France*, Cahiers Libres (La Découverte, 2020); Sarah Mazouz, *Race*, Le Mot Est Faible (Anamosa, 2020).

91. I capitalize the names of all racialized categories for several reasons. One is to have one coherent rule, regardless of whether the category describes ethnicities or religions (which are always capitalized), or racial groups (which are sometimes not). It is also a way to emphasize the fabricated nature of these categories and avoid reifying them as essential biological or cultural differences. Many scholars argue for capitalizing "Black" but not "white," because the capital W is often used by white supremacists. While I understand these concerns, I follow Eve Ewing in capitalizing both, to avoid reifying Whiteness as the norm, or contributing to its seeming neutrality, which would risk obscuring the way it works as a racial category that confers measurable benefits; Eve L. Ewing, "I'm a Black Scholar Who Studies Race: Here's Why I Capitalize 'White'," *Medium*, 2020.

Chapter 1

1. Gwenael Bourdon, "Le rescapé de Clichy livre sa version du drame," *Le Parisien*, December 15, 2005.

2. Véronique Le Goaziou and Laurent Mucchielli, *Quand les banlieues brûlent . . .* , 2nd ed. (La Découverte, 2007).

3. Les réactions, *Nouvel Obs*, November 17, 2005.

4. See, for example, Dominique Strauss-Kahn's statement to Europe 1 radio, reported in *Le Monde*, October 31, 2005, "Emeutes de Clichy-sous-Bois: Les interventions de Nicolas Sarkozy sont contestées, même à droite."

5. Marwan Mohamed and Laurent Mucchielli, "La police dans les 'quartiers sensibles': Un profond malaise," in *Quand les banlieues brûlent . . .* , by Véronique Le Goaziou and Laurent Mucchielli, 2nd ed. (La Découverte, 2007).

6. Sophie Béroud et al., eds., *Engagements, rébellions et genre: Dans les quartiers populaires en Europe, 1968–2005* (Éditions des archives contemporaines, 2011); Abdellali Hajjat, "Rébellions urbaines et déviances policières," *Cultures et Conflits*, no. 1 (2014): 11–34; Saïd Bouamama, "Extrême gauche et luttes de l'immigration postcoloniale," in *Histoire politique ees immigrations (post)coloniales: France, 1920–2008*, ed. Ahmed Boubeker and Abdellali Hajjat (Éditions Amsterdam, 2008).

7. Alfred Archer et al., "Celebrity, Democracy, and Epistemic Power," *Perspectives on Politics* 18, no. 1 (March 2020): 27–42; José Medina, *The Epistemology of Resistance: Gender and Racial Oppression, Epistemic Injustice, and Resistant Imaginations*, Studies in Feminist Philosophy (Oxford University Press, 2013); Kristie Dotson, "Conceptualizing Epistemic Oppression," *Social Epistemology* 28, no. 2 (2014): 115–38; Miranda Fricker, *Epistemic Injustice: Power and the Ethics of Knowing* (Oxford University Press, 2007).

8. Linsey McGoey, *The Unknowers: How Strategic Ignorance Rules the World* (ZED, 2019).

9. I develop this argument more fully in Magda Boutros, "The Epistemic Power of the Police," *Theoretical Criminology* 28, no. 4 (2024): 495–515.

10. Andy Clarno et al., *Imperial Policing: Weaponized Data in Carceral Chicago* (University of Minnesota Press, 2024), 39.

11. Clarno et al., *Imperial Policing*, 42.

12. Fabien Jobard, *Bavures policières: La force publique et ses usages*, Textes à l'appui (La Découverte, 2002); Jérémie Gauthier, "Origines contrôlées: Police et minorités en France et en Allemagne," *Sociétés contemporaines* 97, no. 1 (2015): 101–27.

13. Dominique Monjardet, "Gibier de recherche, la police et le projet de connaître," *Criminologie* 38, no. 2 (2005): 13; Didier Fassin, *Enforcing Order: An Ethnography of Urban Policing*, English ed. (Polity Press, 2013).

14. Commission nationale de la déontologie de la sécurité, "Rapport Annuel 2010 de La Commission Nationale de Déontologie de La Sécurité," April 26, 2011.

15. William Westley, "Secrecy and the Police," *Social Forces* 34, no. 3 (1956): 254–57.

16. Police code of ethics (*Code de déontologie de la police et de la gendarmerie nationale*).

17. See, for example, Sihem Souid and Jean-Marie Montali, *Omerta dans la police* (J'ai lu, 2012). See also the racist violence denounced by Amar Benmohamed and the retaliation he suffered as a consequence: "Pour la Défenseure des droits, le policier lanceur d'alerte 'a été victime d'une mesure de représailles' de sa hiérarchie," *Streetpress*, January 9, 2023.

18. Laurent Bonelli, *La France a peur: Une histoire sociale de "l'insécurité,"* Poche / Sciences humaines et sociales (La Découverte, 2010).

19. Dominique Monjardet, "Le chercheur et le policier: L'expérience des recherches commanditées par le ministère de l'Intérieur," *Revue française de science politique* 47, no. 2 (1997), 212.

20. Bonelli, *La France a peur*; Laurent Mucchielli, "L'expertise policière de la "violence urbaine," sa construction intellectuelle et ses usages dans le débat public français," *Déviance et société* 24, no. 4 (2000): 351–75.

21. Fabien Jobard, "Comprendre l'habilitation à l'usage de la force policière," *Déviance et Société* 25, no. 3 (2001): 325–45.

22. Jobard, *Bavures policières*, 18.

23. Renée Zauberman, "Gendarmerie et gens du voyage en région parisienne," *Cahiers Internationaux de Sociologie* 105 (1998): 415–38; Michel Wieviorka and Philippe Bataille, *La France raciste*, L'Epreuve des Faits (Seuil, 1992); Dominique Monjardet and Catherine Gorgeon, "La socialisation professionnelle des Policiers : Étude longitudinale de la 121ᵉ promotion des élèves gardiens de la paix" (Institut des Hautes Études de la Sécurité Intérieure, 2003).

24. René Lévy, *Du suspect au coupable: Le travail de police judiciaire* (Librairie des Méridiens; Médecine et Hygiène, 1987), 145.

25. Louis Gruel, "Levy René, du suspect au coupable: Le travail de la police judiciaire," *Revue française de sociologie* 32, no. 2 (1991): 303–5.

26. Commission nationale de la déontologie de la sécurité, "Rapport Annuel" (Paris, 2004); Didier Lapeyronnie, "Révolte primitive dans les banlieues françaises: Essai sur les émeutes de l'automne 2005," *Déviance et Société* 30, no. 4 (2007): 431–48; Michel Kokoreff, "Sociologie de l'émeute: Les dimensions de l'action en question," *Déviance et Société* 30, no. 4 (2006): 521–33.

27. Fabien Jobard, "Police, justice et discriminations raciales" in *De la question sociale à la question raciale? Représenter la société française*, ed. Éric Fassin and Didier Fassin, Cahiers libres (La Découverte, 2006).

28. I use Steven Epstein's definition of credibility, as the believability of claims or claims-makers, their ability to enroll supporters behind their arguments and to be seen as the sort of people who can voice the truth.

29. Howard Becker, "Whose Side Are We On," *Social Problems* 14, no. 3 (1967), 242.

30. Fabien Jobard, "Propositions sur la théorie de la police," *Champ pénal*, no. 9 (January 30, 2012).

31. Fricker, *Epistemic Injustice*.

32. AFP, "Emeutes de Clichy-sous-Bois: Les interventions de Nicolas Sarkozy sont contestées, même à droite," *Le Monde*, October 31, 2005.

33. Gwenael Bourdon, "Le rescapé de Clichy livre sa version du drame," *Le Parisien*, December 15, 2005.

34. Cited in Jobard, "Propositions sur la théorie de la police."

35. Jobard, "Propositions sur la théorie de la police."

36. Ivan du Roy and Ludovic Simbille, "Décès suite à une intervention policière: Les deux-tiers des affaires ne débouchent sur aucun procès," *Basta!*, July 16, 2020.

37. Gérard Davet, "La "légèreté" des policiers dénoncée dans le drame de Clichy-sous-Bois," *Le Monde*, December 7, 2006.

38. Archer et al., "Celebrity, Democracy, and Epistemic Power," 30.

39. Michaël Meyer, "Policer l'image: Nouvelles trajectoires professionnelles et risques médiatiques dans la communication policière en Suisse," *Politiques de communication* 1, no. 1 (2013): 59–94; Julie Sedel, *Les médias et la banlieue*, Broché, Poch'BDL (le Bord de l'eau INA éd., 2013).

40. Jérôme Berthaut, *La banlieue du "20 Heures": Ethnographie de la production d'un lieu commun journalistique*, L'ordre des Choses (Agone, 2013), 20.

41. Paul Le Derff, "Faire voir, faire parler, faire taire: La publicisation des faits policiers mortels en France (1990–2016)" (Université de Lille, 2023).

42. Clément Schouler, *Vos papiers!: Que faire face à la police?* (L'Esprit frappeur, 2001).

43. Bendan Kemmet and Geoffroy Tomasovitch, "Le livre qui scandalise les policiers," *Le Parisien*, November 30, 2001.

44. National Assembly, Question number 0577G by Jean-Pierre Schosteck, December 7, 2001.

45. The public controversy and lawsuit also focused on the drawing on the cover of the book, which depicted a police officer with a pig's nose, which was deemed an insult to the police.

46. Cour d'Appel de Paris, Arrêt du 18 janvier 2007.

47. Frédéric Vézard and Bernard Mazières, "A situation exceptionnelle, mesures exceptionnelles, " *Le Parisien*, October 16, 2001. See also the speech of Justice Minister Pierre Méhaignerie at the National Assembly on June 10, 1993 (if there were discriminatory stops, this would lead to nullifying the procedure and in the judiciary imposing sanctions); or the response of Interior Minister Jean-Pierre Chevènement to question number 1631 addressed on November 10, 1999 (there is no *contrôle au faciès*).

48. Amnesty International, "France: Shootings, Killings, and Alleged Ill-Treatment by Law Enforcement Officers" (Amnesty International, October 11, 1994); Amnesty International, "France: The Search for Justice: The Effective Impunity of Law Enforcement Officers in Cases of Shootings, Deaths in Custody, or Torture and Ill-Treatment" (Amnesty International Publications, April 5, 2005); Amnesty International, "Public Outrage: Police Officers above the Law in France" (Amnesty International Publications, 2009).

49. Amnesty International, "Public Outrage: Police Officers above the Law in France," 6.

50. Commission nationale de la déontologie de la sécurité, "Rapport Annuel 2010 de La Commission Nationale de Déontologie de La Sécurité."

51. Assemblée Nationale, Question numéro 64688 de Chantal Robin-Rodrigo, May 10, 2005.

52. Assemblée Nationale, Question numéro 64688 de Chantal Robin-Rodrigo, May 10, 2005.

53. Based on the police statistics published in the "tableaux 4001," retrieved from data.gouv.fr.

54. Assemblée Nationale, Question numéro 64688 de Chantal Robin-Rodrigo, May 10, 2005.

55. Fabien Jobard, "La puissance du doute," *Vacarme* 4, no. 21 (2002): 15–22; Emmanuelle Cosse and Fabien Jobard, "Dammarie-Lès-Lys : Les militants de l'incertitude," *Vacarme* 21 (2002).

56. Mogniss H. Abdallah, *Rengainez, on Arrive! Chroniques des luttes contre les crimes racistes ou sécuritaires, contre la hagra policière et judiciaire des années 1970 à nos jours* (Libertalia, 2012).

57. Mogniss H. Abdallah, "L'affaire Youssef Khaïf dans les médias," *Vacarme* 18, no. 1 (2002), 57.

58. "Des policiers en colère," *L'Obs*, September 28, 2001.

59. Abdallah, "L'affaire Youssef Khaïf dans les médias," *Vacarme* 18, no. 1 (2002), 57.

60. Abdallah, "L'affaire Youssef Khaïf dans les médias," 57.

61. Brigitte Vital-Durand, "Un 'coupable' finalement acquitté," *Libération*, September 29, 2001.

62. "Justice à sens unique," *Le Monde*, September 30, 2001.

63. Angles Morts, *Permis de tuer: Chronique de l'impunité policière* (Syllepse, 2014), 30.

64. Abdallah, "L'affaire Youssef Khaïf dans les médias."

65. Interview with activist, cofounder of the collective Stop le contrôle au faciès.

Chapter 2

1. James Goldston and Rachel Neild, "Ethnic Profiling Fails Europe," *Open Society Foundations*, June 26, 2006, sec. Voices.

2. Goldstein and Neild, "Ethnic Profiling."

3. Goldstein and Neild, "Ethnic Profiling."

4. Oriane Calligaro, "Une organisation hybride dans l'arène européenne: Open Society Foundations et la construction du champ de la lutte contre les discriminations," *Politix* 121, no. 1 (2018): 151–72.

5. Interview with program director at OSJI, March 29, 2018.

6. Interview with Rachel Neild, OSJI, March 29, 2018.

7. Interview with Rachel Neild, OSJI, March 29, 2018.

8. Pseudonym.

9. Including Police et Citoyens, Stop le contrôle au faciès, En finir avec le contrôle au faciès.

10. Tim Bartley, "How Foundations Shape Social Movements: The Construction of an Organizational Field and the Rise of Forest Certification," *Social Problems* 54, no. 3 (August 2007): 229–55.

11. Pseudonym.

12. Field notes, informal conversation with some of OSJI's grantees, August 24, 2017.

13. Interview with Samia (pseudonym), October 5, 2016.

14. Interview with activist, September 13, 2016.

15. The closely related term *délit de faciès*, literally "the crime of having the wrong appearance," is commonly used to talk about all kinds of discrimination, in accessing employment, housing, or entry into nightclubs.

16. Wendy H. Wong, *Internal Affairs: How the Structure of NGOs Transforms Human Rights* (Cornell University Press, 2012).

17. Interview with Adam (pseudonym), July 26, 2022.

18. Open Society Justice Initiative and Jurix, "Ethnic Profiling in the Moscow Metro" (Open Society Institute, 2006).

19. In 1996, his findings were successfully used in court as evidence that the New Jersey police discriminate against Black drivers, in *New Jersey v. Soto*.

20. René Lévy, *Du suspect au coupable: Le travail de police judiciaire* (Librairie des Méridiens; Médecine et Hygiène, 1987); Fabien Jobard and Sophie Névanen, "La couleur du jugement: Discriminations dans les décisions judiciaires en matière d'infractions à agents de La Force Publique (1965–2005)," *Revue Française de Sociologie* 48, no. 2 (2007): 243–72.

21. Interview with Fabien Jobard, August 28, 2018.

22. Interview with Sarah (pseudonym), September 8, 2022.

23. Sally Engle Merry, *The Seductions of Quantification: Measuring Human*

Rights, Gender Violence, and Sex Trafficking, Chicago Series in Law and Society (University of Chicago Press, 2016), 5.

24. Charles R. Epp, Steven Maynard-Moody, and Donald Haider-Markel, *Pulled Over: How Police Stops Define Race and Citizenship* (University of Chicago Press, 2014).

25. Jérémie Gauthier, "Origines contrôlées: Police et minorités en France et en Allemagne," *Sociétés contemporaines* 97, no. 1 (2015): 101.

26. Interview with René Lévy, October 19, 2016.

27. Interview with Sarah, September 8, 2022.

28. Interview with Fabien Jobard, August 28, 2018.

29. In the study, "youth culture clothing" included hip-hop, tecktonic, punk, and gothic styles; "casual" clothing indicated normal everyday attire; and "business" was defined as well-dressed.

30. Issa Kohler-Hausmann, "Eddie Murphy and the Dangers of Counterfactual Causal Thinking about Detecting Racial Discrimination," *Northwestern University Law Review* 113, no. 5 (2019): 1204.

31. Open Society Justice Initiative, "Profiling Minorities: A Study of Stop-and-Search Practices in Paris" (Open Society Institute, 2009).

32. Open Society Justice Initiative, 19.

33. Open Society Justice Initiative.

34. Interview with Fabien Jobard, August 28, 2018.

35. Fabien Jobard et al., "Measuring Appearance-Based Discrimination: An Analysis of Identity Checks in Paris," *Population* (English ed.) 67, no. 3 (2012): 349.

36. Interview with Fabien Jobard, August 28, 2018.

37. The largest daily *Le Monde* titled "The reality of contrôles au faciès is established," right-wing *Le Figaro* wrote "French police largely practice délit de faciès," left-wing *Libération* declared "Contrôles au faciès: The Police Caught Red Handed in Paris," and 24-hour news channel BFMTV wrote "The practice of contrôle au faciès is scientifically proven."

38. Pseudonym.

39. "Stop le contrôle au faciès teaser officiel 'Mon 1er contrôle d'identité,'" YouTube, November 14, 2011.

40. Collectif Contre le Contrôle au Faciès, "Les maux du déni cinq ans de contrôles abusifs rapportés par les victimes et leurs familles, 2011–2015," 2016, 16.

41. Interview with Kiara (pseudonym), November 10, 2016.

42. See the coalition's website: https://enfiniraveclescontrolesaufacies.org/Le -controle-au-facies-c-est-quoi.

43. Interview with Sarah, March 6, 2018.

44. Interview with Sarah.

45. Interview with Kiara, November 10, 2016.

46. Field notes, lawyers' meeting November 21, 2017.

47. "Récépissé: Débat sur LCI avec Sihame Assbague, porte parole du collectif," YouTube, October 10, 2012.

48. See, for example, *L'obs*, July 3, 2013, "Contrôles au faciès: 'Tu sors de chez toi, t'as la pression.'"

49. Margaret E. Keck and Kathryn Sikkink, *Activists beyond Borders: Advocacy Networks in International Politics* (Cornell University Press, 1998).

50. Pseudonym.

51. Pap Ndiaye, *La condition noire: Essai sur une minorité française*, Folio actuel 140 (Gallimard, 2009).

52. Audrey Célestine, "French Caribbean Organizations and the 'Black Question' in France," *African and Black Diaspora: An International Journal* 4, no. 2 (July 2011): 131–44; Marine Haddad, "Des minorités pas comme les autres?: Le vécu des discriminations et du racisme des ultramarins en métropole," *Revue Française de Sociologie* 59, no. 4 (2018): 649–76.

53. Interview with Adam, August 10, 2017.

54. Célestine, "French Caribbean Organizations and the 'Black Question' in France."

55. Crystal Marie Fleming, *Resurrecting Slavery: Racial Legacies and White Supremacy in France* (Temple University Press, 2017).

56. Julien Talpin et al., *L'épreuve de la discrimination: Enquête dans les quartiers populaires*, Collection "Le Lien Social" (Presses Universitaires de France, 2021).

57. Field notes, legal empowerment project meeting, June 13, 2017.

58. NGO internal documents.

Chapter 3

1. Pseudonym.

2. Interview with Malik (pseudonym), youth counselor, March 15, 2018.

3. Interview with Paul (pseudonym), youth counselor, March 21, 2018.

4. Interview with Oscar (pseudonym), resident, April 11, 2018.

5. Even though the Tigers brigade is part of the national police force rather than the municipal police, the mayor has leverage to pass on residents' grievances or to ask the police to address specific issues.

6. Interview with Adam, September 21, 2016.

7. Insee, "La ségrégation sociale entre collèges: Un reflet de la ségrégation résidentielle nettement amplifié par les choix des familles, notamment vers l'enseignement privé," Insee Analyses, September 2018.

8. Interview with Malik.

9. Interview with Malik.

10. Jaime Amparo Alves, *The Anti-Black City: Police Terror and Black Urban Life in Brazil* (University of Minnesota Press, 2018), 214.

11. This definition builds on the notion of "grounded knowledge"; see Loka Ashwood et al., "Linked and Situated: Grounded Knowledge," *Rural Sociology* 79, no. 4 (2014): 427–52.

12. See, for example, Action des Chrétiens pour l'Abolition de la Torture (ACAT), "L'ordre et la force: Enquête sur l'usage de la force par les représentants de la loi en France" (ACAT France, 2016).

13. Interview with Paul, youth counselor, March 21, 2018.

14. Interview with a plaintiff's mother, June 26, 2018.

15. Interview with Malik, youth counselor, April 5, 2018.

16. Interview with Oscar, plaintiff, April 11, 2018.

17. Interview with Oscar.

18. Criminal complaint, lawyers' archives.

19. Trial observations, February 22, 2018.

20. Field notes, April 4, 2018.

21. Field notes, April 4, 2018.

22. Aline Daillère, "L'amende forfaitaire, arme du (non-)droit," *Champ pénal*, no. 26 (December 21, 2022).

23. Interview with Oscar, plaintiff, April 11, 2018.

24. Collectif Place aux Jeunes, archives.

25. Interview with Malik, youth counselor, April 5, 2018.

26. Interview with Paul, youth counselor, March 21, 2018.

27. Interview with Victor (pseudonym), member of the collective Place aux Jeunes, January 31, 2018.

28. Collective Place aux Jeunes, archives, Lettre à la Chargée de mission au Cabinet de la Maire du 12ᵉ, February 10, 2017.

29. Interview with Mathilde (pseudonym), member of the collective Place aux Jeunes, April 11, 2018.

30. Interview with Christelle (pseudonym), plaintiff's mother, May 25, 2018.

31. Collective Place aux Jeunes, archives.

32. Report on the event "Making Place for Youth," Collective Place aux Jeunes, archives.

33. Report on the event "Making Place for Youth."

34. Interview with Joseph, plaintiff, May 24, 2018.

35. Report on the event "Making Place for Youth," Collective Place aux Jeunes, archives.

36. Interview with Victor, member of the collective Place aux Jeunes, January 31, 2018.

37. Field notes, January 16, 2018.

38. AFP, "Violences policières: Quatre jeunes hommes condamnés pour dénonciation calomnieuse, *Le Monde*, May 31, 2022.

Chapter 4

1. Interview with Ramata Dieng, January 9, 2017.

2. Interview with Fatou Dieng, July 25, 2022.

3. Louise Fessard, "Mort de Wissam El-Yamni: Histoire d'un fiasco judiciaire et d'une police intouchable," *Mediapart*, April 3, 2017.

4. The officers who arrested Adama were part of the gendarmerie, one of the two national police forces in France, which is historically linked to the military.

5. Assa Traoré and Elsa Vigoureux, *Lettre à Adama* (Seuil, 2017).

6. Interview with Assa Traoré, September 22, 2016.

7. Interview with Ramata Dieng, January 9, 2017.

8. Angles Morts, *Permis de tuer: Chronique de l'impunité policière* (Syllepse, 2014).

9. Interview with Ramata Dieng, January 9, 2017.

10. Interview with Ramata Dieng.

11. Interview with Farid El Yamni, July 20, 2022.

12. Celeste L. Arrington, *Accidental Activists: Victim Movements and Government Accountability in Japan and South Korea*, Studies of the Weatherhead East Asian Institute, Columbia University (Cornell University Press, 2016); Sandrine Lefranc et al., eds., *Mobilisations de victimes* (Presses Universitaire de Rennes, 2009); Frank J. Weed, "The Victim-Activist Role in the Anti-Drunk Driving Movement," *Sociological Quarterly* 31, no. 3 (1990): 459–73.

13. Lefranc et al., *Mobilisations de victimes*; Arrington, *Accidental Activists*.

14. Angles Morts, *Permis de tuer*.

15. Angles Morts, *Permis de tuer*.

16. Interview with Farid El Yamni, May 11, 2017.

17. Interview with Assa Traoré, September 22, 2016.

18. Interview with a member of the committee Truth and Justice for Babacar Gueye, June 20, 2018.

19. Ruth Wilson Gilmore, *Golden Gulag: Prisons, Surplus, Crisis, and Opposition in Globalizing California*, American Crossroads 21 (University of California Press, 2007); Jaime Amparo Alves, *The Anti-Black City: Police Terror and Black Urban Life in Brazil* (University of Minnesota Press, 2018).

20. Vincent-Arnaud Chappe and Narguesse Keyhani, "La fabrique d'un collectif judiciaire: La mobilisation des cheminots marocains contre les discriminations à la SNCF," *Revue française de science politique* 68, no. 1 (2018): 7–29; Lefranc et al., *Mobilisations de victimes*.

21. Gilmore, *Golden Gulag*.

22. Patricia Hill Collins, *Black Feminist Thought: Knowledge, Consciousness, and the Politics of Empowerment*, 2nd ed., Routledge Classics (Routledge, 2009).

23. Sandra Harding, "Rethinking Standpoint Epistemology: What Is 'Strong Objectivity'?," *Centennial Review*, 1992, 35.

24. Frantz Fanon, *Black Skin, White Masks*, new ed. (Grove Press; distributed by Publishers Group West, 2008); Lewis Gordon, "Fanon on Decolonizing Knowledge," in *Fanon and the Decolonization of Philosophy*, ed. Elizabeth Hoppe and Tracey Nicholls (Lexington Books, 2010).

25. Phil Brown and Edwin J. Mikkelsen, *No Safe Place: Toxic Waste, Leukemia, and Community Action* (University of California Press, 1990).

26. Anthony Pregnolato, "Rébellions urbaines et mobilisations contre les violences policières dans la région parisienne (2005–2018)" (PhD diss., Université Paris Nanterre, 2021).

27. Fabien Jobard, "La puissance du doute," *Vacarme* 4, no. 21 (2002): 15–22.

28. Angles Morts, *Permis de tuer*.

29. "Mort d'Adama Traoré: L'hypothèse de l'asphyxie sous le poids des gen-

darmes," *Le Parisien,* July 30, 2016; "Mort d'Adama Traoré: Un pompier contredit la version des gendarmes," *Le Monde,* September 14, 2016; see also "Deux mois après la mort d'Adama Traoré, toujours autant de questions," *France 24,* September 16, 2016.

30. Interview with a member of the committee Truth and Justice for Ali Ziri, February 22, 2017.

31. On the investigation in this case and others, see Action des Chrétiens pour l'Abolition de la Torture (ACAT), "L'ordre et la force: Enquête sur l'usage de la force par les représentants de la loi en France" (ACAT France, 2016).

32. Interview with Farid El Yamni, May 11, 2017.

33. Action des Chrétiens pour l'Abolition de la Torture (ACAT), "L'ordre et la force: Enquête sur l'usage de la force par les représentants de la loi en France" (ACAT France, 2016); Amnesty International, "France: Des policiers au dessus des lois" (Amnesty International Publications, 2009).

34. Maurice Rajsfus, *La police hors la loi: Des milliers de bavures sans ordonnances depuis 1968,* Collection "Combien de Divisions?" (Cherche Midi, 1996).

35. Interview with Amal Bentounsi, January 24, 2017.

36. Paul Le Derff, "Faire voir, faire parler, faire taire: La publicisation des faits policiers mortels en France (1990–2016)" (Université de Lille, 2023).

37. Farid El Yamni, *Wissam Vérité* (Éditions du croquant, 2021).

38. El Yamni, *Wissam Vérité.*

39. Interview with Farid El Yamni, May 11, 2017.

40. El Yamni, *Wissam Vérité.*

41. Field notes, November 5, 2016.

42. This was part of a broader effort of antiracist activists, see Soline Laplanche-Servigne, "Quand les victimes de racisme se mobilisent: Usage d'identifications ethnoraciales dans l'espace de la cause antiraciste en France et en Allemagne," *Politix* 108, no. 4 (2014): 143–66.

43. At the time of writing, the Traoré and Gueye families were awaiting the decision of France's highest court after they appealed the nonindictment decision.

44. Monica C. Bell, "Police Reform and the Dismantling of Legal Estrangement," *Yale Law Journal,* no. 126 (2017): 2054–150.

45. Interview with Fatou Dieng, February 5, 2018.

46. Rachida Brahim, *La race tue deux fois: Une histoire des crimes racistes en France (1970–2000)* (Éditions Syllepse, 2020).

47. Traoré and Vigoureux, *Lettre à Adama.*

48. Interview with Ramata Dieng, November 9, 2017.

49. Crystal Marie Fleming, *Resurrecting Slavery: Racial Legacies and White Supremacy in France* (Temple University Press, 2017).

50. Field notes, September 30, 2017.

Chapter 5

1. Trial observations, Paris, February 21, 2018.

2. Mariana Valverde, *Law's Dream of a Common Knowledge,* The Cultural Lives of Law (Princeton University Press, 2003).

3. Michael McCann, *Rights at Work: Pay Equity Reform and the Politics of Legal Mobilization*, Language and Legal Discourse (University of Chicago Press, 1994); Michael McCann and George I. Lovell, *Union by Law: Filipino American Labor Activists, Rights Radicalism, and Racial Capitalism*, Chicago Series in Law and Society (University of Chicago Press, 2020); Stuart A. Scheingold, *The Politics of Rights: Lawyers, Public Policy, and Political Change*, 2nd ed. (University of Michigan Press, 2004); Robin Stryker, "Half Empty, Half Full, or Neither: Law, Inequality, and Social Change in Capitalist Democracies," *Annual Review of Law and Social Science* 3, no. 1 (2007): 69–97.

4. Sheila Jasanoff, "The Eye of Everyman: Witnessing DNA in the Simpson Trial," *Social Studies of Science* 28, no. 5–6 (1998): 713–40; Sheila Jasanoff, *Science at the Bar: Law, Science, and Technology in America*, A Twentieth Century Fund Book (Harvard University Press, 1997); Valverde, *Law's Dream of a Common Knowledge*.

5. Susan Bibler Coutin, "Smugglers or Samaritans in Tucson, Arizona: Producing and Contesting Legal Truth," *American Ethnologist* 22, no. 3 (1995): 549–71; Irene van Oorschot and Willem Schinkel, "The Legal Case File as Border Object: On Self-Reference and Other-Reference in Criminal Law," *Journal of Law and Society* 42, no. 4 (2015): 499–527.

6. Interview with lawyer, September 26, 2017.

7. Action des Chrétiens pour l'Abolition de la Torture (ACAT), "L'ordre et la force: Enquête sur l'usage de la force par les représentants de la loi en France" (ACAT France, 2016); Amnesty International, "France: Des policiers au dessus des lois" (Amnesty International Publications, 2009).

8. For an analysis of the ways different branches of law matter in lawsuits against racialized policing in France, see Magda Boutros, "Legal Mobilization and Branches of Law: Contesting Racialized Policing in French Courts," *Law and Society Review* 56, no. 4 (2022): 623–45.

9. Miranda Fricker, *Epistemic Injustice: Power and the Ethics of Knowing* (Oxford University Press, 2007).

10. Fabien Jobard, "Propositions sur la théorie de la police," *Champ pénal*, no. 9 (2012).

11. Cour d'Appel de Versailles, July 1, 1999; Selmouni v. France, European Court of Human Rights, case no. 25803/94, July 28, 1999.

12. Kim Lane Scheppele, "The Ground-Zero Theory of Evidence," *Hastings Law Journal* 49, no. 2 (1998): 321–34.

13. Open Society Justice Initiative, "Profiling Minorities: A Study of Stop-and-Search Practices in Paris" (Open Society Institute, 2009).

14. Cour de Cassation, 1re chambre civile, 10 juin 1986: JCP G 1986, II, 20683.

15. This rule was established by the European Court of Human Rights, which argued that if the burden of proof was entirely on plaintiffs, it would be in practice extremely difficult for applicants to prove indirect discrimination (D. H. and others vs. The Czech Republic, European Court of Human Rights, 2007).

16. The French laws stipulating a shared burden of proof had a limited scope of application, which did not include policing, but the lawyers argued that this rule

was a general principle of EU antidiscrimination law that should apply to all fields.

17. Interview with Felix de Belloy, January 30, 2017.

18. D. H. and others vs. The Czech Republic, European Court of Human Rights, 2007.

19. Interview with Slim Ben Achour, July 7, 2016.

20. Cour de Cassation, Chambre Civile 1, decisions number 1239 to 1246 of November 9, 2016.

21. In French law, the state can be held accountable for simple fault (*faute simple*) or grievous fault (*faute lourde*), with the latter referring to more serious violations.

22. Cour d'Appel de Paris, Pôle 2, Chambre 1, decision number 13/24299 of June 24, 2015.

23. Julia Pascual, "Contrôles au faciès: Après la condamnation de l'Etat, la police devra changer ses pratiques," *Le Monde*, November 9, 2016.

24. Interview with Slim Ben Achour, March 26, 2017.

25. Interview with Emmanuelle Boussard-Verrechia, January 24, 2018.

26. The state was condemned in 2021 for discriminatory stops targeting three high school students during a school trip, Paris Court of Appeal, June 8, 2021.

27. Interview with Slim Ben Achour, March 26, 2017.

28. Interview with Slim Ben Achour.

29. "Des adolescents portent plainte pour violences policières," *Le Monde*, December 17, 2015.

30. "Des adolescents parisiens dénoncent de graves abus lors de contrôles à répétition," *Mediapart*, December 18, 2015.

31. Pseudonym.

32. Field notes, lawyers' meeting, June 9, 2017.

33. Emmanuel Blanchard, "Les 'indésirables': Passé et présent d'une catégorie d'action publique," *GISTI*, Figures de l'étranger: Quelles représentations pour quelles politiques? (2013): 16–26.

34. "Paris: Des images inédites de la police lors de patrouilles dans le 12ème arrondissement," *Le Monde*, February 14, 2018; "Paris XIIᵉ: Le harcèlement policier au quotidien," *Mediapart*, February 13, 2018.

35. Field notes, trial hearing observations, February 21, 2018.

36. Field notes, trial hearing observations.

37. Field notes, trial hearing observations.

38. Field notes, trial hearing observations.

39. "Sursis requis au procès des violences policières contre des mineurs dans une cité de Paris," *Libération*, February 23, 2018; "Dialogue de sourds au procès des violences policières dans une cité de Paris, " *Le Monde*, February 23, 2018.

40. "Le procès d'une drôle de 'Brigade du tigre,'" *France Inter*, February 22, 2018.

41. Field notes of lawyers' meeting, October 13, 2017.

42. Civil lawsuit filed in June 2019.

43. Civil lawsuit filed in June 2019.

44. Tribunal Judiciaire de Paris, decision of October 28, 2020.

45. Tribunal Judiciaire de Paris, decision of October 28, 2020.

46. Défenseur des droits, decision number 2020-102.

47. Anthony Pregnolato, "Les violences policières en procès: Mort d'Amine Bentounsi; La condamnation exceptionnelle du policier Saboundjian," *Lien social et Politiques*, no. 84 (2020): 163.

48. See, for example, Luc Rouban, "Les fonctionnaires face à l'élection présidentielle de 2017" (Centre de recherches politiques de Sciences Po, 2016).

49. Field notes, trial observations, March 9, 2017.

50. Field notes, trial observations.

51. Interview with lawyer, April 14, 2017.

52. The victim was repeatedly described as "fugitive robber."

53. For example, *Le Parisien*, titled "A man Incapable of Questioning Himself."

54. "Affaire Bentounsi: 'Ce n'est pas le procès de la police,'" *Le Monde*, March 10, 2017.

55. Ivan du Roy and Ludovic Simbille, "Décès suite à une intervention policière: Les deux-tiers des affaires ne débouchent sur aucun procès," *Basta!*, July 2020.

56. Sheila Jasanoff, "Just Evidence: The Limits of Science in the Legal Process," *Journal of Law, Medicine, and Ethics* 34, no. 2 (2006): 328.

57. Interview with Farid El Yamni, July 20, 2022.

58. "Affaire Adama Traoré: Une expertise réalisée à la demande de la famille met en cause les gendarmes," *Le Monde*, March 4, 2021.

59. "Affaire Adama Traoré: La longue bataille des expertises médicales," *Le Figaro*, June 3, 2020.

60. "Affaire Adama Traoré: Ce que disent les expertises successives depuis 2016," *Radio France*, February 8, 2021.

61. "Mort de Gaye Camara: La légitime défense remise en cause," *Disclose*, January 18, 2021.

62. Nathalie Revenu, "Gaye Camara, tué par un policier à Epinay: La reconstitution 3D qui ébranle la thèse de la légitime défense," *Le Parisien*, January 20, 2021.

Chapter 6

1. David S. Meyer, "Protest and Political Opportunities," *Annual Review of Sociology* 30, no. 1 (2004): 125–45.

2. Jean-Marc Berlière and René Lévy, *Histoire des polices en France: De l'Ancien régime à nos jours*, Ed. revue et mise à jour, Nouveau monde poche, histoire (Nouveau Monde, 2013).

3. David J. Hess, *Undone Science: Social Movements, Mobilized Publics, and Industrial Transitions* (MIT Press, 2016).

4. Sally Engle Merry, *The Seductions of Quantification: Measuring Human Rights, Gender Violence, and Sex Trafficking*, Chicago Series in Law and Society (University of Chicago Press, 2016).

5. Steven Epstein, "The Construction of Lay Expertise: AIDS Activism and the Forging of Credibility in the Reform of Clinical Trials," *Science, Technology, and Human Values* 20, no. 4 (1995): 408–37.

6. David J. Hess, "The Potentials and Limitations of Civil Society Research: Getting Undone Science Done," *Sociological Inquiry* 79, no. 3 (2009): 306–27; Vololona Rabeharisoa, Tiago Moreira, and Madeleine Akrich, "Introduction: Evidence-Based Activism; Patients', Users', and Activists' Groups in Knowledge Society," *BioSocieties* 9, no. 2 (2014): 111–28.

7. Epstein, *Impure Science*, 351.

8. Twenty-four-hour news channel BFMTV wrote: "The practice of contrôle au faciès is scientifically proven."

9. Open Society Justice Initiative, "Profiling Minorities: A Study of Stop-and-Search Practices in Paris" (Open Society institute, 2009).

10. Fabien Jobard and René Lévy, "Racial Profiling: The Parisian Police Experience," *Revue Canadienne de Criminologie et de Justice Pénale* (2011).

11. "La police mise en cause pour ses contrôles au faciès," *Le Monde*, June 30, 2009.

12. "Contrôles au faciès: La réponse de la police," *Mediapart*, July 4, 2009.

13. Interview with Fabien Jobard, August 28, 2018.

14. Human Rights Watch, "'La Base de l'humiliation': Les Contrôles d'identité En France," 2012.

15. "La base de l'humiliation: Les contrôles d'identité en France épinglés," *Libération*, January 26, 2012.

16. "Study Says Blacks and Arabs Face Bias From Paris Police," *New York Times*, June 29, 2009.

17. "Eric Besson reconnaît la réalité des "contrôles au faciès," *Le Monde*, December 9, 2009.

18. "Le séminaire à Matignon aurait tourné au défouloir," *L'Obs*, February 10, 2010.

19. "Contrôles au faciès: La réponse de la police," *Mediapart*, July 4, 2009.

20. Twitter, @canalplus, September 21, 2012.

21. Cited in Jobard and Lévy, "Racial Profiling."

22. "Ardisson attaque Zemmour en diffamation," *Libération*, March 24, 2010.

23. "Propos sur 'les Noirs et les Arabes': Eric Zemmour condamné," *Le Parisien*, February 18, 2011.

24. Interview with Kiara, cofounder of Stop le contrôle au faciès, November 10, 2016.

25. James Goldston and Rachel Neild, "Ethnic Profiling Fails Europe," *Open Society Foundations*, June 26, 2006, sec. Voices.

26. Stop le contrôle au faciès, *Dossier de Presse*, November 21, 2011.

27. Interview with Jean-Marie Fardeau, Human Rights Watch, September 14, 2016.

28. François Hollande election manifesto, 2012, "Le changement c'est maintenant. Mes 60 engagements pour la France."

29. Open Society Justice Initiative, "Equality Betrayed: The Impact of Ethnic Profiling in France" (Open Society Foundations, 2013).

30. "Contrôles d'identité: Valls inquiète la police," *Le Figaro*, May 31, 2012.

31. "Le gouvernement veut empêcher la multiplication des contrôles au faciès," *Le Monde*, June 1, 2012.

32. Journal Officiel du Sénat, October 4, 2013, Réponse du Premier Ministre.

33. Journal Officiel du Sénat.

34. "Matricule des policiers: 'Une mesurette qui ne changera rien,'" BFMTV, October 17, 2012.

35. Stop le contrôle au faciès, April 7, 2013, "Des cameras sur l'uniforme des policiers: On se moque de nous!"

36. Proposition de loi relative aux contrôles d'identité, présentée par M. Yves Pozzo di Borgo, Sénateur, 16 octobre 2012.

37. Assemblée Nationale, Compte rendu intégral, June 2, 2016.

38. "Après la mort de Rémi Fraisse, la classe politique se déchire," *France Info*, October 28, 2014.

39. The parliamentary commission did not interview any family of victims from the Truth and Justice movement.

40. Olivier Fil-lieule and Fabien Jobard, *Politiques du désordre: La police des manifestations en France* (Éditions du Seuil, 2020).

41. Interview with Amal Bentounsi, January 24, 2017.

42. She was invited twice to the one of the most watched talk shows in France, *Touche pas à mon poste!*.

43. Interview with Amal Bentounsi, January 24, 2017.

44. For example, *Le Monde* called it a symbolic case (*une affaire devenue un symbole*).

45. See also Soline Laplanche-Servigne, "Quand les victimes de racisme se mobilisent: Usage d'identifications ethnoraciales dans l'espace de la cause antiraciste en France et en Allemagne," *Politix* 108, no. 4 (2014): 143–66.

46. For a more detailed analysis, see Anthony Pregnolato, "Rébellions urbaines et mobilisations contre les violences policières dans la région parisienne (2005–2018)" (PhD diss., Université Paris Nanterre, 2021).

47. This march was strongly criticized by some leaders in the Truth and Justice movement, who perceived it as watering-down their grievances and being primarily "a march for Whites."

48. Interview with a member of the committee Truth for Adama, December 31, 2018.

49. "Les policiers se mobilisent contre "la haine anti-flic," *Le point*, May 4, 2016.

50. "Assa Traoré condamnée pour 'atteinte à la présomption d'innocence,'" *Le Parisien*, March 2, 2021.

51. Articles 122-5, 122-7, and 122-4, code pénal.

52. Until then, there were two legal regimes governing police use of lethal force. The laws applicable to the *police nationale*, which police urban areas, were

the same as those applicable to any citizen acting in self-defense. The gendarmerie on the other hand, the agency policing rural areas, was regulated by the Defense Code and allowed gendarmes to use lethal force in four situations: when they are subjected to violence or threats of violence by armed individuals, when they cannot defend the territories they occupy any other way, when they cannot stop individuals any other way, and when they cannot stop vehicles in any other way. This bill sought to align the legal regime of the *police nationale* on the rules applicable to gendarmes.

53. For example, Ligue des droits de l'Homme, "Une police anonyme autorisée à tirer," February 7, 2017.

54. See, for example, the judges union statement, Syndicat de la Magistrature, "Projet de loi sécurité publique: refusez ce débat expédié!," February 7, 2017.

55. Défenseur des droits, Avis 17-02 du 24 janvier 2017 relatif au projet de loi n° 310 relatif à la sécurité publique.

56. At the National Assembly, on November 2, 2016, he asked the Interior minister about police impunity in this case.

57. Field notes, informal conversation with Amal Bentounsi, February 1, 2017.

58. Assemblée nationale, February 7, 2017.

59. Loi n° 2017-258 du 28 février 2017 relative à la sécurité publique.

60. Marie Clais, "La Note de l'ONDRP," Rapport annuel 2017, October 2017.

61. Police Nationale, "Rapport Annuel de L'IGPN 2016" (Inspection générale de la police nationale, 2017).

62. Ivan du Roy and Ludovic Simbille, "'Refus d'obtempérer,' 'malaises' en detention . . . 52 décès liés à une intervention policière en 2024," *Basta!*, June 26, 2025.

63. Sébastian Roché, Paul Le Derff, and Simon Varaine, "Homicides policiers et refus d'obtempérer la loi a-t-elle rendu les policiers irresponsables ?," *Esprit*, September 2022, online.

64. Thibaud Le Meneec, "Violences policières: Comment Emmanuel Macron a fait évoluer son discours depuis 2017," *FranceInfo*, April 24, 2023.

65. Ronan Maël, "Des milliers de policiers s'échangent des messages racistes sur un groupe Facebook," *Streetpress*, June 4, 2020.

66. For an analysis of this broader rhetoric, see Jean Beaman and Jennifer Fredette, "The U.S./France Contrast Frame and Black Lives Matter in France," *Perspectives on Politics* 20, no. 4 (2022): 1346–61.

67. Déclaration de M. Christophe Castaner, ministre de l'intérieur, sur les accusations de racisme dans les forces de l'ordre, leur formation à la lutte contre le racisme et les discriminations et les sanctions prises à l'encontre des auteurs d'actes racistes ou discriminatoires dans les forces de l'ordre, à Paris le 8 juin 2020.

Conclusion

1. With some important differences in the places and profiles of participants between the two uprisings. See Oberti Marco and Maela Guillaume Le Gall, "Analyse comparée et socio-territoriale des émeutes de 2023 en France," October 10, 2023.

2. "Mort de Nahel M. à Nanterre: Emmanuel Macron sur une ligne de crête entre la gauche et les syndicats de policiers," *Le Monde*, June 29, 2023.

3. "Mort de Nahel tué par un policier: Darmanin dénonce des images 'extrêmement choquantes' et appelle au calme," *Libération*, June 28, 2023.

4. Notre pays est en deuil et en colère, public statement, July 5, 2023.

5. An analysis of the press coverage of four major newspapers, *Le Monde*, *Le Figaro*, *Libération*, and *Le Parisien*, during one month following the death of Zyed and Bouna in 2005, and one month following Nahel's killing in 2023, shows that in 2005, there were five articles containing the term "violences policières" and fifty-seven articles containing the words "police" and "racism"; in 2023 there were respectively 329 and 259.

6. Fabien Leboucq and Ludovic Séré, "Affaire Nahel pourquoi la police tue," *Libération*, June 29, 2023.

7. Fabien Leboucq, "Racisme et violences dans la police: Les multiples occasions manquées d'une réforme," *Libération*, July 3, 2023.

8. An analysis of the press coverage of four major newspapers, *Le Monde*, *Le Figaro*, *Libération*, and *Le Parisien*, during one month following the death of Zyed and Bouna in 2005, and one month following Nahel's killing in 2023, shows that the term "racisme systémique" appeared zero times in 2005 and forty-two times in 2023.

9. Patrick Simon, "Pas de racisme systémique en France, vraiment?," *Libération*, July 14, 2023.

10. Emmanuel Blanchard, "La France a une histoire longue de la racialisation de l'emprise policière," *Le Monde*, July 4, 2023.

11. Fabien Jobard, "Politiste: 'Le législateur a consacré l'ascendant de la police sur la jeunesse postcoloniale,'" *Le Monde*, July 5, 2023.

12. Didier Fassin, "Mort de Nahel: État de légitime colère," *Libération*, June 28, 2023.

13. "'Le nombre de tirs policiers a diminué depuis 2017': Pourquoi cette affirmation de Gérald Darmanin est fausse," *Le Monde*, June 28, 2023.

14. "Le vrai du faux: Y a-t-il vraiment eu cinq fois plus de tirs mortels de policiers à la suite d'un refus d'obtempérer depuis la loi de 2017?," *FranceInfo*, June 30, 2023.

15. "Mineur tué à Nanterre: La loi de 2017 sous le feu des critiques," *Le Figaro*, June 28, 2023.

16. Sébastian Roché, Paul Le Derff, and Simon Varaine, "Homicides policiers et refus d'obtempérer la loi a-t-elle rendu les policiers irresponsables?," *Esprit*, September 2022, online.

17. Andy Clarno et al., *Imperial Policing: Weaponized Data in Carceral Chicago* (University of Minnesota Press, 2024).

18. Simone Browne, *Dark Matters: On the Surveillance of Blackness* (Duke University Press, 2015).

19. Ana Muñiz, *Police, Power, and the Production of Racial Boundaries*, Critical

Issues in Crime and Society (Rutgers University Press, 2015); Clarno et al., *Imperial Policing*.

20. Clarno et al., *Imperial Policing*.

21. This argument is developed in a (yet unpublished) paper by Michael Zanger-Tishler, doctoral candidate in sociology and social policy at Harvard.

22. Miranda Fricker, *Epistemic Injustice: Power and the Ethics of Knowing* (Oxford University Press, 2007).

23. Jocelyn Simonson, "Copwatching," *California Law Review* 10, no. 2 (2016): 391–445; Bärbel Harju, "Dialogue 'Stay Vigilant': Copwatching in Germany," *Surveillance and Society* 18, no. 2 (2020): 280–83; Michaël Meyer, "Copwatching et perception publique de la police: L'intervention policière comme performance sous surveillance," *ethnographiques.org* 21 (2010).

24. Marcelo Hoffman, *Militant Acts: The Role of Investigations in Radical Political Struggles*, SUNY Series in New Political Science (State University of New York Press, 2019), 15.

25. For example, Fabien Jobard, "Police et pouvoir en régime de visibilité," *Délibérée* 12, no. 12 (2021): 19–23.

26. Edouard Bouté, "La mise en visibilité des forces de l'ordre sur Twitter pendant le mouvement des Gilets jaunes," *Questions de communication* 39, no. 1 (2021): 185–208.

27. Glencora Borradaile and Joshua Reeves, "Sousveillance Capitalism," *Surveillance and Society* 18, no. 2 (June 17, 2020): 272–75.

28. Harju, "Dialogue 'Stay Vigilant': Copwatching in Germany," 281.

29. Sandra Harding, "Rethinking Standpoint Epistemology: What Is 'Strong Objectivity'?," *Centennial Review*, 1992, 35.

30. Steven Epstein, *Impure Science: AIDS, Activism, and the Politics of Knowledge*, Medicine and Society (University of California Press, 1998).

31. "Mort de Nahel: 'De jeunes hommes trouvent la mort pour un défaut de permis parce qu'ils ont la peur du policier,'" interview with Amal Bentounsi (collectif "Urgence notre police assassin"), *Dailymotion*, BFMTV.

32. Brut, "La mère de Nahel témoigne aux côtés d'Assa Traore," June 28, 2023.

33. "C a vous, Mort de Nahel: Les mots poignants de sa mère—La Story de Mohamed Bouhafsi—C à Vous—29/06/2023," YouTube.

34. "'Que la vérité soit faite': Emmanuel Macron réagit à la mort de Nahel, tué à Nanterre," YouTube, BFMTV.

35. Jaime Amparo Alves, "From Necropolis to Blackpolis: Necropolitical Governance and Black Spatial Praxis in São Paulo, Brazil," *Antipode* 46, no. 2 (2014): 323–39.

36. Awa Gueye et al., "Entretien avec des membres du réseau d'entraide vérité et justice: Awa Gueye, Mélanie Ngoye-Gaham et Hadja Bah; Entretien Réalisé Par Magda Boutros, Anthony Pregnolato, Paul Le Derff," *Champ pénal* 26 (2022).

37. "Mort de Nahel: La chorégraphie très classique des réactions politiques," *FranceInfo*, June 29, 2023.

38. United Nations High Commissioner for Human Rights, press briefing, June 30, 2023.

39. "Mort de Nahel: Accusée de violences et de racisme, la police de nouveau sous le feu des critiques," *France 24*, July 1, 2023.

40. Aline Daillère and Magda Boutros, *Amendes, évictions, contrôles: La gestion des "indésirables" par la police en région parisienne*, Défenseur des droits, Collection Éclairages, 2025.

41. "Comment réformer la police? Le débat à gauche entre Manuel Bompard et Philippe Brun," *Mediapart*, July 7, 2023.

42. Fabien Jobard, politiste: "Le législateur a consacré l'ascendant de la police sur la jeunesse postcoloniale," *Le Monde*, July 5, 2023.

43. Violences urbaines: "'Bien sûr que si,' il y a un 'lien' avec 'l'immigration,' assure le chef de file des Républicains au Sénat, Bruno Retailleau," *FranceInfo*, July 5, 2023.

44. Émeutes: "Marine Le Pen dénonce 'la haine de la France' des jeunes casseurs," *Le Figaro*, July 6, 2023.

45. Alliance Police Nationale, June 30, 2023, Maintenant ça suffit!

Index

The authorized representative in the EU for product safety and compliance is:
Mare Nostrum Group
B.V Doelen 72
4831 GR Breda
The Netherlands

www.ingramcontent.com/pod-product-compliance
Lightning Source LLC
Chambersburg PA
CBHW030351270326
41926CB00009B/1046